SUNSHINE ON THE WATER

My Random Jaunts Around Asia

By

Geoffrey Leo

This book is dedicated to:

Taylor, Codey and Dominic, Ronnie and Freddie, and Mia

And in loving memory of:

Alan Leo 1947 to 2017

All profits from this publication will be donated to Compton Care, Wolverhampton's centre for palliative care.

Acknowledgements

Once again I would like to thank all those individuals and organisations that have delivered me safely and mostly soundly to hundreds of destinations worldwide. The vast majority of these people have been low paid and seasonally employed by small organisations dependent on tourism and operating in developing countries. We must also give thanks to these people for continuing the work of conservation and protection of threatened habitats. Without their tireless work and the money tourism provides, the world would have already lost so many precious ecosystems and historical artefacts.

Introduction

Oh, the mysterious East!

These are my adventures whilst gallivanting around Asia.

In my mind I am an explorer, an adventurer, seeking out new experiences, discovering new countries and civilisations, boldly going, etc. To my wife, however I am merely some hapless tourist gallivanting from place to place on holiday.

I am haunted by Paul Simon's Homeward Bound, and find myself with tickets for destinations in airports and railway stations, lost with my thoughts escaping, touring on one night stands. I simply get itchy feet if I spend more than one or two nights in any place around the world, however exotic.

In this episode I am in the Near East; Asia on the Mediterranean, visiting Turkey and the Sinai, then to Jordan for Petra ("the rose red city half as old as time itself") and to meet Lawrence's Aqaba on the Red Sea, an arm of the Indian Ocean. There is Africa to the south and the Arabian peninsular north where I discover Oman and the eastern reaches of the Sahara. Then onto the Jewel of the British Empire, India, to be brought to tears by the beauty of the Taj Mahal, and galvanised by the search for tigers. I have sailed the islands of the Maldives and toured the island of Serendipity, ancient Ceylon, now Sri Lanka. Moving back north I travelled in Nepal, trekking the Annapurnas and flying around Everest. On the vast steppes and deserts of Central Asia, in Uzbekistan I took the Silk Road to Samarkand. Then there was walking the Great Wall of China. Now in the Far East I visited Thailand (formerly Siam) to see the Bridge Over The River Kwai and Burma (now Myanmar?) to travel The Road To Mandalay. Onto Anghor Wat and the Killing Fields of Cambodia and being impressed by the rise from the ashes of war torn Vietnam. I journeyed into the South China Sea to climb Mount Kinabalu and see the orangutans at Sepilok on the island of Borneo before ending these expeditions searching for dragons on the magical islands of the Flores Sea.

None of these expeditions are long, I have to promise to be home in less than a fortnight, for to Kaz I am a humble teacher gadding about pretending to be an adventurer.

Then there's mother, "Why on earth do you want to go to these godforsaken places (because they are there). Just promise me you won't do anything silly or dangerous."

Comprising 48 countries on the Earth's largest land mass (there are 65 people for every one Brit), Asia is wholly in the Northern Hemisphere apart from some of its southernmost islands. It stretches from the icy tundra of Siberian wastes, to the eastern coast of the Mediterranean, the ancient Levant; from the steamy tropics of India and former French Indochina, via the Malay peninsular and the huge island archipelagos of Indonesia and the Philippines to the final oriental jewel that is Japan, the land of the Rising Sun.

During my American adventures I was struck by the carefree attitude of poor people travelling to and from work in battered buses, and how content they appeared with their simple existence. There was so much laughter on these buses.

Throughout Asia there is so much serenity and beauty, often associated with water features. These could be moats, pools, lakes, cascades, streams, rivers, seas or great oceans. Whenever the sun glistens off the water it makes you smile. You should never underestimate the joyous power of Sunshine On The Water.

I begin my second round of Random Jaunts, those around Asia, in Cairo, Africa.

Contents

From Sinai to Petra

I met Andrew in the Windsor Hotel, Cairo. He was a pleasant, single, thirty something Scot with a soft Edinburgh burr who now lived and worked in London, "Something in the City," as he described himself. The Windsor was an old colonial style hotel which had both Churchill and Michael Palin as previous guests. All of the rooms were spacious if dull and rather drab; it was atmospheric. Every floorboard creaked and you swayed in the corridors like a madhouse fairground ride.

Someone had had an idea to furnish the lounge bar with wooden beer barrels fashioned into chairs and tables. The effect looked good, but the chairs were uncomfortable. You certainly couldn't endure a good session in there. Andrew and I decided therefore to find a bar nearer the Nile in a modern business person's hotel where we could perhaps watch a football match and more comfortably discuss our plans.

We found Harry's Pub on Zamalek Island, beneath the Marriott Hotel. Over cold beers Andrew explained how after taking in the sights of Cairo; the Museum, Great Pyramids at Giza, Sphinx, step pyramid of Saqquara, and the Muhammed Ali Mosque, he would be striking out into the Western desert, deep into the Sahara, to the Siwa Oasis. Very adventurous, I thought.

I was impressed. I had previously "done" Cairo, and the Nile cruise from Luxor to Aswan. This trip (I had arrived in Cairo by Jumbo the previous day) I was venturing into the Sinai desert, then north to Jordan. We agreed to meet up back in the Windsor in a week's time to compare notes. I was taking an overnight bus across the Suez canal, east to Nuweiba, so at nine left Andrew to nurse his beer and finish watching Chelsea with a group of friendly Yemenis.

I took a taxi to the Ramses Midan bus station, outside which stands an impressive statue of Rameses II, and found my bus. The overnight coach had a conductress, and she settled me in with a blanket, pillow, and refreshment box which included a sandwich and fruit drink. I was ready to cross the eastern desert, the Suez canal, and enter Asia.

The Suez Canal was built in the nineteenth century. It links the Mediterranean, an arm of the Atlantic Ocean, to the Gulf of Suez, the left finger of the Red Sea which is an arm of the Indian Ocean,. It enables people and cargoes to travel from Europe to Asia, avoiding the six week journey around the Cape of Good Hope. It simply cuts through the desert, there are no mountains to cross, so no expensive, time-consuming locks. It is 120 miles long and has needed continuous widening and dredging over its history to accommodate bigger and bigger shipping. Over 50 ships transit the canal daily and it is estimated to make Egypt more than $5 billion per year.

The French built it, under De Lesseps who was then commissioned to build the Panama Canal and failed. Strangely, the Victorian British were against its construction, Palmerston seeking to thwart it as he feared Ottoman control would endanger our overland route to India. Ultimately it became an invaluable asset to our empire, and soon we had acquired 44% of its shares. The rest, as they say, is history.

Sadly, I never saw it, I slept well on the bus and was delivered to Nuweiba, an important port on the Sinai peninsular, around dawn. Saying a fond farewell to the driver and conductress I hoisted the back pack, walked about 30 minutes from the bus station to the village of Tarabin and rented a hut on the beach. The contrast here between the sandy barren mountains of the Sinai, the beach and the shimmering blue of the Gulf of Aqaba was amazing in the heat of the rising sun There were no other colours other than the black tents of the Bedouin, and the straw huts of Mooncamp. Anwar brought me strong syrupy coffee and some honeyed breads for breakfast and together we gazed at the ocean as crabs scuttled between their holes on the sandbank to my right. He told me of his friend Kemal, a deaf mute who each morning summoned a dolphin, "You wait, his singing brings her to shore."

If it is colour you want, then the most vibrant lies just beneath the surface of the warm, calm water. The electric blue-greens, oranges, reds and yellows of the coral covered rocks are only yards offshore, and I was quickly up and snorkelling amongst them. And the fishes, sergeant-majors, damsons, butterflies, picassos, parrots and wrasses and much more There is a riot of life and colour and I felt very alive after the crowded, dirty streets of Cairo.

Later I was dozing amongst the dark warm blankets in my hut when I heard a shout and peering out of the doorway, my eyes adjusted to the bright sunlight. There, no more than 50 yards off shore, a thin robed man stood tall in the prow of a rowing boat. Anwar was operating the single scull and Kemal begins ululating.

I grabbed my mask and snorkel and raced across the sand and into the water to join about ten others who were treading water behind the boat. Kemal continued his yodel-like bellowing, possibly his only vocal method of communication, and stopped every so often to scan the waters around.

Sure enough a fin appeared and circled the boat. It was a signal to those in the water to don their masks and follow. In my rush my mask strap snaps, and I am left having to push the mask onto my face, struggle with the snorkel and only use my one free hand to manoeuvre in the water.

I splashed away in the general direction when I suddenly saw her. She was a blue-grey porpoise, only about four feet long, and no more than five yards away, and she circled me, breached to breathe, and then the waters became murky. I must have gasped, because I took in a lot of water. I cleared my mask and lungs, and tried again to find her. There were glimpses in the choppy water and I could see the notches on her dorsal fin, and at one stage I was so close I could nearly reach out and touch her, but the mixture of the errant mask, water slopping into my snorkel and fatigue were gradually drowning me, and as she dipped and swam to the open sea, I struck out rather wearily for the shore.

After coughing up half the Red Sea I dried, changed and walked back to the port, and sat in a dark, stinking departure shed awaiting my three pm departure. As I had left Anwar asked if I should like to climb Mount Sinai. "You betcha!" I excitedly agreed, and went to shake his hand. Anwar mistook my excitement and went for a high-five, and I realised his intent and turned my handshake into a fist pump. Anwar ended up grasping my fist, highly embarrassing. Sheepishly I thanked him for his offer and hospitality and promised to look him up as soon as I returned.

The Seacat was a wonderfully efficient powerboat which only took an hour to reach Aqaba with views of Saudi Arabia to our right, now bathed in the sun that sinks into the Sinai in late afternoon. Unfortunately it was two hours late leaving Nuweiba, due to the endless forms everyone has to fill out, and another hour in Jordanian customs awaiting new visas.

Clearing customs I shared a taxi with a pleasant American lady into the town and secured a room for overnight before venturing into the town centre.

Aqaba, how historic. Its strategic position controls the Gulf and only required sea defences, according to the Ottomans, who reasoned any attack from the land side impossible. The great hero of Arabia, T. E. Lawrence proved them wrong, and united the Arab tribes to defeat Turkey.

Unfortunately, after the Great War, France and Britain got together and drew lines on the map of Arabia to give these tribes countries. That has caused no problems at all! We have evidently never understood the concept of Nomadic.

I found Aqaba, and the whole of Jordan, to be much more laid back than Egypt, which at times, I'm afraid, appears to be full of spivs and wide boys.

Annoying Egyptians

Egyptians are a wonderfully friendly and welcoming people. Just never go shopping, because the shopkeepers can be rather aggressive in their methods of sales persuasion. I've known many holiday makers and tourists who will not leave their hotel complex, and it is not for fear of terrorism or any other form of violence. It is because of the constant harassment. You cannot take a relaxing stroll down a street, or go idly window shopping. You will be accosted. And it will be at every shop and restaurant.

The worst though is when you are nowhere near any shops. You may have just arrived in a town, got off the bus, or left a boat, and may hesitate to find your bearings or consult a map. A very helpful gentleman will appear at your side and welcome you and engage in simple conversation. Where are you from, they will ask, thank you for visiting Egypt, they will say, is this your first time, they will assert. It doesn't matter how experienced you are at parrying this attack, they will continue with a smile. I've tried being Russian, claiming to be deaf, insisting I'm in a hurry, or simply crossing the street. They will pursue you, helping you find your destination, and gaining your confidence. Eventually they will operate their sting. Please, come to my (perfume, carpet, papyrus, jewellery) shop, they will insist you do them the honour of taking tea. This is fatal. As soon as you are in the shop, the shutters come down, the doors are locked and you are in a struggle to keep hold of your wallet. We can deliver, what is your address? Is the answer to the 'can't get it into my luggage' objection. They will overcome anything you can throw at them. And if you still will not buy at the end of their polished presentation they will become aggressive and belligerent and claim you have insulted their Egyptian hospitality. I have known people to be physically manhandled, something you wouldn't get away with anywhere else in the world. I was once chased down a street in Aswan by a man insisting I had entered into a contract to buy a belt! At Giza I had to seek the assistance of the Tourist Police to remove one of these harassing individuals. The police woman who came to my aid then tried to sell me hashish. In Cairo a distinguished looking gentleman accompanied Kaz and myself to a Nile Delta cruise boat, and insisted on buying our tickets. This, I learned later, included a small commission for himself, and a bung for the captain. I have heard many similar stories and it is sad that this type of activity spoils it for the majority, who are honest individuals. It can serve only to harm the tourist trade, which always seems to hang on a knife edge anyway.

I wandered Aqaba's town squares which were very clean, and made my way down to the esplanade, alongside which were many cafes and restaurants. Inside and seated outside were the men of the town, in the evening I saw few women. The men were all attired in the long white robe, kandura, worn with the kaffiyeh red and white check headdress, secured with the igal, coiled rope. They were busy at discoursing, playing backgammon, or puffing on their sheesha pipes. There was a very relaxed atmosphere, nobody harassed me or looked upon me suspiciously, and everyone I spoke to was most courteous, and genuinely interesting to talk to.

I ate a grilled chicken dinner, and found my bed by ten, first real bed in 40 hours. This morning I had been in a different country swimming with a 'dolphin' (who nearly drowned me) named Ollin.

Following a street breakfast of falafel on pita with mango juice, I found myself seated on a half full minibus waiting to leave for Ma'an on the King's Highway. I was heading for Wadi Rum, another favourite of Lawrence, but the bus dropped me off well short. Luckily, Havad, an American/Israeli medical student was also deposited here.

A wadi is a dried river bed, and around Rum rise huge jebels, mountains. Together we hitched a lift on the back of an open truck which drove us (bounced us) about 20 miles through the wadi to where it really opened up, at the Government Rest House. The scenery, of pink, yellow and brown rock formations was never less than spectacular, there was even the odd (very odd, and always scrawny) tree.

At the Rest House we negotiated a trip into the desert and an overnight stay in a Bedouin tent. The Bedouin are renowned for their generosity and hospitality. A jeep took us deeper into the wadi and deposited us at a Bedou camp with its characteristic low slung black tents. We stepped inside and rested awhile. I have to admit the flies and musty stench

11

were quite off putting. Presently Ahmed, a boy of no more than thirteen years guided us on a trek into the desert and a climb up to Lawrence's Spring. The view back down into the wadi and across and all around to the jebels was a pure click moment, impossible to describe or catch on film. The emptiness, peace, and breathtaking size of the whole vista were something you can only desperately try to consign to memory. We scrambled for some time along the escarpment and among the granite and sandstone boulders before descending back down to the desert floor. You could truly see the place through the awe inspired eyes of Lawrence himself.

Presently we returned to the camp, and as Havad slept, I guiltily sneaked out and hitched a jeep ride back to the Rest House where I secured a mattress for the night on the roof.

I had forsaken the Bedouin hospitality for the promise of a cold beer and proper toilets. Sorry Havad.

Following a spaghetti and hot sauce dinner, and a chat with a group of climbers who waxed lyrical about the "verticality" of their day's adventures, I settled in under the stars, which is never a bad thing. I recall counting several shooting stars as the Milky Way became almost crystal clear over my head and the French community singing gradually died to a gentle snore. Tomorrow, Petra.

"The Rose Red city, half as old as time itself" was probably established around the fourth century BC by the Nabateans, a nomadic Arabian tribe able to harness the scarce water sources. They saw the value of establishing a permanent community on this trade route, a natural pathway from the Dead Sea to the Gulf of Aqaba. Originally called Raqmu, the Romans gave it the Greek name meaning rock (as in Saint Peter), and it achieved the above quote from a poem by John William Burgon. It is most famous for its use in the Indiana Jones adventure, "Raiders of the Lost Ark", and then only for the Treasury facade (there is only a small burial chamber inside, not the cavernous system imagined in the film).

I rose at dawn, quickly breakfasted and secured a car for the two hour journey which I shared with Johannes, a tall, blond Dane. I found a hotel room, dumped my heavy bag and loaded my day sack. I was ready for Petra and it was not yet nine o'clock

Wadi Musa (where Moses struck the rock with his staff to bring forth water) is where you buy your ticket and I then walked into the mile and a half Siq. This is a very narrow and precipitous gorge leading to where it suddenly arrives at the Treasury. You can hire a horse, but it only carries you from some way after the entrance to a good way before the exit. But what an exit. I had to repeat it twice. One moment in the dark, almost claustrophobic rock cleft, the next it opens up to this marvellous pink edifice carved out of the sandstone rock itself.

The Khazneh, thought to be the mausoleum of King Aretus IV, was probably built in the first century AD. It is 130 feet high, and its Corinthian pillars and intricate friezes are topped by a funerary urn, thought to have contained treasure. There are bullet holes in this urn where 18th century soldiers had tried to release the fabled contents.

Here, everybody turns right, but I lingered after having seen the tomb room and climbed the rock-face to the left. Here in the cool shadows was a pool fed by dripping fronds of greenery. Climbing here gives you a completely different aspect of the treasury facade, but now it was time to descend to explore the city itself. I took the route to the right, and then turning left the whole city itself opens up in a huge basin. I saw instantly examples of the civilisations that had left their mark.

All around in the cliff-sides were the carved tombs of the Nabateans. In the foreground was a Roman amphitheatre in which dust devils swirled, and beyond, a Roman road flanked by ancient shops, then a Greek temple. There were Crusader castles, Christian churches and Ottoman mosques. You need two days here, but I had to do it in one, so without rest, I set about the task.

In a moment of genius I decided to climb the hidden rock steps I had found beyond the necropolis and to my left. These took me precariously up through a narrow siq to the Nabatean high point. Here,

13

among the tombs, obelisks and sacrificial altar (it had a blood drainage hole like an autopsy slab), I could see over the whole city, and plan my exploration campaign accordingly.

I descended and avoiding the crowds climbed the other side to the ancient tombs. Here were caves, ancient dwellings which had the smoothest colourful rainbow like curves of layered rock, red, white, yellow, blue, not unlike the multi coloured sand jars you could buy from Alum Bay on the Isle of Wight.

I explored these then skirted around the Roman arch and street to the Crusader castle. From here I took the southern route back to the outer siq before winding my way through the centre back to the dust eddies of the amphitheatre to rediscover the Treasury. I lingered awhile before trudging wearily back up the Siq to Wadi Musa. I had only one regret, a failure to negotiate the trail on Jebel Harum to Aaron's tomb, and I had missed the Ad Deir monastery (OK two regrets), but all in all I think that with limited time I had managed to do justice to Petra.

I taxied back to my hotel, dined on saffron rice with chicken and vegetables and slept well. I was back in Aqaba having bussed via Ma'an by 11am the next morning, Easter Sunday. I was ticketed, visa'd, stamped (twice) and taxed to leave Jordan by midday. The Turbo Cat raced us down the Gulf of Aqaba with mountains of the Sinai to the right, and Jebels of Saudi to our left, on both sides great heights plunging into the blue sea. I had to buy yet another visa to re-enter Egypt, and was delivered to the Mooncamp of Tarabin by 5pm.

"I hope you have had a good rest," Anwar said, once he had greeted me with a hug like a long lost relative, "We leave for Jebel Musa at eleven tonight to arrive at the summit for dawn."

I took to my bed! That isn't to say I went to bed in my hut. Sun beds on the Sinai are mattresses laid out on the sand sheltered by a gazebo style tent to keep off the harsh rays of the sun, Bedouin style. So I lay on the sand, with a fair bit of activity around. There were families of Egyptians and Israelis, mixing and mingling quite happily enjoying the seaside. This is Passover holiday, an event that Muslims, Jews and

Christians all observe. It celebrates the Angel of Death passing over Moses' people, to inflict death on the first born of the Egyptians. This final of ten plagues inflicted by God, persuaded the Pharaoh to let the enslaved Israelites leave on their Exodus.

You may recall from your scripture lessons that God then parted the Red Sea to allow Moses and his Israelites to cross. The sea flowed back to destroy the Pharaoh's army which was chasing them. After this miracle, they wandered in the Sinai for some time looking for the promised land (of milk and honey) before Moses was called by God to collect the Ten Commandments from the top of Mount Sinai.

While he was away his impatient children built a golden calf to worship. Moses saw this and hurled the stone tablets down the mountain to destroy it. Hence he had to return to the mountain to receive them again. They were subsequently carried around in the Ark of the Covenant which now resides in Ethiopia (see Random Jaunts Around Africa).

Back to my beachside bed. Anwar's camp is dry, which probably accounts for the peaceful fun that families were enjoying around me. There is a lot to be said for sobriety, it is very sobering.

As night fell Anwar brought me three girls. "These are German tourists who also want to climb Moses' mountain," he explained. We dined together on a table Anwar had prepared with foul (a spicy soup of pulses) and falafel, simple but tasty with breads and oily dips. The girls introduced themselves as Gretchen, Beatrice and Andrea, students from Munich.

The car came to collect us and I have to admit I slept for most of the two and a half hour journey into the interior. We were dropped off at St Catherine's Monastery where we could, if we so desired, hire a camel to take us nearly to the top. There were a lot of people milling around. I suppose following in Moses' and God's footsteps is a popular tourist pursuit, hence dozens of camels making their living here. (forget footsteps, the Monastery is officially dedicated to the God-Trodden Mount Sinai)

15

We started our trek at 3am. I quickly discovered the same problem climbing at night as during the day. There are beautiful views (at this hour, of the half-moonlit, star strewn sky), but Murphy's Law guarantees as soon as you lift your eyes off the trail to take in and admire your surroundings, you will trip over a root or rock, or indeed on this occasion bump into a camel, which are bad-tempered at the best of times.

Our task began with a gentle uphill climb, but soon we had to zig-zag as the going became much steeper. Camel riders slowly swayed past us with that distinctive camel plod, and there was the occasional bellowing grunt, which I imagined came from the camels, although the German girls were starting to struggle. It is five miles to the top, an ascent of 2,300 feet. At the 9,000 foot peak is a chapel. The last half hour is up a strength sapping 700 carved steps.

We eventually arrived at the camel terminus where they could unload their burdens, and everyone has to climb the steps. Near the summit was a final Bedouin tent cafe, and we stopped for refreshments, tea taken seated on cushions. I could never have been a Bedou, when attempting cross-legged I always fall backwards (even for story-time when I was in primary school).

We summitted and in the cool, eerie silence everyone found themselves a vantage point. The four of us climbed onto the roof of the small stone chapel and dangled our legs precariously over the edge, a sheer drop to the valley below. Strange that I remember thinking to myself this was the sort of silly risk I promised my mother I would never take.

We were seated, facing south, and the sky was beginning to brighten to a light blue away to our left. The light blue began to change to orange then to a deep red. The centre of this redness became brighter and brighter until the disc of the sun revealed itself to signal the dawn. As the sun rose the vista in front of us changed by the second. What was darkness became shadow, and those shadows gradually crept smaller and smaller towards the sun, revealing the heights of surrounding mountains, their uneven, rounded, rocky shapes and their colours, a reddish orange sandy hue. The sky (the moon and stars were long gone) was an unbroken blue, not a cloud dared spoil the panorama.

When the sun had first broken, there was some applause. Some people began singing, for others there were tears. It wasn't just the beauty, there was also the significance of this place, its holiness.

Eventually we began our descent and were able to admire (risking stubbed toes) in broad daylight, the moonscape of a few hours previous.

Back at the car park there was a refreshment marquee for weary climbers, and we breakfasted at 8am before visiting the monastery named for the martyr, Saint Catherine, broken on a wheel before she was beheaded.

Built in the sixth century, the monastery's remains were discovered in the grounds by monks in the ninth century having been brought here by angels. The complex more resembles a fortified citadel with defensive perimeter walls, possibly a result of the wars seemingly having raged forever in this troubled land. Think of it; Israelites and Philistines, Egyptians and Babylonians, Pharaohs, Romans, the creation of Islam which brought in the Crusaders, and onwards to finally include (inevitably not final) today's territorial squabbles.

The monastery was built on the site of the Burning Bush, from which Moses received the message from God to bring his children out of slavery in Egypt, to find the land of milk and honey. And the Bush still exists, and has grown out into a mighty circle, as it has supposedly evolved from perhaps 3,000 years of generations. It is a blackberry bush, a simple bramble, common enough in the woods and hedgerows of home, but a rarity in this desert. (or is it a parasitical growth having killed off the original?) I loved the mighty shrub, and the wall against which it grows, which is festooned in its nooks and crannies with prayer messages written, carefully folded and pushed in; the wishes of centuries.

Inside, in the dark coolness were scores of ancient wooden icons, and the World's oldest continually operating library. In the nineteenth century the Codex Sinaiticus was discovered here, the oldest preserved hand written manuscript of the Bible; both testaments. It is thought to have been written in the 4th Century. And where is it now? It was sold by Stalin (how come he had it) to the British Museum. An older one has since been found, on palimpsests, reused parchments whose previous writings were erased by lemon juice. Its invisible ink properties means that the original writings can still be deciphered.

We left the monastery and wearily made our way back to where Yasser, our driver was waiting. Grinning, he said he had one more surprise for us, and sure enough after an hour on the road, he stopped and ushered us out of the air-conditioned car into the unmitigating heat, "Boots off" he insisted, and together we climbed an adjacent sand dune, the windward side, rocky. I scraped my bare foot and suddenly there was blood on the sand. "Don't worry, I will fix it at the bottom," Yasser said dismissively.

At the top there were wonderful views of the desert and its dunes all around. Yasser lined us up and we held hands, Gretchen, Yasser, Beatrice, me and Andrea. There was no sound, just a gentle warm breeze, and Yasser waited until we had all caught our breath. We were facing the lee slope, where the fine sand is blown and gathers, it was at least a 45 degree angle, if not steeper to the bottom, and probably the same temperature.

"Ready?", Yasser grinned, his eyes flashed as he looked around at us. We nodded. And he launched himself, "Go!" he shouted belatedly.

We galumphed after him, loosing hands and feet sinking into the soft sand. We careered down at a rate of knots. Arms flailing and legs spiralling in a blur, just like those old comic book images. And all of us finished the last few yards head over heels, tumbling into a collective British, German and Egyptian heap, laughing so much we nearly convulsed trying to catch our next breath.

"Again," Yasser shouted.

"No!" I gasped. "Mend my broken bits and take me home".

Yasser cleansed my wounds; a grazed left foot, right knee and both elbows, dressed them in iodine, and we returned to Anwar's camp where I just took to the sea and floated my pains away. Great adventures.

That night Anwar took me into Nuweiba where I caught the overnight bus back to Cairo. The next evening I was relaxing in the bar of the Windsor Hotel and Andrew walked in. I bought him a beer.

"How was the Siwa Oasis?" I asked eagerly.

"Not been there yet," he answered.

"What about the pyramids, did you enjoy Giza and its history?"

"The hotel's arranging a car for me tomorrow" he replied a little more confidently.

"I suppose you must have spent your time in the museum" I ventured,

"Yes, it's definitely on the list," he smiled. "Another beer?"

The next morning I flew home by Egypt Air Jumbo jet. The one and only time in my life I had been upgraded to first class, a wonderful way to travel, with one problem. Egypt Air is dry. Very sobering this sobriety.

Post Script

I enjoyed the Sinai so much that many of our future family holidays were spent in Sharm, Dahab, and Taba; meeting up with old friends, snorkelling, and venturing into the interior to marvel at the stars, walk canyons, and stay in the Ain Quseib oasis.

I have had two strange adventures which found their way into my journal.

Adventure One

We were in Dahab, home of the famous Blue Hole diving site, and where the Gulf of Aqaba is at its narrowest, and where it can be quite breezy.

"Today lying around the pool, overlooking the sea, and I was reading Tolstoy's Anna Karenina. Next to us was a young German mother who was playing with her tiny baby. She was obviously taking great care to shield her from the sun as they sat together on a sun lounger. As happens on these occasions there were a series of coincidences. She gets up to find some sun lotion from her bag. I put my book down and sit up to look at the sea. A freak gust of wind suddenly lifts the baby's sun lounger six feet into the air and tips her off. She is falling head first onto the marble, and I'm up, out of my seat and reach out and catch her in mid-air. In the right place at the right time. I gave her a little cuddle, well who can resist a three month old baby in their arms, and handed her back to mum who was shocked but effusively grateful. I returned to Anna, whose ending wasn't quite so fortunate."

Adventure Two

This time we were visiting a public beach in Sharm El Sheik, the southernmost point of the Sinai desert. This is a favourite location for snorkellers because of the wonderful coral gardens and tropical marine life of the protected Ras Mohamed Marine Reserve. The Red Sea is an arm of the Indian Ocean, but being quite cut off, there is no great tidal flow. There is however more than in the Mediterranean, possibly a range of about two feet. So there can be a slight current. On this occasion the current was going North to South, so drift snorkelling to the right of the beach jetty was easy, but meant swimming quite strongly back. I was with Kaz lying on sunbeds on a cliff overlooking the beach with its 50 yard jetty which took swimmers over the coral shelf to the drop off. At the end of the pontoon were about 30 people coming in and out of the water.

"I noticed a woman struggling to swim back against the tide. Her companion threw her a life preserver ring on a rope and went in to try to haul her back. Soon they were both in difficulty but the people on the jetty were oblivious to their struggling. I was too far away. Surely someone would do something. I realised everyone was blissfully unaware. It had to be me.

I shouted something to Kaz and ran to the edge of the cliff, bounded down the carved steps, across the beach then onto the jetty. I was at full pelt, and when I reached the end of the jetty I pushed through the crowd and dived into the sea and was with the stricken couple in moments. They were two elderly Russians, and I indicated to them to both hang on to the ring, and I towed them in by the rope. It took a few minutes against the current, and it was a struggle, but eventually I made it to the jetty and pulled them up onto it where they could recover.

I got to my feet and unleashed a torrent of abuse to the watching crowd who once again appeared unaware there had been any problem. Unbelievable!

I retrieved my flip-flops and trudged back to Kaz who was beaming. "What's so funny?" I asked.

"It was just like Baywatch," she replied grinning.

All day long, I was the Hoff!"

Oman's Desert Adventure

Muscat

In the early 1990's I was offered a position introducing and organising Business Studies courses in Muscat, the capital of Oman. I considered it, of course, and had virtually discounted it as I didn't want to work away from my family. However, before I could reply, the offer was withdrawn. I spent subsequent years wondering what might have been. So when the opportunity arose to visit Oman, I jumped at the chance with a little more positivity than I had given the job offer.

The Sultanate of Oman is strategically placed to control the Strait of Hormuz on the Gulf. This is one of the busiest oil shipping lanes in the world, an arm of the Arabian Sea and part of the Indian Ocean. For most of the last 200 years Oman has maintained a special relationship with the UK due to its geographic importance and our mutual empire interests.

I have a theory about countries, especially those of the Middle East, that if you rarely hear of them in the news, then they should be comparatively affluent, stable and peaceful. Such is the case with Oman. It is bordered by the Yemen, embroiled in constant civil strife, Saudi Arabia with its arcane laws, and a variety of Emirates. It lies at the mouth of the Persian Gulf which also serves Kuwait, Iraq and Iran. Pakistan is also a maritime neighbour. It must be doing well to maintain such a low profile.

I flew overnight and began my visit before breakfast at the Sultan

Qaboos Grand Mosque, a beautifully impressive new building which at that time housed the largest single carpet in the world. At an impressive 5,200 square yards and weighing over 20 tons, it takes a lot of hoovering. There is also a huge central crystal chandelier and many side chandeliers. The whole place is sensational, full of colourful opulence and sheer indulgence with its white Indian marble, massive dome and imposing minaret. It can accommodate over 20,000 worshippers, and shows (if proof were needed) that there is big money in religion.

Virtually the whole of the indigenous population of Oman adhere to Islam and the house of Ibadi, so there is a tolerance of other religions. This is handy as this mosque, and most of Muscat's new hotels and malls would have been built by imported labour, mostly Indian Hindus. I particularly enjoyed the gardens and their symmetrical beds of flowering shrubs.

My modest hotel room now being ready I checked in and grabbed three hours kip before hitting the sights. Mohammed on the desk organised a car and barely had I chance to collect a chicken tikka wrap than Mo turned up in a gleaming white Toyota to whisk me away. First stop, unusually for a modest hotel car, was a luxury hotel. The Kampinsky is a deluxe five star establishment with an opulent white marbled reception and wonderful views from the manicured gardens along the coast, but it felt a little patronising as in "this is where you could have stayed".

I left and was saluted by the doormen. Mo then drove me to the port of Mutrah. Here I walked along the corniche, a beautifully clean balustraded esplanade, and climbed to an old Portuguese fort to look down on the harbour. Out of the sun glistening water were leaping shoals of tiny fish, and then followed the reason, a huge six foot tuna exercised a perfect arc in hunting them. I walked with Mo to the fish market where I saw hundreds of sharks, including juvenile hammerheads, their dead eyes staring menacingly up at me from iced wooden blocks. We continued to wander the tiny, winding souk streets and then finally on our itinerary was another 16th century Portuguese fort. More excellent clambering around its crenelated parapets.

We returned to the hotel and Mo had sold me a sunset cruise, why not, I reasoned. He picked me up early evening and took me back to the port of Mutrah where I joined more tourists on a tourist boat. We sailed past a posh hotel and two forts and I had this nagging feeling of deja vu, either that or jet lag. It had been a very long day.

However, there was something else significant about the sunset cruise. We are in Ramadan, and although Oman is tolerant, they request their visitors to observe certain rules, one being to restrict alcohol consumption until after sunset. So once the sun had dipped beneath the horizon, and with the sky reddening as we headed back to our mooring, the crew broke out the ice cold beers. A perfect end to that very long day.

Tiwi Beach

Breakfast in the hotel was surprisingly good with plenty of fresh fruit, delicious breads and cakes, and some wonderful curry options, as well as the usual eggs of all types, toast and jam. You do not find bacon and sausage in Arab, Jewish, Hindu or Buddhist countries as the pig is not deemed suitable to eat (or any sentient creature for some). There are sometimes substitutes, like turkey rashers or chicken sausage, but few people find these adequate, so I prefer to eat as the locals. Curry for me, morning, noon and night.

I had signed up for a tour which was due to pick me up after check out. Two white Toyota land cruisers duly arrived at 8:30, and I was surprised and delighted to be greeted by the petite tour leader, Clare, a lovely tanned and permed blonde from the Cotswolds. She introduced me to my fellow adventurers. There was Sumi, an Asian Londoner; Peter, a solicitor from the Potteries; Sandy a Joyce Grenfell look and soundalike, Celia who rejoiced in the nickname Patsy after Joanna Lumley's Character on AbFab, Andrew whose floppy hat, wispy beard and piercing blue eyes brought him the appellation Vincent (after Van Gogh), Alexa who in the spirit of alternative naming became Hyacinth and husband and wife team, James and Tanya.

The nine of us were to be looked after by Clare who introduced us to our two Indian drivers, Sarfraz and Mandip. She explained Omanis wouldn't undertake such work, would definitely not work for a woman, and that Indian migrant workers were often used during Ramadan as the fasting rules could make local drivers tired and unsafe (incidentally, if that does happen to drivers, they are allowed to eat, as are schoolchildren if the fast might interfere with their studies. As I have said, a tolerant nation).

We first drove to the Binmah Sinkhole to swim in the green warm water that filled this steep white walled canyon, then onto a beach where the drivers prepared lunch whilst we snorkelled in the warm blue water. Large wrasse, parrotfish, and memorably, cuttlefish were all on view. This was luxury, with the deserted white beach, our very own piece of the Indian Ocean, and being waited on hand and foot. In the absence of trees or any shade, a tarpaulin was stretched across the two vehicles, with tables and chairs set beneath accordingly.

After lunch we drove to Wadi Shab and trekked for nearly an hour up into the dried river gulch, clambering over and around some difficult rock formations. You could see that when the rains came, they gushed down the mountain in a series of precipitous water falls. Eventually we came across an aqua marine pool and Clare bade us get in and follow her. We swam and paddled into some hidden caves. On one stretch I had to go through a hole in the rock only wide enough to fit my neck, losing footing here would have meant supporting myself by my jawbone. It was also dark, but then opened up into a vast cavern. There was greenery here and rope swings hung from ancient branches, obviously created for local children who had been using this place as a playground for centuries.

It was a carefully negotiated return journey, and twice I fell on slippery marble surfaces, bruising naught but my ego. We then drove to Tiwi Beach where the drivers had set up our overnight camp.

They cooked our fish curry dinner whilst we chatted as the sun set. The stars came out as we ate and I marvelled at the upside down crescent moon. There were many stories to tell and games to play as we

25

enjoyed our evening on the beach and became better acquainted. You could say there was much laughter on the beach.

I thoroughly enjoyed listening to Sumi, who had been awarded the British Empire Medal for her services to the health industry, something we found out, she didn't broadcast. Somewhere in her past she had married a Belgian Count, now long gone, so for the rest of the tour she became our Contessa. She certainly had nobility in her genes. She delighted in telling us she was a member of FANY, who provided driving services and intelligence operations during the Second World War, and now provide response teams for civil or military incidents in London.

Of course there are opportunities for innuendo and double entendres, but FANY stands for First Aid Nursing Yeomanry.

Later we walked along the beach hoping to come across turtles, either laying or hatching, but although we saw many tracks, and several dancing crabs, we saw no turtles. However for the first time in my life I experienced that rarity of the ocean, its bioluminescence. As the gentle waves broke on the shore, there were sparkles of blue light spread throughout the surf along the whole length of the beach. These are blooms of plankton, usually created far out into the ocean, but will occasionally be washed to the shore to create this wondrous phenomenon. I felt privileged.

Back in camp, in the shadows of the camp fire, Peter snook off with a torch, a spade, a lighter and a roll of toilet paper.

"We know where you're going," chirped Clare.

There are certain luxuries that deserted beaches cannot cater for, and certain embarrassing functions from which there is no hiding place. And in less than one day we had become acquainted enough as a group to begin to take the piss, as it were.

Sur

Up at dawn to swim in the ocean. It feels unbelievably hedonistic to write that sentence. But the sand felt like a cushion beneath my feet, there were the softest of soft waves lapping the shore, the sun was rising huge and warming on the horizon, the breeze was a gentle zephyr, and the sea was like wading into a warm bath. Looking back at the beach there were two white cars and six black tents, the Eastern Hajar mountains in the background, and two men busying themselves cooking my breakfast.

Our morning rituals complete we walked south along the beach whilst the drivers packed up. Presently we came upon a small village, and a number of unkempt but happy children came running to greet us. They delighted in having their photos taken then seeing themselves on the screens. In the background stood several mothers wearing traditional clothing. Some wore the Niqab with a pointed black mask covering their faces, a Batula. It is reminiscent of the visors of medieval knights' armour, and is very rural, worn now only amongst the older generation.

Sadly the children held out their hands as we left, but we could not help them. Previous tourists have given them sweets or money, which encourages begging, both dishonourable and demeaning. Their parents wouldn't have thanked us. You have to be cruel to be kind.

The drivers eventually caught up with us and we drove up onto the coast road and into the town of Sur, which lies on the eastern most point of Oman. Sur has been a powerful port over the centuries, linking this area with East Africa and India, but lost its strategic importance with the opening of the Suez Canal, and the demise of the slave trade. Now its strength lies in building boats, mostly wooden dhow types used up and down the coast for fishing. We visited a boat building yard and its impressive white lighthouse before finding a viewpoint high above the now crashing surf of the ocean. Here we lunched sheltering under the shade of a copse of palm trees.

From Sur to the western most point of the Sahara, at Nouadhibou, Mauritania, is over 5,000 miles. Twice the width of Australia, and desert all the way (if you part the Red Sea). We were now heading inland.

Whilst provisioning for the desert a pump attendant accidentally fuelled one of the cars with petrol instead of diesel. I wondered how we would cope. Back home you call upon the AA, RAC or Green Flag to ride to the rescue. Surely this would be a crisis too far and we would be left stranded awaiting a backward service system to provide us with a replacement vehicle later rather than sooner. They'll have to send a car from Muscat we thought.

Cue a group of tourists hanging around, kicking their heels, tutting over their predicament. Cue Sarfraz on his phone, barking out a series of orders, and in ten minutes we had a perfect substitute Toyota arrive into which we transfer all of our belongings, and off we go. Amazing.

There was one more task to complete. Deflating the tyres by 25% to allow better traction in the desert. "Seat belts on!" urged Clare, seriously.

Thus began our switchback afternoon. Into the desert and we started climbing dunes and slipping and sliding down the other side; slewing across the desert floor, and up and down more dunes. It was a real stomach churner as there were thumps and lurches, squeals of fright and excitement, slides and bounces, with the driver's occasional cry of "Oops!" interspersed with equal portions of laughter and screams.

Several times I'd banged my head off the roof, and stood up almost vertically, desperately trying to apply the non-existent brake under my right foot, or grasped the door handle white-knuckle style, praying not to be flung out. How neither car hadn't somersaulted I'll never know.

We did manage the occasional rest, when one or other of the cars got stuck, and everyone had to get out whilst the other hauled the former out. This happened at least three times, and is why you always venture into the desert with at least two vehicles.

Eventually the fun had to stop, and Sarfraz and Manjit adopted normal driver mode, and we found a campsite about four miles inland.

Surprisingly after sunset the evening grew cool, and fleeces were brought out when we took tea and coffee. At dinner we were joined by an army of scarab beetles, and our lights attracted more moths and other flying insects. Following the meal we took a torchlight walk into the desert and saw many animal tracks; fox, gazelle, jerboa, skink and more. All this was conducted under the most marvellous night sky full of stars and clusters, with the Milky Way flowing overhead.

The cool evening brought in moisture and during the night my tent became awfully damp inside. With it becoming wetter and wetter I found it difficult to sleep. My imagination ran wild when actual snuffling outside the tent turned into imaginary slithering and sliding inside the tent. I was convinced a snake had got in. Unsurprisingly I overslept and eventually emerged to an unsympathetic chorus of "So what happened to the dawn swim?" Thank you Contessa, I was being attacked by a snake.

Following breakfast and ablutions we were driven down to the ocean to frolic in the heavy surf while the sun melted away the grey mist and the village children laughed at our childish antics.

Wahiba Sands

We drove north to cross the Wahiba Sands, or the Sharqiya Desert. It is known as a Sand Sea due to the wave effect of the giant dunes which cross it and have been formed by wind and erosion over millions of years. To stand on a dune and admire its perfect wave peak undulating into the distance is other worldly.

There was a tree, not an especially grand tree, but it did have the distinction of being the last tree for a hundred miles, and so, passing this we drove into the desert. The driving was not dissimilar to yesterday with bumps and grunts aplenty, and the occasional Sarfraz "Oops!" which we had learned always prefixed a sickening, bone crunching, bouncing pitch of the tortured vehicle.

It was soon time to stop for lunch where the tarpaulin was stretched across the two cars to provide the only shelter in the sweltering heat. This was when we ventured from the vehicles and climbed the dunes for the first time. Absolutely stunning views, nothing but golden waves of dunes as far as the eye could see, in every direction.

Later we set up camp overlooking a valley, before the oasis of Al Minitrib. Whilst enjoying a coffee with the sunset, there came the sounds of a commotion in the kitchen area. Investigating the hubbub we found Mandip in a bit of a state. He complained he had seen a scorpion which was now hiding. We began a search and ultimately James discovered the interloper when he lifted up a corner of a blanket. Peter tried to get his size 12's to it, convinced it was a large plastic toy set there by Sarfraz to put the willies up his mate. Confronted by the possibility of being squelched, the creature scuttled away under one of the cars.

That night the meal of soup, curry, rice and melon was eaten in a mood of uneasiness not knowing the location of our friend. Later the torches were scanned wider and latrine holes dug broader in the hope nothing exposed could suffer the cruellest of stings.

The next morning after breakfast and decamp I suggested we raced up and down a dune. Patsy revised this to walk up, rest, then race down.

We gave Sarfraz and Mandip our cameras and walked up to the summit. The nine of us, including the Contessa who was old enough to have known better, stood in a line, held hands, shouted Geronimo, and launched. We galumphed down the soft, steep slope, and convulsed with laughter landing arse over tit at the bottom.

Sadly all of the camera phones had turned off and the boys hadn't a clue how to switch them back on, so the escapade remained unrecorded.

We drove out of the desert. It was goodbye to the golden red and orange sands, and hello to a grey and rocky landscape with lots of examples of obducted oceanic lithosphere formations, according to James, a geologist. This area of the world (like everywhere else, it seems) was once under the sea, hence there are a multitude of sea creature fossils. The lithosphere, beds of limestone, were created by the skeletons of myriads of said animals. Over millennia the forces of plate tectonics forced up the lithosphere to create hills and mountains, hence the obducted, curved shapes evident in the exposed rock.

We came to a small town, Sinaw and stopped to wander its souk and I sampled a mango ice cream. With my background I am obliged to test ice cream wherever I go. It is an onerous chore, but I feel I am up to the task.

On our way to Nizwa we visited a ruined village, bombed by the RAF in 1955. This was not an example of colonial suppression, more a favour for the Sultan. A dispute had arisen between the Sultan who ruled the coastal area, and the Imam who ruled the interior, over who should make the money from Oman's oil reserves. The Sultan requested British help to suppress the Imam's rebellion and we obliged. We still maintain good relations with this country and even the so-called Arab Spring, so fomented by the BBC, had little effect here.

Nizwa

Nizwa is the ancient capital of the country and lies on an important crossroads between the mountains and the sea. There is also a natural spring here, so the creation of a falaj, irrigation system, has made the area an important source for agriculture, specifically date palms.

We checked in to the Falaj Daris Hotel, sampled the first sumptuous bed for four nights (and first real toilet), swam in the refreshing pool, and anticipated sun down with relish. But never have the late afternoon hours dragged so much. It genuinely felt like an age as the seconds slowly ticked away. Finally the moment arrived and I was able to phone down to reception for a truly mouthwatering order.

"Could we have ten large, cold beers, please?"

"Yes sir, it is after sunset, I will send them to you immediately"

I will never forget the look on the waiter's face as I opened the door and he handed me a carrier bag with ten large, cold cans of beer, and he looked up to see the eager, beaming faces of the whole group crowded into my bedroom.

"You wonderful, wonderful little man," exclaimed the Contessa as he fled before she could smother him with kisses. But not before I had asked for a repeat order.

Thanks to Ramadan these were the best beers I'd ever drunk, the first for four days, and a true "Ice Cold In Alex" moment.

The next morning after breakfast we visited Nizwa's famous goat and cattle market. First there were the outskirts, and the goading of the animals off or onto Toyota pick-ups. It was a scene to behold. Imagine stubborn immobility turned instantly into blind panic, then turned back just as quickly. There was much shouting and waving of sticks, and the wide-eyed terror of the poor flailing creatures.

But this was nothing compared to the scenes inside the market. There was a multitude of Omani men, all dressed in long white robes and sporting the colourful, brimless Kufi cap, crowded inside and outside the market circle. Those inside were racing around and around clockwise, driving their steers before them in a circle of frantic showcasing. Add to this the cacophony of noisy bartering as the whirling mass of humanity and livestock swirled about. It was a completely mad and breathless occasion.

We left the market amazed at what we had just witnessed and wandered the souk up to Nizwa Fort, Oman's favourite national monument.

Constructed in the 17th century on a site fortified since the 13th, it has protected the town from multiple sieges. It was built over a spring and has evolved to contain huge food stores and multiple booby traps to ensnare potential invaders, including murder holes from which boiling date oil could be poured onto an unsuspecting enemy.

After a lunch of samosas and fresh dates (nothing so bland and sticky as the "EatMe!" Christmas essential) we visited the village of Jabrin and its castle. Very impressive in itself, but the best were the views over the fertile valley to the Bahla Fort which is so populated with Jinns that superstition forbids foreigners from entry.

Later, following another session of hotel room beers, we walked to a restaurant and ate traditionally. Sadly this meant sitting cross-legged on the floor picking from a variety of bowls, a sort of meze. Nothing wrong with the food, nor the company, nor the service; it is just that I cannot sit like that without falling over. So ultimately, with my back against the wall and legs stretched out in front, I was able to feed myself. It was however uncomfortable, and having to stretch to spoon up portions, I managed to spill sauce over trousers and shirt. Be that as it may, the paneer cheese cooked in a cashew gravy was one of the tastiest curries I've ever had, even if the stains ruined some of my favourite togs.

On our final day together we drove north towards Muscat, first stopping at another village laid waste by the RAF, then a village built into the mountainside which had a perfect example of an irrigation falaj. This is the life giving and life preserving heart of any community. If your falaj dries up, you move on, therefore it is the responsibility of the whole community to maintain the falaj and the harmony of the village.

We eventually came to Jebel Shams, the Mountain of the Sun, and climbed to its southern summit, at almost 10,000 feet it is the peninsula's third highest mountain, and the highest in Oman. With the heat and the scrambling, it was a laborious ascent, but well worth it for at the top there were marvellous views into the canyon below, Oman's very own Grand Canyon. The rocks in and around the canyon were very craggy, with many examples of obducted oceanic lithosphere formations. It was difficult to reconcile that this mountainous landscape was but a few miles away from the smooth sand dunes of the Wahiba Desert, but we did try to do so whilst eating a packed lunch provided by the good people of the Falaj Daris Hotel, sadly now bereft of beer.

There was a three hour air-conditioned but somnambulant drive back to Muscat. It was dark, so we approached a sprawling, glowing city shining with new money and confidence. I felt that this was a country I could definitely work in. At dinner it was time to say farewells to a grand group of people. Sarfraz and Mandip had not only been excellent drivers, but good company (and cooks); Clare had been a wonderful guide, Patsy, Hyacinth, Vincent, Joyce, et al, lovely fellow travellers, but my star had to be Sumi the Contessa, FANY and all.

33

I flew home early next morning.

Turkey's Turquoise Coast

I hadn't been to Turkey since I sailed down the Bosphorus, into the Sea of Marmara and out into the Mediterranean via the Dardanelles and past Gallipoli, in November 1969. It had been a school cruise aboard HMS Uganda, on which I had my sixteenth birthday, and we had already visited Venice, Athens and Istanbul, and were on our way to Crete and our final port of call, Gibraltar.

Istanbul, I'll always remember for the Topkapi Palace, the Blue Mosque, and its markets of fake brands. I bought a gold "Rolex" watch with green leather strap for the price of a pint which served for over 40 years, and saw me into retirement (replaced the strap four times, and then the hands fell off). These were all on the European side, and I do recall that we walked across one of the Istanbul bridges just to set foot in Asia.

This time, and many years later, I flew direct to Izmir, on the west coast of the 90% of Turkey that lies in Asia. This was Anatolia, also known as Asia Minor. A taxi took me to a cheap overnight hotel and I stepped out into the sunlight early the next morning to be greeted by the most hustling, bustling, hot and dusty, atmospheric wannabe European city.

From a chaotic bus station I caught the bus for the resort of Kusadasi. Alighting the bus and everyone was surrounded by excitable "pansyon" owners eagerly seeking occupants, with their well-thumbed brochures thrust into your face. I chose a kindly looking old man who hadn't been badgering people.

With the promise "five minutes from beach", he ushered me out of the bus station and into an old Ford Consul. Haydar drove some bumpy blocks down towards the coast and parked outside a white villa with landscaped open dining areas and a large, blooming vegetable garden. Before I had time to see my room he proudly showed me his tomatoes and peppers. Mrs Haydar, or Mama, as she was universally known rescued me. She wore a light blue hijab, and had smiling, sparkling eyes behind a sunburnt face.

Mama showed me to my room, explained that all her guests took meals together, then led me to the kitchen to introduce me to the huge fridge full of large bottles of Efes beer and the honesty book.

As we were talking I heard a motorbike pull up, and a huge young man jumped up onto the patio to be greeted warmly by his mother. Mama introduced Genghis, an amazingly handsome young man, well over six feet, whose body had had more than a passing acquaintance with the local gym. He reminded me of Khan from the StarTrek movie the Wrath of Khan, played by Ricardo Montalban, but even more chiselled.

"You've seen the beach, Geoff? I'll take you to the beach, leap on the back." he instructed and smiled with a huge row of gleaming white teeth.

So before you could say "beam me up Scotty" I was roaring down the back streets of Kusadasi on a huge Kawasaki with Genghis Khan. Just five minutes away, apparently.

Ladies Beach, as it is called, was horrendously crowded, so I didn't stick around. The sun was such that shade beckoned more sensibly. Before I left, however, I watched something I had never seen before in Europe, the Americas, nor Africa. Turkish women, dressed from head to foot in black robes, bathing in the sea fully clothed. It just seemed weird.

Later after a dinner of meatballs and stewed aubergines, I asked Haydar where his son was. "Oh, he has gone out with his English girlfriend" he answered.

"What is her name?" I ventured innocently.

Haydar beamed, "She has a different name every night".

Also seated around their beautiful marble table were two lovely young Sami women, very pale complexions and both with sky blue eyes and very light, very straight, long blond hair. They assured me they had never herded reindeer and were proud to come from Finland and be called Finnish. They were both language students from the University of Helsinki who bemoaned the fact that Finnish children are made to learn the Sami language as a second language in school, and not English.

"Sami is only spoken by 70,000 people. The world speaks English," they complained.

It was a pleasantly warm evening drinking Efes, chatting with the two Fins, a German couple and some Americans. Mama and Haydar left us to it and between us we put the world to rights.

The next morning Genghis, who looked surprisingly fresh at breakfast, pillioned me to the bus station and I caught a local dolmus minibus to the ruined city of Ephesus, after which the beer is named (Efes). This was one of the aspects of Turkey I admired. Throughout Greece, her neighbour, you can find isolated monuments and temples. In Turkey you had whole cities, and in this one was the Temple to Diana, or Artemis, one of the Seven Wonders of the Ancient World.

Ephesus is 150 miles south of Troy and was once an important port allied to a variety of great civilizations; Persian, Greek, Roman, going up to Byzantine and Ottoman, but by the middle ages the Mediterranean had receded leaving a mosquito infested swamp, which ultimately led to its desertion and ruin. It is remembered now for the letter Saint Paul allegedly wrote to its inhabitants from his Roman gaol in 65AD imploring Christians to get along with each other. The city had a heyday of only 2500 years.

The day I visited was very hot and outside the entrance small Turkish boys hassled tourists with the offer of a bottle of cold water for a dollar. Inside, scrambling around the ruins kept me occupied for most of the day, and although Artemis' temple itself has been all but decimated, the double tiered Celsus library was impressive, as were the whole of the city's streets. I remember finding a live tortoise, probably just a baby at about four inches from head to tail.

It is sad to think that most of these ancient cities were ruined because subsequent generations plundered them in search of building materials. Marble sculptures, it is said, were ground down to make plaster. Those rescued can be found in the British Museum.

That night we all enjoyed a meal of Mama's spiced chicken and potatoes accompanied by balloon bread flamboyantly created in his garden oven by a singing Haydar (...you with the stars in your eyes!). The Sami girls, Anna and Leena said they were leaving for Fethiye via Pammukale the next morning, and I asked if I could join them as I needed to travel to Kas on the south coast.

Haydar drove us to the bus station after a breakfast of cheese and salamis and home grown salad, and helped us buy tickets, and we bade him goodbye promising to return.

On the bus we found the back seat for the four hour journey inland. After a while the conductor sauntered down the bus to check tickets. Never have I seen such a swagger and attempt at haughty disdain. At the front of the bus was seated a Greek Orthodox monk, complete with large beard and huge black hat. He had fallen asleep but the conductor shook him hard by the shoulder until he awoke with a start.

"Ticket" the man snarled, almost spitting the word. The monk proffered the small slip of paper. The conductor snatched it from him, tore it extravagantly and thrust it back to him. We watched agog and thought perhaps the official might have taken a dislike to the Christian cleric travelling through a Muslim country, but we were mistaken. The conductor treated every seated passenger the same. Demanding a ticket with a snarl, snatching it, ripping it with a flourish and thrusting it back. By the time he reached us we were relishing the little piece of theatre, and he didn't disappoint, he even managed the slightest grimace as he administered his ticket tear.

We stopped at the village of Nazilli and bought some drinks and cheese pies for lunch which we ate on the bus. Aware of our responsibilities we gathered the used cans and paper bags and put them into one black plastic bag. When Atilla, as we had named the conductor, approached the back seats, Anna gave him the bag so that he could dispose of it appropriately. This he did by opening the window and throwing it onto the kerbside as we sped by.

As you might imagine, all of his antics led to a good deal of laughter on the bus, well, more Scandinavian giggling, which became subdued when we saw a bear chained to a tree at the side of the road. Used and abused for dancing, we had thought that this least palatable of Turkish traditions had been outlawed and died out.

Turkey, like many countries around the world has a somewhat well co-ordinated transport system. Large buses take people intercity, and at the bus stations, mini buses, called dolmus, are on hand to take people to the suburbs. Such was the case at the town of Denizli. As we got down from our bus there were young boys hanging off the doors of numerous dolmuses shouting "Pamukkale, Pamukkale, Pamukkale!". Everyone came here to go to Pamukkale.

Before we could grab a bus a mature Australian couple approached, "Can you tell us how we can get to Parm-you-car-lay?" drawled the Crocodile Dundee lookalike.

"Oh! Pamukkale," I confirmed, "Just follow us."

There are thermal springs here, and over millennia the calcium rich waters have bubbled up and cascaded down the hillside creating warm pools, and gleaming white limestone deposits as the water drips from stalactite to stalactite. The effect is to appear like a cotton wool castle, which is what Pamukkale means. The hot pools at the top of the hill, in the settlement of Hieropolis are cluttered with submerged Roman walls and columns from when it was a tourist attraction 3,000 years ago. Cleopatra is said to have bathed here. We played all afternoon on the natural slides and swimming pools, one of the most beautiful and unusual natural phenomena I've ever encountered. Sadly the pollution of many years of human activity has started to turn the castle light brown. I believe it is now a UNESCO World Heritage Site. They will protect it by preventing people from enjoying it. It is the tourism conundrum.

We overnighted in a simple 'pansyon' at the foot of the Cotton Castle, and walked back up the limestone levels the next morning before taking a dolmus to the interestingly named ruined city of Aphrodisias next to the village of Geyre. Here is a temple renowned for its orgies (before the Christians arrived), and I was particularly impressed with its circus, or stadium which could easily have held Ben Hur style chariot races, and its theatre which would have witnessed gladiatorial contests. This had been a city dedicated to hedonism.

In the evening we boarded a bus to Fethiye. The road east, whilst being nothing like the expressways of Izmir, had been a well maintained single carriageway taking in villages and arable farmland; a well trod route.

The road south from Denizli, however was a different kettle of fish. Winding through a rugged landscape, barely tarmacked in parts. We wound up and then down in a switchback of parched hillsides. "What are these called?" I asked the driver, no luxury of a conductor on this route. He thought for a while as he negotiated another hairpin bend, "Mountains," he replied disdainfully.

We found digs in a three storey hotel overlooking the harbour and dined in a seafront restaurant where we spotted a huge leatherback turtle grazing the seaweed from rocks between two moored fishing boats.

In the morning the girls took a ten island cruise. I passed as I was soon to board a gulet. Instead I climbed to the Lycian tomb of Amyntas, a fourth century mausoleum carved into the cliff face behind the town. In itself the tomb is impressive with its columns and Gothic facade, not unlike those of Petra, but the views from the cliff out over the town of Fethiye and into the bay itself were magnificent. I could count the islands the girls would be visiting, one of which had apparently entertained Cleopatra. She certainly got around.

Back at the hotel I asked about a local beach, anxious to relax and swim and perhaps snorkel.

"Celis beach is no good for you, very boring, too many spiny urchins. You must take the dolmus to the most beautiful beach in all of Turkey, Olu Deniz."

The near empty bus took me up out of town, turned right through a series of Mediterranean pine groves and then down into the next cove. About 200 yards from the beach the road ran out, and there were one or two tavernas in wooden shacks advertising lunch deals. I followed the dirt track down and found the most perfect little lagoon. This was classic unspoilt beach bum fare. The pine trees shaded the circular beach perfectly, the soft sand led into shallow, warm, perfectly calm water. Olu Deniz means dead pool, and apart from the abundance of life beneath the surface, this stretch of water looked so peaceful.

I strolled around the lagoon, the scent from the pine intoxicating, the shrill rhythmic screech from the crickets melding with the shimmering heat to create the perfect Mediterranean moment. I then swam and snorkelled around the rocks opposite where there was the narrowest of openings to the sea. I shared the water with several turtles and shoals of colourful wrasse.

I'll never forget that first day at Olu Deniz, I've been back several times since and it is now built up with a brightly lit and noisy main strip backed by many large hotels, and people jumping off Mount Babadag to the east and floating down in a tandem harness, paragliding. I've done it myself, my pilot was Sara, a 21 year old junior national champion. The views down to the lagoon and to Saint Nicholas' Island beyond are breathtaking. I know it is high where you start, nearly 6,000 feet, and there should be some sort of adrenalin effect as you jump off the mountain, but you just bob along when suddenly the world opens up beneath you. I was coping very well, then Sara began her acrobatics. I remember a less than dignified landing on the beach, on my backside.

Turkey is famous for its genuine fake shops. At Olu Deniz there is a Saintbury's, Azda, I.idl., Primarni, McKebab, Houze of Frazer and

Harrools (second o and l touching to create a d). All of the restaurants advertise televised sports, bar dancing and live "Tranny" shows, as well as traditional belly and fire dancing. There is a "white" Michael Jackson (his dream fulfilled?), a bald Elvis, and many other tribute acts. At the bottom of the strip you find ice cream vendors loudly inviting customers with a Turkish "Yesss Pleaze", and a wide corniche full of street theatre and excursion sellers.

Whilst you admire the development of the resort, especially for the Turkish economy I regret that the blue lagoon itself is now filled with sunbeds and parasols, there is not an inch of beach to be seen. No buildings, it is a protected National Park after all, but huge swathes of forest cleared for car parks. Fittingly, having paved paradise, the taxis are yellow.

Back in time, and back at the hotel I thanked the receptionist for her recommendation. Anna and Leena returned gushing about their multi-island excursion. They had swam in a pool frequented by none other than Cleopatra, and Anna had found what she thought might be a piece of encrusted jewellery. "It could even have belonged to the Pharoah queen herself," she joked, and when I left the next morning she presented me with the memento. How kind.

The three inch, blue-green artefact has spent many years on my mantelshelf as a reminder of a lovely friendship and a curious moth incident. We had returned for dinner to the same harbour restaurant and probably shared one too many glasses of moon juice, as the locals called their home made red wine. We staggered back to the hotel and bade each other a very good night. As I prepared for bed I could hear the drunken giggles on the other side of the wall then suddenly they both screamed. "Geoff, Geoff, come to help us," they began laughing again, so I knew there was nothing serious.

I quickly donned my boxer shorts and knocked on their door. Anna opened the door. I immediately realised she was wearing nothing but a grin.

"There is a huge moth, look!" and she pointed to the curtain alongside the balcony door. Sure enough a large grey monster was clinging to the material. I looked around for something to catch it and saw Leena lying on the bed as overdressed as her friend and looking up at me pleadingly for deliverance. I gulped and hoped the moth might fly off, imagining the leaping about chaos it could cause. Instead I just advanced towards it, quickly grasped it in my two hands and threw it out of the balcony door. I turned and brushed off my hands.

"Oh! Thank you Geoff, thank you" gushed Anna as she lay down on the bed with Leena. "If there is anything we can do for you?" she slurred and grinned.

"Anytime" I grinned back, and turned and closed the door behind me. "Don't forget to lock it, I might change my mind" I called behind gritted teeth.

I've gone over the incident many times in my mind since that drunken evening, but the dream always seems to end there.

I was thinking of the Finnish girls as years later I showed their artefact to a colleague. "It's probably a piece of coprolite," he assured me. "Could easily have belonged to Cleopatra," he mused.

I was quite excited at the prospect. "How very wonderful. What's coprolite?" I asked optimistically.

"Fossilised poo."

*

I was taking the bus from Fethiye to Kas where I was meeting Kaz for a cruise on a gulet.

Kaz was flying in to Dalaman, then transferring to the Sea View Hotel where I had agreed to meet her around lunchtime.

My bus was a little late and I had some difficulty finding the hotel which I had been assured was in the centre of town within sight of the sea, which proved a little optimistic. However she was there as I breathlessly mounted the steps up to reception, and she smiled broadly, happy to see me. I was similarly pleased to see her as I knew she was extremely nervous about staying on a boat. She is a martyr to sea sickness, and has nightmares about drowning. As you might imagine, she was over the moon when I booked us a week on a gulet.

We spent the afternoon sun bathing on a comfortable shaded double bed overlooking the sea and dined at a cosy restaurant in the town square and I regaled Kaz with my adventures thus far. She hates moths, so I kept that story from her.

We walked to the harbour and boarded Semercioglu 3 the next morning and were greeted warmly by the captain, Circa and his crew of two. The wooden schooner was twin masted with four double, en suite cabins below, next to the galley. Above and astern was a seating and eating area with a lovely big varnished wooden table, and up top a sunbathing area and the bridge. At the prow a ten foot opportunity to walk the plank, and my favourite hang-out for that Titanic moment (the pose, not the iceberg). There was also an indoor area for those cooler nights, and where the crew slept. It had a library of games from Monopoly to Cluedo, cards, chess and backgammon. There was also a Jenga, a tower of alternating wooden blocks from which you have to eject individual blocks without upsetting the whole. How you played that in a rough sea, is anybody's guess.

Our cabin barely had room for us once the cases were in. Had we wanted to swing one, a cat would have been impossible. Being as the cat referred to was the cat o' nine tails of ancient maritime folklore, it may not have been appropriate. We're neither of us into that sort of thing anyway.

We relaxed into our new home as the other guests arrived. Phil and Ali, hotel owners from Harrogate, Toby and Amanda from Surrey and Sally and Paul from the Wirral. As we became acquainted Circa set sail (or to be more precise started up the engine) and we were soon out of Kas harbour and encountering a small swell. This drove Kaz onto a sunbed for the remainder of that day's cruise.

"Stay up top," I advised, "fresh air, sunshine, and face the way we've come." That and the sea sickness tablet she'd taken seemed to do the trick.

Presently our open ocean excursion was over and Circa steered us into a secluded cove and dropped anchor. We were surrounded by grey/white hillsides dotted with green, thorny scrub and blue pine trees. Cicadas screeched, the sun beat down, and the water of the lagoon was turquoise clear. The crew lowered a set of steps from the stern and broke out a selection of swimming aids; floats, fins, masks and snorkels. We got the hint and within minutes were bobbing about in the warm water continuing our getting-to-know-you conversations. The women particularly enjoyed sitting astride the colourful noodles and chatting whilst the blokes swam around the boat then snorkelled at the rocks.

Once our bodies were sufficiently pruned, we left the water, dried off and began drinking ice cold beer to await dinner.

This was some kind of heaven.

Dinner was served; a salad of tomatoes, cucumber, lettuce and onions with goat's cheese, and olives in a honeyed dressing, followed by stuffed aubergine with potato and minced beef, finished with baklava, all accompanied with a full bodied home made red wine. The whole was a classic Greek dinner and we discussed how the Turkish and Greeks detest each other with a vengeance (which stems from the barbarity of the Ottoman Empire, and has continued with the Turkish annexation of Northern Cyprus), yet are so alike in their culture, customs and cuisine. Although you would never tell them that.

In the gathering gloom, a brilliant night sky began to appear, and by 9pm there was a full Milky Way overhead, and the occupants of this boat were playing a number of silly table games; "I'm going to the moon and taking with me" (an object with the initial of your name, and only players who see the connection can also go to the moon), passing scissors which are crossed or uncrossed, but it is your legs that the crossing refers, some silly whoops bunny hand activity which ends with the arms folded, players have to copy but always fail to go as far as the arm folding. There were the guess-who games using post-it notes with celebrities or historical characters, charades with movies or songs, and the inevitable pub-style quizzing. Oh, the mirth. The night gets sillier as the alcohol flows. It is at times like these you have to feel sorry for teetotallers, or worse, designated drivers, who so often fail to see the joke.

People are thinking of staggering downstairs to their beds when Circa produces a bottle of Metaxa style brandy and succeeds in finishing us all off.

Regardless of hangovers, everyone is up around dawn to dive into the welcoming waters lapping around the boat. An excellent way to start the day. A quick towel, clean teeth, and we're ready for breakfast.

Breakfast, especially a first one, is always a slightly embarrassing situation for me. I don't eat eggs. And the presumption, all over the world, is that breakfast means eggs. No other food has such an internationally accepted ubiquity. People look at you (fellow diners as well as waiters) as if you must be mistaken, or worse, mad.

The fact is I have never been able to eat eggs. I'm not allergic, I just cannot stomach the smell ("They don't smell!" Oh, yes they do), nor the texture of the evil little splodges, whether fried, boiled, poached, scrambled or omelettes.

Don't get me wrong, I understand I am at fault here, and I am quite happy to cook with them, my mother loved my scrambled eggs, I make wonderful pancakes (which I do eat), and lemon drizzle cake is my speciality.

I can say without eggs in several languages (sin huevas, sans oefs, senza uova, ohne eier) and my local Chinese takeaway knows me as "Friedricenoegg", all one word.

By way of an apology to Tara, who I mocked for ordering risotto with no rice in Colombia, I once ordered a Spanish omelette with no egg in Germany, and received a wonderful plate of spiced potatoes, tomatoes, onions and mushrooms with cheese.

There is a plus side to this madness. Touching a large piece of wood, I confess that in all my travels around the world I have never had tummy troubles, whilst sometimes watching my fellow egg-eating travellers drop like flies. So, I have this theory....

The table of the Semercioglu 3 groaned with cooked meats and cheeses, breads and fruit, preserves and pickles. Thank goodness they never tried to substitute bacon and sausage with turkey rashers and chicken sausages, awful fare. But what do I know, I can't eat eggs!

Breakfast concluded we left the shelter of the little cove and sailed along the coast until mooring at a lone jetty. Leaving the boat we climbed a hill and came across a whole ruined village with tombs dating back to Lycian times. Exploring and clambering around this magnificent dereliction overlooking the silver sea took well over two hours so lunch was awaiting on our return.

After lunch as we dozed in the sunshine someone put on a George Michael tape, Ladies and Gentlemen, a tongue-in-cheek title based on his alleged activities. It had two discs, "For Feet" and "For Heart". And on the latter I was immediately captivated by the haunting "You Have Been Loved". His melodic voice and the long held soft, silky notes seemed to harmonise our location perfectly, gently swaying on the sea, surrounded by wooded hillsides. So peaceful.

It just so happens another track on the album is "A Different Corner" which is our tune. I met Kaz whilst researching stables where I could have riding lessons. I chose hers for the whinnying telephone ring tone. I could have moved on, turned a different corner, and we never would have met. But I didn't. It was the neighing which captured me. This would have been the most perfect romantic moment had Kaz not looked so green.

And so life aboard a gulet progressed; swimming before breakfast, a land excursion, swimming, lunch, sailing, another land excursion, finding a secluded cove, swimming, drinking, dinner, silly games and bed.

Then one afternoon, about 5pm, we were sailing from Kalkan towards Olu Deniz, opposite Patara beach. My diary entry:

"There's dolphins!" shouted Sally.

There's a moment's hesitation, then a collective realisation as everyone is shaken from their torpor, and we rush to the port prow of the wildly pitching gulet. All thoughts of mal de mer and hanging on for grim death are dispelled as seven sets of eyes scan the blue expanse.

We didn't have long to wait as a 10 foot bottlenose breached about 100 yards away and parallel. She breached again, closer and we could see her as clear as day, her grey sheeming, perfectly streamlined body gliding just beneath the surface. She was so close her eye was definitely trained on us.

Circa rushed forward and began beating a metal peg on the suspended anchor to reproduce their clicking communications. Suddenly she was beneath us and her partner had joined her and there were two bottlenose dolphins swimming beneath our prow, surely two of God's most beloved creatures having graced us with their company.

And there they stayed, occasionally breaking off to breach and breathe and check on our attention for what seemed fully two or three minutes, while we blundered about clumsily trying to locate cameras.

And then they were gone. We stayed, of course, clutching the rail and searching the waves in hopeful, quiet contemplation, counting both our bruises and blessings.

"How often do you see dolphins?" I asked Circa.

"Oh, once, maybe twice a year". We realised how blessed we'd been.

Circa took us to Gocek, and suggested we look around the small harbour town and maybe take coffee to watch the world go by while he re-provisioned (we had hit his Efes stocks rather hard). Walking along the small jetty we came across Phil and Christine Lane who were lounging on the back deck of their tiny yellow cruiser, the FriskyChris, which at only 15 feet looked like the sea going equivalent of a two berth caravan.

With his white beard and bronzed body, Phil looked like a skinny Captain Birdseye whilst his wife put me in mind of a smiling Sue

Barker.

In the course of conversation I asked what had brought them here, expecting a two week boat hire, but their tale was a lot more interesting. They were from Plymouth, and a year from retiring his job as a clerk in the Civil Service, Phil studied for his navigation and sailing competence skills at night school. They bought their boat, painted and named her, and sailed their local waters in preparation. With perfect conditions they chose to cross the channel to St Malo and followed the French inland waterways to the Canal Du Midi, entering the Mediterranean at Narbonne. They had spent the last four years tootling around the Tyrrhenian, Adriatic and Aegean seas, preferring to Winter on this Turquoise Coast, occasionally indulging in the luxury of a few nights in a local hotel whilst FriskyChris was berthed in a sheltered marina.

It sounded the idyllic way to live out a much deserved retirement, but personally I couldn't see how I could turn my back on the grand kids and family occasions, social groups like the rugby club and golf mates, and generally our British way of life (The Pub). How can you have a conversation about the weather when it's always good? I'm still vilified for missing my nephew's wedding because of a cancelled flight from Peru, not being there when the dog needed the vet, and missing England's World Cup final against South Africa when the TMO fatefully cancelled out Mark Cueto's try. Had I been there we would have won.

Anyway, it is very easy to envy Phil and Chris's life in the Levant on a boat, but what about our takeaways, our rainy bank holidays, gardening, fish and chips in Barmouth, evenings in the pub, the Six Nations, Wimbledon, family barbies, riding the horses and walking the dog.

That evening Circa moored us in another secluded cove and rowed Toby, Paul and myself to the shore. We had spotted a craggy hillside behind which the sun was due to sink and challenged ourselves to climb it to see the other side of the island at sunset. It took us over an hour of scrambling, and half way up we found a cave containing the graffiti of millennia.

At the top we couldn't see the other side of the island, might not have been on an island anyway, but what we could see was an incredible panorama. Stretching westward was a range of mountains as far as the distant horizon with the sun sinking behind; wonderful. Looking back down into the bay, our boat appeared a tiny illuminated speck on blue-black canvass . For them the evening had already begun, for us a tricky steep descent lay ahead as it suddenly dawned that it gets dark after sunset. Dinner was delayed.

Breakfast accompanied swimming in the cove and Circa set sail for Gemiler Island This lies opposite Olu Deniz and is the fabled resting place of Saint Nicholas, of Santa Claus fame. It is a beautiful long, narrow island full of the ruins of several medieval churches and related buildings, and we spent a very pleasant morning clambering over the ruins and their rocky surroundings. After lunch I introduced everyone to the lagoon I'd discovered the week before and had been telling them of all week. They had listened in disbelief when I related its beautiful setting. They were no longer in disbelief.

And so our cruise continued on to Marmaris. Thankfully Circa showed us the sprawling tourist trap before heading back across the straight to another quiet bay. We dined within sight of the lights of the metropolis, and loved the firework display to celebrate Republic Day and the memory of their beloved Mustafa Kemal Ataturk, founder of the modern republic. He introduced universal suffrage, education for all, and a form of nationalism which helped align Turkey with the tolerant West instead of the totalitarian Soviets or the fundamentalism of the Arab world, for which his nation would be forever grateful. He also banned the fez, for which Tommy Cooper was also, forever grateful.

We left Marmaris next morning and headed back to Fethiye where we disembarked and said our goodbyes to the friends we had shared the last week. Whilst we awaited our bus Kaz and I wandered the vibrant market place. There was a smelly fish souk, meat stalls with varieties of fly covered carcasses hanging listlessly, vegetables from small holders, doubtlessly organic, souks for clothing and household goods, but my favourite was the herbs and spices souk. Browsing the mountains of colourful powders, we were accosted.

"Mr and Mrs, where are you from?"

The omnipresent question which is almost certainly the harbinger of pressure to buy a carpet or perfume or whatever from "my factory, please just give me five minutes".

"Please, will you take tea with us?" asked the spice shopkeeper.

How can an English couple refuse such a question.

Thus we met two of the most pleasant yet argumentative young Turkish men.

The first asked about my football team as he poured four glasses of steaming hot apple tea. I mumbled something about the Wolves.

"Ah! The best team in Turkey is Fenerbahce," he exclaimed.

"No it is Galatasaray" his competitor from the herb aisle shouted back.

And so it continued while we sipped the most refreshing drink I have ever tasted. A perfect blend of sweet, fruitfulness and thirst quencher. I always have a box in the house for those long hot days of Summer!

"Fenerbahce...Galatasaray...Fenerbahce...Galatasaray..." It was like Wimbledon as the praise for each others' football team went back and forth with laughter and mock confrontation. Each man's chest puffed out in pride, arms gesticulating wildly.

We left with them still arguing and a bag of saffron which cost all of 50 pence.

The journey back to Kusadasi involved an overnight in Bodrum, the least said of which, the better. And when we arrived at Haydar and Mama's 'pansyon' we were greeted like long lost family, hugs and tears and kisses, and they hadn't even met Kaz.

They had completely different clientele than I remembered, of course, and at dinner we regaled them of our adventures "Down South".

Haydar was amazed, "Mostly people come here for just a week on the beach" he announced to all who would listen "You have made Antalya proud," and he smacked me on my back and gave Kaz a hug.

"Where is Genghis?" I asked, keen to meet up with my old buddy.

Mama was serving a chicken dish with home grown vegetables to her guests seated around their wonderful marble table.

"He is in town with his English girlfriend" she announced, proudly.

A Maldives Cruise

When you fly west, to the Americas, say, you go back in time and have time to catch up. Often your sleep is disturbed because you need to go to bed too early and can often awake at midnight ready for breakfast. It can be unsettling, but not as uncomfortable as the jetlag you suffer coming the other way, returning.

Fly east and you are journeying into the future. The next day comes upon you too quickly and you miss out on a good night's sleep. This can take days to catch up and if you are not careful you can miss out on what's going on around you for some time.

This is especially true when all of those wonderful Asian airlines like Emirates or Etihad and many more entertain you with great music, wonderful movies, fantastic food and free booze for the length of the flight.

Leaving Blighty at 6pm, flying for ten hours of pure indulgence (and I've been known to devour up to a dozen quarter bottles of wine before landing) and arriving sozzled at midday can play havoc with the body clock, let alone meeting reps and fellow travellers who have the misfortune of being sober and refreshed.

This happened on our trip to the Maldives and Alan has never forgiven me, nor let me forget how much I let him down by simply being too social on the flight. Apparently enjoying a disco party in first class isn't the done thing.

I had wanted to visit the Maldives because of the country's position south-east of India, out in the Indian Ocean. It is an archipelago of coral atolls, and is perfect for snorkelling and exploring reefs. It also happens to be a popular honeymoon destination, many of its islands being pristine resorts

I had no wish to be stuck on an island however, when a week cruising offers the opportunity to visit many islands. On this adventure, my brother Alan, five years my senior, and head of the family's ice cream manufacturing business, decided to join me.

We hadn't travelled much together. This was his first time out of Europe, his first experience of long-haul luxury, his first journey beyond a single time zone, and come to think of it, his first expedition beyond the Costa Del Sol....ever. This was going to be a culture shock.

It didn't start well. I'd failed to secure anything direct from a local airport therefore we had to travel to Gatwick by train. Four dreary stop-start, chugging hours into Euston, an hour on the murky, unfriendly tube across London, then another hour into Gatwick. No wonder our nerves were frayed.

But we eventually landed at Male airport, midday next day and were seated at the dock just outside Arrivals, awaiting our boat. We were relatively refreshed. I was wondering whether to work hard on sobering up or simply hit the nearest bar to top up.

Ranjeev, ("Call me Bobby") met us, a tall, slightly built young man with a ready smile and a captain's hat. He also wore a white singlet and white shorts. He beckoned a crew member to load the water taxi with our luggage, and we boarded for the exhilarating five minute express to our floating hotel moored somewhere out in the harbour.

Our boat was the blue and white Dhoni, the Gulfaam, a little like a Turkish Gulet, but smaller and much more basic. It is most similar to an Arab dhow, and is traditional to the Maldives. Fellow passengers had also joined that morning and we introduced ourselves to kiwi sisters Anna and Rachel ("G'day, how're ye doin' d'yer like rugby or cricket, we play both! D'ja wanna beer?), Toby from Nottingham, a serious looking bespectacled thirty something, and Alice, a slim kindergarten teacher with a blonde bob, relishing imminent retirement, from Surrey.

As the engines fired up Bobby explained a few boat rules. Barefoot only on board, flush no paper, that sort of thing. He briefed us on meal times, and introduced the crew who were from Sri Lanka, "We can't have a local crew. Their fasting, praying and alcohol avoidance would get in the way"

Maldivians he continued, are Sunni Muslim, quite tolerant and moderate, but strictly adhering to Islamic tenets like Ramadan, calls to prayer, avoidance of pork, and abstinence.

Our cabin was below deck and tiny, barely room for bunk beds and a single wardrobe. I took the top by virtue of Alan's inability to climb, and I had a single porthole next to my pillow. Bathroom facilities were shared.

The skies were clear as we left the harbour, but with poor weather forecast, Bobby set sail for the south atoll to hopefully avoid the worst of it. To our collective joy we immediately spotted a school of spinner dolphins off the port bow. These are smaller than the more common bottlenose but have the delightful habit of leaping from the water and spinning like an ice skater, several revolutions before re-entry.

Bobby explained the nature of the Maldives archipelago as we ate lunch with the Gulfaam ploughing towards Felidhoo. There are 26 atolls making over 1,000 islands, mostly uninhabited, enclosed by a huge coral reef. Some islands are merely sand bars, and none achieve a height over 15 feet, averaging only four feet, making the country uninhabitable due to forecasted sea level rises by 2100. It is not only man made conditions which threaten the country. El Nino phenomena can and do kill the coral, and tsunamis can and have flooded the islands.

There is a population of less than half a million, and the capital, Male inhabits King's Island in the south of the northern atoll. The all encircling coral reef happily keeps out the larger predators like great white sharks and Chinese tankers. At most times the white water created by the crashing Indian Ocean can be both heard and seen on the distant horizon.

We were scheduled to visit several islands and their villages, but mostly we would be exploring the pristine seas, corals and wildlife with mask, snorkel and fins. I discovered we'd also be using doodles, which are worm like flotation devices, as Alan chose this moment to inform me he was not a strong swimmer and had never previously snorkelled.

I was impressed, however, when I came out on deck and saw Alan had climbed onto the roof of the boat and was trying to shin up the mast. In the channel between atolls, there was quite a swell, and the small boat, travelling at top speed, was pitching quite violently. This, I thought was dedication to the task of spotting dolphins. As he precariously reached to the topmost point, I saw him raise his right arm. Then I realised he was risking life and limb simply for a better phone signal. He would be trying to talk to his girlfriend, Nora, back home in Blighty.

We reached the Felidhoo atoll, Bobby anchored in a cove sheltered by palm trees and fringed by the whitest narrow sandy beach, and everyone geared up for our first dive.

The sun shone in a clear blue sky as I entered the warm water. The ocean at these latitudes never goes below 27 degrees, a comfortable warm bath temperature. And immediately I am in a world I know and love. In the silent world beneath the waves there are corals of all shapes and colours, and hordes of brightly coloured fish.

The living corals are iridescent blues and greens, pale reds and pinks, golden yellows. There are onomatopoeic shapes; brain, fire, plate, fan, mushroom and mosaic varieties. Shoaling around are damsels and dominoes. Slightly larger butterflies and sergeant-majors move serenely between the fronds. Wrasses and parrots feed off the corals, and larger grunts, surgeons, unicorns, groupers and puffer fish wander aimlessly. There are barracuda at the surface, cornets and triggers further down. One of my favourites is the Picasso fish, seemingly designed in a cubist studio, whilst the most popular are the clownfish (Nemo's) to be found swimming in and out of the venomous brown tentacles of the anemone.

There are occasional eels, especially the foreboding jaws of the moray, swinging menacingly to and fro. Rays like flatfish, hide in the sand, blue lipped clams await open jawed affixed in the coral. There are graceful angels and maned lions. Tiny, electric blue cleaner wrasses service the bigger fish, and if you are lucky turtles may sweep majestically by.

And all of these are here and you think it is wonderful, and then you find the drop off where the colours and shapes gradually disappear into the dark blue black abyss. I can float above this wonder world for hours, and frequently do.

There is no sound as you bob up and down in the waves, floating. Just the reassuring sound of your breathing, and occasionally, I swear I can hear the whispered golden tones of David Attenborough:

"...as the parrotfish effortlessly nibbles the coral, you can hear it crunch, and it ejects the sand that has been creating the beaches of the world for aeons"

Over the next six days we averaged three dive sites a day. I was always first in and last out, Bobby called me the king of the snorkellers. Extra to the above I saw a reef shark, giant stingrays, a shoal of angelfish that almost devoured me, and huge napoleon fish. We undertook some drift dives where we were dropped off in a current, then picked up a mile or so down tide. Just fold your arms and go with the flow. We dived off sand bars which were actually beneath the surface at high tides, and from islands with five star resorts. At another dive I attempted to follow a turtle and was reminded why I cannot scuba when my left ear blew with a horrific bang at a depth of only 10 feet. It sent me quite fuzzy and the drum wept every night from then on (So much so I worried about the cabin pressure for the flight home. I needn't have). And every so often, between dive sites we would be joined by dolphins. I became a little blasé and sometimes just leapt off the boat to swim with them, leaving Bobby and the rest to turn around to rescue me from my own mad folly.

That first evening we anchored in the little harbour of Felidhoo and walked into the village. There was limited tarmac, just dirt roads between the houses built of local materials, stone coral, palm wood and lime. They were painted ice cream colours and had gardens for mango trees and yams. Mostly life is lived outside, with plastic chairs by the front step for socialising. You only go into the dark indoors for the cool, and to sleep. Children do what children do all over the world, play football in the dirt, and there were tiny shops with dark interiors selling essential goods.

There was a Bodu Beru performance. Excuse my cynicism but this appears to be available wherever you go in the world of tourism. Bobby assured us it was a traditional dance. What actually happened was a great deal of drumming and wailing, followed by frenzied dancing. It all looked terribly staged, and then the poor western observers were encouraged to join in. This was the point at which the rest of the villagers were reduced to uncontrollable laughter with the ritual humiliation of their visitors.

My brother and I remained firmly in the corner, upper lips stiffening according to our British psyche. However, there does come a time in all of these events when eventually I give in, taking the advice often shouted across social media to "dance like nobody is watching". Sure enough I got up to jig with the usual result. It doesn't matter what I try to do, samba, tango, merengue, or even Bodu Beru, I always end up doing the little dance perfected by Hank Marvyn's Shadows, one up, one across, one back, repeat, with jazz hands and an imbecilic smile.

Back on the boat, relaxing under the stars, we chatted over drinks and discovered we had two people at complete opposite ends of the literary spectacle. Rachel apparently devoured books. She loves reading and will happily consume a book a day. Toby on the other hand never reads. How can you possibly visit paradise and have your head buried in a book, is his argument. And true to form, I never saw him take his eyes off the wonderful views that our Dhoni offered throughout our time together.

He did confess later that week that he had read the Harry Potter books. "Well that's quite impressive" admitted Rachel.

"But it's not strictly true, is it?" I challenged. Toby had been speaking with me earlier.

"I've watched all the films on the tele," he announced, "And with the subtitles on, so it's the same thing, isn't it."

There was a pause then Anna, Rachel and Alice fell about laughing.

Alan thought Toby had a point.

I have neglected to mention that another part of our daily routine was tea and cakes served every afternoon at 4:30. Tiffin, I believe it was called in the days of the Raj. Very civilised.

One night I felt quite fatigued but was unable to sleep. I found the slight rolling of the boat and the gentle lapping of the water on the hull very relaxing, but inevitably my night najjers began. I became convinced we would be attacked by vicious pirates, and kidnapped for ransom. So I was out and up on deck for 3 o'clock to admire the full moon. Its light hid most of the stars, but was unable to hide a huge shooting star which arched the width of the heavens. The feeling of solitude out in the middle of the ocean was wonderful, even if pirates were hiding behind the nearest coral island waiting to pounce.

For each dive, Bobby would indicate we were anchoring, and everyone, or all those who wanted, kitted up. This included selecting your mask and snorkel, and choosing correct fitting fins, and readying your camera in its waterproof satchel. We would then jump in, and either Bobby or a crew member would signal to follow. Initially everyone simply played follow the leader, but as we became more experienced at the different reefs, we could strike out on our own to find the best reefs, drop offs, or outcrops. If you floated still in the water the fish would become used to you and just go about their business. If you happened to hover at a cleaning station then the wrasses would identify you as a marine creature in need of a cleansing munch, and come over to nibble at your fingers or toes. If you wanted to create a feeding frenzy and attract all kinds of fish, then nothing works better than squashed banana. They go crazy. But you have to beware, there are some sizeable types, especially trigger fish, which are perfectly capable of taking chunks out of you, let alone a bit of fruit.

On one dive I was treading water waiting for the others when I absent mindedly looked away from the boat. Inexplicably Anna chose that moment to jump in, backwards, and her nether regions landed plum on my head. It was quite a shock as all I felt was a massive bang, and I was sent reeling, deep underwater. Luckily the force had come from the fleshier parts of her ample backside, and although she nearly knocked me out, I managed to splutter back to the surface. I heard her muffled apologies, such are the nature of communications out of a snorkel, and I tried to smile, an expression which was similarly distorted.

The weather was still glorious one morning when after our usual breakfast of curried dahl and chapatis we headed for an uninhabited island. This was where I discovered the popular belief in the desert island paradise is an unfortunate misconception.

Here is the article I wrote following this Damascene moment:

The Paradox of the Desert Island Idyll

We all have images of what a desert island looks like. There's the cartoon image of a small island of sand with the single palm tree and the castaway with ragged clothes and long straggling hair and beard. Sometimes there are shark fins circling, or a message in a bottle floating by. The joke could be "I spy, something beginning with T!"

A little more depth of thought gives us Robinson Crusoe's island with Man Friday's footprint in the sand, or Tom Hanks' Cast Away, a study of isolation and survival, or the black and white original film of Golding's Lord of the Flies with Piggy, Ralph, and the rest of the angelic choristers turned vicious hunters. There have been many depictions of tropical or coral desert islands in books and films, and generally the image is one of an apparent perfect location, the sort most of us seek out for a relaxing holiday; palm fringed white beaches with warm blue sea, and wall to wall sunshine.

In fact, any island on our crowded planet which can sustain life will be populated. Somehow humans will have found it and domesticated it. Even in the furthest reaches of the Pacific Ocean, the most isolated islands on earth are populated. One, Easter Island, lost its people when they foolishly cut down all the trees to help create their Moai stone statues they worshipped. They had religion but could no longer sustain or shelter themselves (that's one theory). Another deserted island is the furthest flung of the British Isles, St Kilda, but this was no-one's idea of a sun kissed paradise. This wind and wave swept island had too small a gene pool, and with no hope of diversity, the whole population had to be relocated to the mainland.

The reality of a tropical desert island is pretty horrific. If the isolation or lack of food and fresh water don't get you, then there are the hidden dangers of these idyllic hideaways; mosquitoes, spiders, scorpions, snakes, and any number of dangerous sea creatures. See Leonardo di Caprio's Beach.

But back to the paradox, the deserted desert islands I have seen in the Maldives and the Caribbean actually suffer from their lack of inhabitants. There is no one to clean the beaches, so unfortunately they become little more than a rubbish tip. It is all our fault of course, we have littered the oceans with detritus, or to give it its lyrical name, flotsam and jetsam. And it is mainly plastic rubbish, because this marvellous invention of the 20th century doesn't break down. More natural litter like paper or cloth or glass or even leather will be broken down by the incessant motion of the sea, and begins to return to some form of natural state. But it still gets washed up on desert islands and becomes part of the rising levels of garbage.

It is plastic, though, which is plaguing our seas. Carrier bags, which I have previously reported colourfully carpeting the shores of Lake Nicaragua, are a problem which the developed world is trying to solve by changing the mindset of shoppers and shop owners. We are using fewer, and we are recycling. Ocean rowers like Peter Bird, however have described the Pacific as being awash with carrier bags. The problem with these is not just litter, turtles mistake them for jellyfish. I once saw a turtle eating a blue carrier in Vietnam, and could do nothing about it.

Other items which can regularly be found washed up on all shores are what the Americans call Q'tips and we know as cotton buds. Used and discarded into toilet pans, there are billions of these plastic sticks scattered throughout the world. I have seen plastic cutlery, bottles of all sorts, throwaway cups, straws, caps, packaging of all types, polystyrene, broken furniture, toys and always, always plastic shoes littering desert islands. Brought in by the tide and gradually moved up the shore, desert islands are awash with mountains of litter in amongst the dead seaweed. As the organic material rots back, the litter, especially plastic, is left; hanging from trees and bushes, filling the cracks between rocks, obliterating the sand, and covering the land. It chokes any fresh water source and causes stagnating pools of rotting mess. There is nothing idyllic about this dystopian reality.

Mankind discovered oil and how it could be used to create energy and power our vehicles and manufacture plastic less than 200 years ago. Since then we have used a lot of it. Whether we have used more than half of it, we don't know. We certainly know there is a finite amount in the Earth, and although we are discovering more every day and can drill for it in Siberia and the Antarctic and even under the oceans, one day it will run out. We can only hope we have harnessed solar, wind and wave power before the fossil fuels run out or life as we know it will become seriously curtailed.

Strange and troubling to think it has taken the earth millions of years to convert billions of organisms which were created by solar power in the first place, into oil and gas; yet it will have taken mankind less than a blink of the eye in geological terms to have used it all up.

But back to our litter problem; by looking at desert islands we can see what all of our shores would look like if we stopped sweeping the rubbish away. It is a fact of life and a very sad one. Sad to think that when I first discovered this desert island paradox, I was visiting some of the most beautiful places on the planet. When will we learn?

Just a suggestion, but should you ever want to holiday in the paradise that is the Maldives, don't go to the island of Thilafushi. Even though it is a tropical lagoon with wonderful beaches and coral reefs, and is probably the highest point of the whole country, it is simply a mountain of rubbish, an artificial island of landfill growing by over 300 tonnes of garbage a day.

Finally we now know that Australia's oceans have been categorised as plastic soup. The stuff can't break down, but can disintegrate into smaller and smaller pellets, so much so, that plastic has now entered the food chain. And where that can lead is scary stuff indeed.

The interior of the uninhabited island we visited today was indeed choked with litter and the centre was a mosquito infested stagnant swamp. We were bitten mercilessly by sand flies. With no inhabitants to clean the beach, the sand at the tideline was a six foot wide line of garbage

The coral reef surrounding it however was the usual wonder world of rich flora and varied fauna. For how much longer?

We had had four days and nights of perfect weather before the wind changed and the skies turned grey and we travelled further south to the village of Dhiggarou which Bobby assured would afford us a sheltered anchorage.

Before nightfall Bobby took his fishing rod in the outboard while we continued to snorkel the local reef. We came back empty handed, but Bobby caught three yellow fin tuna which the crew made into a wonderful meal with rice and salad.

It began to rain as bedtime approached. I played chess with Alan and after three games he accused me of cheating. "You play too aggressively!" he complained. I wouldn't have thought you could play chess anything but competitively, the point being to trap the opponent's King and force annihilation. At least he didn't throw the pieces overboard. We played draughts after that, with no huffing.

By one in the morning a full blown monsoon was in force. There was no thunder or lightning, but the wind and rain were buffeting our little boat. In our bunks we were gripping onto the sides as the pitching of the boat threatened to tip us out of bed. Alan became quite fretful and wanted to know whether Bobby had sent a mayday signal, and when the helicopters were arriving to lift us to safety. I tried to explain that Air Sea Rescue didn't operate 5,000 miles from home, but he became quite belligerent. At one stage I had to restrain him from opening the door to go up on deck. Fist waving, he insisted something be done.

"They've got to send help. They can't leave us here to die!" he shouted.

I tried to reason with him. Out in the remote tropics there is no "they". We've just got to sit it out till morning, I explained, but he collapsed back into his bunk, head in hands, crying "We're doomed, doomed!"

The battering we were taking kept us awake most of the night with Alan frantically listening out for the tell tale sound of the choppers, which of course, never came. A pity, as I would have loved to watch him being winched away. He was the perfect weight for someone 6 feet 4, unfortunately he's only 5 foot 6.

Following the night of the big storm we never again spotted dolphins. As we approached Hilhidhoo reef, however, we did see a squadron of manta ray beckoning with their wings above the waves, and off the beach at Fulhidhoo we came upon a fever of sting rays resting on the ocean floor.

Sometimes after dark the crew would shine spotlights over the stern and and throw in scraps to create a feeding frenzy of fish, some of which were encouraged to join us for dinner. One afternoon we came to an island populated only by a scientific research station. Here we saw a dozen baths containing thousands of clown fish. Was this for research or had someone identified a profit opportunity, exporting Nemos across the world?

We sailed as far south as the Meemu Atoll, calling at islands like Kudiboli and Kuda Anbaraa dividing our time between sun bathing and snorkelling, playing games, or just eating and drinking. Or we would join Toby, endlessly gazing at the enigmatic turquoise horizons, seeing the white ocean outside the reef, crashing like an invading force fruitlessly scaling the walls of some ancient fortress.

We moored for our final evening in the southern atoll on the island of Fenboa Finolhu the crew set up a barbecue on the beach and we played games around the campfire and danced the Macarena and something called the Cha Cha Slide. The Kiwi sisters won all the games, mainly because they made the rules up as they went along and were incredibly competitive. But also as they preceded the playing with a wonderful Haka, all foot stomping, rolling eyes, tongues out and threats to kill and consume their opponents.

Toby and Alice were the best dancers, the teacher having taken a shine to the partially literate savant, and Alan kept scouring the skies in between looking for a better phone signal. I was struggling with both earache and feet blisters caused by sand flies, and to make matters worse I also nursed a broken right little toe having stubbed it falling down the steps into our cabin.

Soon enough it was time to return to Male, and our last dive was on the Embudhoo reef. One more chance to marvel at the colours, corals, and brilliant diversity of life in the ocean. One more opportunity to witness what we are threatening to destroy with our careless misuse of our planet.

On our last night together, over dinner, the conversation turned to Muslim lifestyle. Alan, who had never travelled to a Muslim country confessed he was impressed at the friendliness and the relaxed nature of the locals. Back home Islamophobia was emerging and, as Alan admitted, the popular image of Muslim culture was one of strict religious adherence and intolerance of others' beliefs. He had learned that this was untrue. Brilliant proof that travel really does broaden the mind.

Bobby told us he was married and his marriage had been arranged. His and his wife's parents had come together to choose the best fits for their children. The others believed this was quite medieval and did not take into account the wishes of the children. Bobby defended the practice, explaining that he and his wife were very much in love, and that failed marriages were very rare in their culture.

I had to side with Bobby. "Look at me, I have three daughters and they have all sought out their own husbands. My son-in-laws are perfectly competent," I explained, "but self selection has brought me one from Kent, and two Baggies fans. That can't be right!"

The Kiwis understood the gist, Alan, Alice and Toby realised my tongue was firmly planted in my cheek, whilst Bobby looked slightly perplexed. After all, he didn't drink.

The next morning we left the boat saying our goodbyes and swapping email addresses. We had some hours to kill so had a walking tour of the capital. There were cars and vans, which seemed unusual. On the islands, bicycles had appeared more than satisfactory. The museum killed an hour, but was little more than adequate, with a few interesting artefacts. All in all, Male disappointed, but this is a country lived in the ocean, it doesn't need impressive buildings. Adequacy is all that is required. The best was to just sit in the small park watching life go by. But isn't this the same for all cities.

We flew back in time, and arrived home the same day. But the rail journey back from Gatwick to Wolverhampton was interminable and fraught indeed. An experience to be avoided. It is no wonder we argued.

Finally, I was pleased to have whetted my brother's appetite for worldwide travel. He could now spread his wings further than Spain. He had Africa, Asia and the America's, even Australia to choose from. So where did he go next? It appears he had enjoyed the Maldives so much that he booked himself on the very same trip, later that year, this time with Nora.

INDIA

The Golden Triangle and Goa

"Have you ever had a lady friend, Major?" asked Fawlty, matter of factly.

"Why, Yes, Fawlty," the Major replied with pride, then added sternly, "I must have been keen, took her to see India!"

"India?" questioned an impressed Basil.

"Yes, at the Oval, but she went to the ladies room before lunch, and I never saw her again" added the Major, rather downcast.

I took Kaz to India. Not the Oval, INDIA!

Because of my travels on four continents I am often asked where is my favourite place, so I have had to give the question some thought.

If I have enjoyed one country or trip more than another it was probably because of the quality of the people I met there. I cannot in all honesty point to a place and say it is my favourite. I also cannot decide between natural or man made wonders. Taj Mahal or Iguazu Falls, Angkor Wat or Okavango Delta, Macchu Pichu or Grand Canyon. How can you categorize, must you have a checklist of oohs and aahs?

I have however decided upon three nuggets of wisdom, three snippets of advice, three adventures I would urge anybody to undertake in their lifetimes. They are not in any order, but the opener is the cheapest and easiest to achieve, and will appeal to youngsters discovering the wanderlust.

Firstly, spend time in Paris. Not just the odd weekend, some real quality time. Stroll the gardens, scour the Left Bank, shrug knowingly at the Impressionists, be a Glum, man the barricades, just don't put a lock on a bridge or wear a yellow waistcoat. Live and speak as the Parisians, not even most French have done that.

Secondly undertake a Nile cruise, experience the river that created civilization, and the marvellous tombs and temples created for over 3,000 pre-Christian years. From the Pyramids at Giza, train to Luxor, ancient Thebes, then sail to Aswan. Immerse yourself in the Pharaohs and their gods, and do it on a small boat, Poirot style (avoid being sidetracked with murder mystery). Egypt, the only country with its own Ology.

Finally, and the subject of this chapter, The Golden Triangle; New Delhi to Agra and Jaipur; tigers, temples and mausoleums. This is the sparkle of the jewel in the crown of the British Empire. India, the greatest democracy on earth, its peoples among the richest and poorest, bordered by the Himalayas and its very own ocean, wetted by monsoon, baked by sunshine, it is the most gloriously cosmopolitan experience. You can't do it all, but I beseech you, do the Golden Triangle.

One of the joys of travelling in India is to go by train. Everyone has seen pictures of trains full to overflowing, with people hanging off or even seated on the carriage roofs, and stations crowded with traders which magically fold up on the arrival of a train. I had a friend who travelled the world as a water polo international referee and journeyed throughout India by train. Bramwell Stone, who also played second row, never occupied a carriage, he only ever shared the footplate with the engine driver and mate "You wouldn't get me back there with the hoi-poloi," he used to say. How very Raj.

I had previously journeyed by train on the Shatabdi Express from Delhi to Jaipur, an excellent experience, included in the ticket was breakfast and there was constantly a tea waller dispensing masala tea, sweet and milky and spicy. I recall moving slowly through Delhi and encountering the post nuclear landscape which were the shanty town suburbs. On my left were the blocks of flats the government had built to relocate the shanty town dwellers. They had initially moved in enthusiastically, then moved back to their shacks equally quickly when they realised they had to pay for rent, electricity, and water. The shacks of corrugated roofs were typically higgledy piggledy, clinging to the contours, with their one constant, the satellite dish.

On that trip I had been impressed by the majestic red kites circling above the city and between the buildings on the wind eddies. But in truth these are a pest, spreading disease from the rubbish tips they inhabit, and depositing great splodges of mess.

One had apparently pooed on my foot and a shoe cleaner immediately appeared with the kind offer of cleaning my sandals. It was only later when recounting this tale in the bar, I realised the trickster had created his own splodge of mess, spat it onto my foot, blamed it on the birds and cleverly relieved me of several rupees. Scammed again.

I had also stayed in a city centre hotel with a penthouse pool and bar, and within easy walking distance of the India Gate, Parliamentary buildings and the site of Gandhi's cremation, a large green area of the city, a favourite for picnickers at weekends, and a hangout for youngsters after school.

Some years later, with Kaz, the circumstances would be a little different.

New Delhi

Our adventure began in a cold February at a frosty Heathrow. We had given ourselves plenty of time and had arrived at the airport a frustrating five hours early, such can be the fickle nature of our motorways. The eventual flight was relaxing however, and we managed to sleep before arriving in a hot and steamy New Delhi after breakfast.

The week before our visit there had been a tragic fire in a four star hotel in the city centre. The government displayed the knee-jerk reaction of bureaucracies everywhere, and closed over 3,000 city centre hotels whilst new regulations were formulated, administered, applied for and implemented. Therefore our itinerary had to be hastily rearranged and from the airport the transfer took us on a convoluted drive, eventually arriving at an OYO hotel somewhere in the Delhi suburbs.

During registration we met four mature ladies, friends from Wymondham, near Norwich. I was keen to tell them of my East Anglian heritage. Perhaps too keen, and they thought I was claiming family ties.

"My mother was from Suffolk, Southwold." I told them.

They appeared non-plussed.

"Actually a village near Southwold, Reydon, do you know it?"

Mumbles which appeared to convey "So what!", so I retreated. These ladies were evidently disinterested in any kinship. Kaz thought they were just rude.

So why was a Suffolk girl living in Wolverhampton? Which might also have been what the Norfolk ladies had thought, had they shown any curiosity.

I am reminded of Spike Milligan's autobiography "Adolph Hitler, My Part In His Downfall". My equivalent, as it is for many contemporaries, could have been "Adolph Hitler, His Part In My Existence".

My father had been too young to join the army at the beginning of World War Two, instead he was called up in 1942 when the threat of invasion was all but over. His fallen arches precluded him from the Infantry so he joined the Royal Engineers. Bill Leo (Our Willy, to his sisters) was given the cushy job of clearing the beaches of mine fields which had been laid years earlier, when we feared Nazi invasion. He began the task very much hands-on, but was soon given a team of German POW's who took on the risky task, totally against the Geneva Convention.

As he moved south, around the East Anglian coast, they came to

Southwold, a popular town with the American air force, even then. My mother, Edna, was used to going to the dances with her elder sister, Phyllis, in village halls like Wangford. By the end of the war she was engaged to my father and they wed in September 1946. They remained in Suffolk awaiting dad's demobilisation

My maternal grandfather had been badly injured at the Somme in the Great War, and was profoundly deaf. He had spent this conflict building airfields across the south of England. When he returned to Southwold he secured a position as a retail assistant in the High Street ironmongers, but was on a low wage. My grandmother insisted he asked for a rise, and when he prevaricated she went into the shop to make her point. Grandad was summarily sacked. That sort of thing happened in those days.

Dad was therefore in a position to move his wife and her family to the Black Country where he secured a council house for his in-laws and a job for grandfather at the Star Aluminium. He set about building the family ice cream business with his brother., and that's when I came along.

Southwold is now one of the most fashionable seaside resorts in the country and I have cousins in Beccles and Halesworth. But I'm from Wolverhampton. Had it not been for Hitler...? Now when I visit Southwold, I am just another one of them grockles.

The Grand OYO 6845 hotel was functional, but no more, and I was hoping for much better for Kaz's first experience of India, and my style of adventures. As soon as we had settled in we embarked on an orientation walk. I needed an ATM and we needed lunch. We were on Nehru Place, in an area known as Kailash Colony. The desk had told us there were banks in both directions, so I turned right out of the hotel, and avoiding a storm drain banged my nose on the hotel sign which protruded out into the street five feet above the pavement.

"Don't worry," I assured Kaz, as I stemmed the blood flow, "This is India, this sort of thing happens all the time."

Later we met Paul and Pip, from Devon, seasoned travellers, originally from Kidderminster and Avi, who was to be our guide.

Avi was a slim, handsome young man, only 23 years old, and as he led us to the local railway station he delighted in informing us he was from Pataliputra, from where the Kama Sutra originated.

We were out in the suburbs, and this allowed us the opportunity to use the modern Metro system. The trains were new, bright and comfortable, and the stations were clean with plenty of mop-wielding operatives ensuring they remained so. Our fellow passengers were mostly youngsters, students going into town for a social evening. They were keen to talk to us and the young men insisted we take their seats. Some photographed or video'd us. It was so incredibly different to London's Tube. Each train also had a ladies only carriage, indicating there is still a sinister side to Indian society, but generally, using the Metro was a joy.

We passed exotically named stations. From Kailash Colony on the Violet line, there was Moolchand, Lajpat Nagar, JL Nehru Stadium, Lodhi Colony and Khan Market. We changed to the Yellow line at Central Secretariat and travelled to Patel Chowk, Rajiv Chowk, and we left at Chawri Bazaar heading for Chandni Chowk, in Old Delhi, a labyrinthine maze of tiny streets and alleys north of the 17th century Jama Masjid Mughall Mosque, today's goal.

We had to pass through a sea of people in each souk. First the bathroom fitments souk, then the steel fabrications, left into the wedding invitations souk, past the fireworks, and brass lamps souk, we tried to pause but were pushed onward and onto the steps of the Mosque to breathe and take in that journey. Amazing. The people, hustling and bustling, constantly on the move. You cannot stop to browse, only to dive into a shop. Cyclists and motorbikes weaved their way through, pushing and shoving people to one side, rickshaws delivering and collecting goods, the constant hubbub and aromas of crushed herbs underfoot. Also at our feet, sometimes impossibly high kerbs to trip you up and cavernous storm drains and potholes to swallow you whole. Overhead a Gordian knot of electrical wiring which looks just impossible, but everything works. There is no-one smoking or chewing or spitting; no shouting or road rage, there is no alcohol, just that sea of colourfully clothed people happily getting along with their simple lives.

We arrived at the mosque and climbed its sandstone steps to enter the red and white marbled building by its northern gate. Inside lay a vast square courtyard with prayer rooms situated in central areas under three domes and two 150 foot minarets at the corners of the western facade. Kaz doesn't do heights or steps so we didn't climb the one I had climbed years before for marvellous views across the city, especially to the extensive Red Fort to the east. It is difficult to believe we had left the tiny streets massed with people to enter this huge, almost empty space. It could accommodate 25,000 people.

There were plenty of people wandering around inside, both tourists and worshippers, but the space was such that it was easy to find places for quiet contemplation, and we wandered happily for an hour marvelling at the intricate tiled artwork, all geometric designs, where people prayed. There were separate prayer halls for women.

The mosque was built in the 17th century by Shah Jahan, everyone's favourite Shah, the Taj Mahal (of which more later) was his. The buildings outside we were about to rejoin had been created to house the 5,000 workers used to build this.

Once we left it was dusk, and we descended back into Old Delhi to the brass lamp souk (should we buy one and rub it and see if a genie pops out?) then left into the covered food souks. Wow! If we had thought the crowds before dark to be mad, the swarm we now encountered was even more intense and now we had fragrances from cinnamon, coriander, frangipani and jasmine to invade our senses together with the steam and smoke from numerous cooking pots. Spaces here were even more confined and the stall holders had nowhere to squat but upon their own selling slab.

We came to a right hand bend, and to the left was a stuffed paratha restaurant. Very simple, just tables with benches and white tiled walls. Every space was taken, and people were queuing to go in, but the queue went down quickly and soon we had been squeezed onto benches at the back of the shop. The menu, written on the wall was simply a choice of what you could have, stuffed into your paratha. In the centre squatted two old men who spent their time kneading and rolling out the circles of dough. Various fillings were applied to each bread which were then thrown into a deep fat frying wok.

Avi interpreted the fillings, cheese (paneer), cauliflower, spinach, aubergine, onion, chilli. I opted for a cheese and a chilli "Are you sure?" warned a concerned Avi, who was probably unaware of the prevalence of curry restaurants and sweet centres that make our high streets so wonderfully multi-cultural. "Oh yes!" I replied knowing I could easily be hoisted with my very own petard if the chillis prove to be extra hot. As it happened, they were fine, in fact, less hot than I was used to.

As our bread cooked, a naafi style metal tray was placed in front of you and another elderly gent carrying buckets full of food ladled chutneys and vegetable curries into the various compartments, and then your parathas arrived to spoon them up with. Delicious. Fast food of the very best kind, all for the cost of a few rupees.

We left and found a main street where there was motorised traffic. Avi was very proud of this street, showing the religious tolerance of this nation. Here, he explained is a mosque next to a Hindu temple, across the street is a Sikh temple next to a Christian church and further down another temple to Jainism.

Avi led us to the Sikh Gurdwara where we first had to take off our shoes and pass them through a hatch to an army of volunteers who were busy cleaning and polishing all visitors' footwear. More people dressed us in scarves and robes, and Avi led us into the prayer hall where a stereotypical old guru with flowing grey beard was singing verses from the holy book. Subtitles in Hindi, Punjabi and English were relayed on huge screens recommending we follow the path of saintly godliness. We were then shown the kitchens where more volunteers were filling pots the size of dumper trucks with food, langar, cooked for every visitor and worshipper,. Having recently eaten

I was inclined to decline the invitation to partake of a tray, but that would have been disingenuous, instead, sitting cross legged and leaning back against a pillar (or I would fall over) I received the offerings, a sharing of God's gifts; dahl with chapati and a sweet white semolina called karah.

We left, returning our robes and collecting our clean shoes. It was a short walk to the metro, and we appeared to travel back with the same happy youngsters we'd met earlier.

Arriving at our Oyo hotel, Kaz enthused how she had been overwhelmed by the whole happy, relaxed, welcoming atmosphere we had encountered. She had found it difficult to comprehend how massed crowds of humanity could be so friendly and accommodating. We all felt humbled.

As we readied ourselves for bed, Kaz with a marsala tea, me with a cold beer, she confided to me "When they put the orange gown and turban on you in the Gurdwara" she whispered quietly, "you looked a right wazzock!"

Early the next morning after a distinctly average breakfast, we left the Oyo hotel on route to Agra. Our bus was a 16 seater for the eight of us and we were separated from the driver's compartment by a glass door. The driver and his mate occupied this cockpit and Avi was lording it in the back. India doesn't have a class system like us, they have a caste system. The upshot is their society works just the same. In every way of life people know they're place, as we were to later discover when we met the wedding planners of Goa. Everyone is beneath them.

We didn't actually leave Delhi until after lunch, there were so many places to see. First Avi took us to a stepwell or Baori. These used to be common all over India. Put simply, instead of a hole in the ground into which you throw and haul up a bucket, water is located and steps built down to the level. From ancient tribal gatherings, a whole system of superstitions grew up around the Baoris. Gods are associated with water, so shrines would be built into the sides. Then they would become meeting places for women, not least because in the shaded

Baori, the air was cool. Men did not like the gossip that was encouraged, neither did the British Raj as collections of people could lead to revolt. The wells could also become dangerous, people slipping into them and drowning in the dead of night, so stories of hauntings would surround the Baori to frighten especially children from using them. Many were subsequently filled in, and few exist today. Those that do are mostly of architectural value, or for tourists.

Humayun's Tomb was our next port of call. The first so-called paradise garden burial for an emperor, with many domes and minarets and geometric designs and cool rooms leading to inner sanctums. By looking at the ceilings you can see the remainder of painted, colourful decorations and can imagine how wonderful these looked when first created five centuries ago.

The tragic Qutub Minar was next on the list. A pattern was beginning to emerge. Avi's main concern was toilets, and knowing how important these can be for the women, he always pointed out where "beautiful" toilets could be found. Kaz informed me there was very little beautiful about them. Queues, stinking, squatting over holes, filthy, and you have to buy individual sheets of paper as you enter. Of course, in many places in India, urination and defecation in the street is still common place.

Then there was the farce of the ticketing. You begin by entering the patting down security zone (separate lines for women) where your bags are also checked. Then, having scrutinised the impossible-to-understand pricing system, you buy your ticket from the official housed behind a miniature dark window. A pristine ticket is issued which is then ripped by the official at the next window before being exchanged for a magnetic disc from yet another officer. Time for another security patting down before giving your disc to the attendant whose job it is to present it to the turnstile which hopefully opens. Once inside, just for good measure, there is another security station to pat you down and examine the contents of your bag, which could well have changed since the last check nearly ten minutes ago.

And so inside the Qutub complex, at the centre of which is a tapering five storied minaret, 240 feet high, with a history involving earthquakes, lightning strikes, cupola follies, and hauntings which have caused at least one suicide.

There are 379 steps spiralling to the top, and in 1981 the internal lighting failed causing a stampede and crush killing 47 people, many of them schoolchildren. Inside is now closed.

One of the things we really enjoyed walking around these sites were the many cheeky green parakeets screeching and swooping to crevices in the buildings, chipmunks nervously running from tree to tree, and the macaque monkeys scampering around in family groups.

The mysterious Iron Pillar of Delhi also stands in this complex. No-one really knows who, how, where or why it was created but King Chandra is a favourite, over 16 centuries ago. It could well have been relocated several times. It is famous because it does not rust, proving the quality of the materials and the forgers who created it. Erich Von Daniken of "God Was An Astronaut" fame claimed it must have been made by extraterrestrials, something he retracted in later life. Suffice is to say it is an iron pillar, and it is mysterious.

We left the Qutub and drove past India Gate, a sort of enlarged Marble Arch, and the site of Ghandi's funeral pyre, before stopping in a suburb which could have been Kensington, for a really overpriced curry. I had to visit an ATM for rupees.

("I'm going to India. Thought I'd better let you know." I had phoned my bank the previous week.

"You no longer need to tell us that you are going away," insisted the young gentleman on the other end of my designated Premier Hotline. "Our algorithms can sort out any anomalies" he reassured.)

That conversation came back to me as I was refused cash from the third ATM I visited that afternoon and received a text message informing me my card was being blocked as it was being used in India, and if that was me, I was to message back the word "YES". That was all well and good, but my phone had used up my credit and buffer zone and wasn't allowing me to message anybody. I can't remember how I got out of that pickle, nor do I really understand how I got into it, but it was clear the bank's algorithms had no idea how to sort out my particular anomaly.

And so we set off for Agra, and the further we left Delhi behind, the more and more litter we encountered.

I'll try to avoid generalisations as I attempt to describe Indian life.

Leaving the cities you find a village or small settlement about every five miles. In between there are fields of crops, and in the fields are women; planting, tending and harvesting; fetching and carrying. Other beasts of burden might include oxen and camels.

In the towns and villages there are immaculately uniformed children going to and from school. They're not regimented, they laugh and play and socialise as they go. On the main streets there are shops and market stalls nearly all staffed by men. Young mothers and older women will be picking over the produce. Young and old men sit around in the shade chatting and no doubt putting the world to rights.

There will be camels stood with their carts, cattle roaming freely, goats grazing and dogs snoozing. The industrious animals are the pigs, whole families of them busying themselves consuming any discarded rubbish. That is why pigs aren't eaten here. Their job is to clean the streets thereby making themselves unclean. The conundrum India now faces is that the rubbish problem has outgrown the pig population.

In the olden days, paper, cardboard, food scraps, excrement and general waste was cleared up by the pigs. Glass and metal could be recycled. Now there is too much plastic; from packaging to bottles, shopping bags to polystyrene cartons. Neither the municipal trucks nor the pigs can cope. Where there are people the streets are carpeted with litter. You might have a nicely painted and tidy little house here, next door to a similarly trim bungalow, but the space in between is choked with litter, and this is nationwide, and dare I say it, worldwide. We can no longer cope with all the plastic we create.

Then you look behind the main street and see the dilapidated buildings, the flaking paint, the overgrown gardens, broken fencing, abandoned rusting hulks of farm machinery, fallen walls, jagged holes where doors and windows once stood, every inch gone over to litter and you have to ask; Is India beginning to lose her pride?

Agra

Nevertheless we arrived in Agra and checked in to the Amar Hotel. There are little niceties. The doorman dressed in semi-military, a proud Sikh, gleaming, beautifully cut clothing and fantastically moustachioed, stands to attention and salutes our entrance as he holds the door. Inside a pretty girl in a pink sari Namaste's our welcome, bows and puts garlands of flowers around our necks, and a young suited gentleman offers us cooling, refreshing fruit drinks. The Amar is very different from the functional Oyo, but they are refurbishing and the pool is out of action. Not so the bar, and such had been the length of our day, that was all that was left to enjoy.

We were in Agra to see the Taj Mahal, the most beautiful building in the World. How on earth can a simple scribe like me attempt to describe something as sublime as the mausoleum that the Shah Jahan built for his favourite wife, Mumtaz, who died aged only 38 at the birth of their 14th child.

I had seen the Taj Mahal 20 years previously, when I was privileged to witness a formidable thunderstorm with lightning forking all around. I passionately believe everyone should strive to see it and that is one of the reasons I had returned with Kaz.

We woke and were away before dawn. Only electric vehicles are allowed within three miles of the grounds of the Taj Mahal to protect it against pollution, and we were driven to join the interminable queue extended by all those levels of officialdom. It is refreshing to see that only about 10% of tourists are foreigners like ourselves. The vast majority of people wanting to see the Taj are Indians.

You enter the complex from the south, walk west along a crenelated corridor to the main gate, then turn to your right, and there she is. The facade so well known worldwide. There can only be a collective jaw-dropping sharp intake of breath as the people around you gaze upon this most seductive of creations. On my first visit I wept in awe at this moment. I looked to Kaz. She had a dreamy smile, her eyes wide and bright with wonder, and an almost holy countenance, a halo of gold. You have to spend time drinking in this moment. We did, together.

As you come down to earth you are struck by its perfect symmetry (there is a working mosque on its west side, and opposite a perfect copy, previously used as a guest house, but constructed solely for that symmetry). It is a shimmering white, a slightly imperfect creamy white which reacts with the sky beyond to produce an ethereal, ghost-like apparition. The gardens to the fore would have delighted Capability Brown, the dimensions of the lawns, hedges and pools in perfect harmony. And there is Diana's bench, on which she posed alone and wistful, a metaphor for her approaching divorce.

Essentially you are looking at a decorated dome atop an adorned building with towered minarets at each corner. There is now an overwhelming desire to reach the building. It is a pity as the gardens in between deserve much more attention, but you promise yourself you will do that on your return. At the foot of the stairs up onto the forecourt you have to put on jay-cloth shoe coverings, then you ascend and can finally rejoice at the intricate decoration of every wall, ceiling and archway. The floral designs made up of a semiprecious stone inlaid to the marble are known as *pietra dura.* You finally enter a huge gate and find yourself alongside the raised tombs of Shah Jahan and his wife Mumtaz. The Shah outlived his wife by 35 years, long enough for him to have her (their) mausoleum built, and for their son, Aurangzeb to depose him and imprison him for his last five years in Agra's Red Fort from where he had a view of this, his great creation.

Having seen and been inside you can now relax and wander around and drink in your surroundings. My favourite aspect of the Taj Mahal is the Yamuna river that flows at the rear. There are herons fishing, cows cooling off, and women washing the family clothes. Stretching from the far bank are green fields of crops, and in the distance to the left a line of traffic heralding the entrance to the old city of Agra and the Red Fort itself.

We strolled around marvelling at the architecture and the artistry and the sheer beauty of this wonderful place. At every angle throughout the gardens and approaches you look up and gasp at the white majesty that adorns every inch of the Taj Mahal.

Eventually and reluctantly we dragged ourselves away and returned to the hotel for a very late breakfast.

The Taj Mahal is impossible to follow, but we had a full day ahead of us. We drove to what is known as the Baby Taj or "Jewellery Box". Located anywhere else it would be acknowledged as a uniquely beautiful edifice. A forerunner of Humayun's tomb in Delhi, it was built as the tomb of Mumtaz's grandfather, known as the Pillar of the State (I'timad-ud-Daulah) and is believed to be the introduction of Pietra Dura. Here of course there are no crowds.

We lunched in a restaurant garden then visited the Red Fort. I was excited to once again see the Peacock Throne. It was pleasant to be in the land of the living. We learned about the blueprint for what we would call a Maharajah's castle. Firstly, of course are the defensive walls and ramparts with towers and ornate gateways, often surrounded by a moat, here provided by the Yamuna River. There is an approach from the river, across a wooden drawbridge, and the Hathi Poi, the Elephant Gate flanked by two life-size, stone elephants. Following a twisting alleyway designed to stall invading armies, there is the main courtyard, the first of three where the public were allowed to gather, socialise and trade. The next, smaller courtyard was where the Maharajah would hold court and where the people could petition him their concerns and disputes, and where the Maharajah could be entertained. Here were also places of execution usually trampling by elephant. Many historic buildings; temples, stores and domiciles surrounded these courtyards, including the harem where the concubines could secretively peer down at the proceedings and entertainments.

Finally the inner court for private entertainment containing a library and the Maharajah's residence. Only the Maharajah, his wives, immediate family and the harem were allowed here. Maharajahs, of course could take many wives, but in an attempt to appease their people they would always take at least three, one Hindu, one Muslim, and one Christian. We also learned the origin of hiding the faces of wives behind the veil. Quite simply it was to prevent them being coveted by visiting rulers who otherwise might go to war to steal their beauty. You may think it an uncivilised practice, but think, if Helen had been veiled , all of those wars between the Greeks and the Trojans could have been avoided. (Mind you, we would have lost so many stories of heroes such as Achilles and Hector, the epic Iliad and the adventures of Odysseus, proverbs 'beware of Greeks bearing gifts', famous lines 'the face that launched a thousand ships', and innumerable tales of wooden horses and vulnerable heels).

We wandered around and around, especially the inner sanctum. There was a marble fountain and a beautifully carved octagonal room from which apparently Shah Jahan wistfully viewed his wife's mausoleum, but we could not find the Peacock Throne.

We asked about it and were informed it had been plundered by the Persians in 1739, and that a replacement had only existed until the mid eighteenth century. From the original throne, via a circuitous route, the Koh-I-Noor diamond had found its way into our Crown Jewels. A coveted spoil of war

I wondered why I had this recollection of having seen it, then later we saw a beautiful tapestry embroidered with the throne on the wall of a local carpet factory. Priceless, we were told, not for sale. (How about if I called it a spoil of war? Swap you for the Elgin Marbles?)

Our incredible day in Agra wasn't yet over. In the evening we had secured tickets for the theatrical performance of the creation of the Taj Mahal, the love story of Shah Jahan and Mumtaz. This was a piece of pure Bollywood. Singing and dancing to a sitar orchestra, a sound and light show of innocent melodrama. Via headphones the story was relayed to us in clipped English, the voices imported directly from the

Noel Coward school of acting.

This magical day finally ended after a rooftop dinner. I haven't spoken a great deal about the cuisine we had been experiencing. Suffice is to say that we ate curry, three times a day.

We left the litter strewn streets of Agra after yet another battle with the ATM's and headed west for the almost mythical deserted city of Fatephur Sikri. Founded by Akhbar the Great in 1571 it was to be the capital of his Mughal empire but fell into disuse when according to legend the water source dried up.

Akhbar's son Jahangir was born in the village of Sikri, a peaceful site some 25 miles from the bustling Agra, on the shore of the Yamuna river. For this reason and to celebrate his victory in Gujurat, Akhbar built Fatephur. He lost interest when he left to campaign in the Punjab after about 15 years, and 20 years later the whole place became abandoned.

Jahangir was the father of the Shah Jahan who built the Taj Mahal.

Like all royal cities, it is made up of three major courtyards, reached through elaborate gates. Mainly sandstone with marble floors, many of the fine buildings were restored during the Raj and it is now populated by monkeys, guides and hawkers. There is a small walled, rather stagnant lake here, and one guy earns his living by stripping off and diving in for a few rupees. To be fair, he makes sure he collects his fee before his performance.

We enjoyed the five storied Panch Mahal Palace built for the ladies of the court, and the Salim Chisti tomb within the Jama Masjid Mosque, but after three days of tombs and palaces, we were beginning to feel a little blasé about them. What we enjoyed most were the beautiful views down onto the scorched Sikri plain which surrounded us.

Near the Sikri plain is the town of Bharatpur and the Keoladeo National Park, an important bird sanctuary. I had rickshaw cycled through both 20 years ago and remembered seeing many fantastic birds, animals, and beautiful flora in the wetlands park, and enjoying the fort and markets in the town. Sadly the park is now off the tourist trail as the floodwaters from the Yamuna have failed, leading to a dramatic fall in the migratory bird species. That of course has affected the tourist trade in the town. I had also stayed in the penthouse of the four towered Maharajah's hunting lodge, as big as a palace, in the Sariska Tiger Reserve, and enjoyed three game drives. I saw monkeys, deer, gazelle, jackals and again beautiful birdlife. But no tigers, they had been forced out of Sariska, the tourist economy following.

Karauli

We drove to the town of Karauli and our next hotel, the Bhanwar Vilas Palace. This was a former royal summer house, with an entrance hall full of stuffed animals and walls covered in historic photos. Above the tiger, were games of polo, besides the antelope heads, cricket teams, and next to the leopard, a hunting party. It reeked 18th century with its ornate, velvet sofas. Our room had a huge four-poster bed and a bathroom of antique ceramics.

We relaxed in the sunlit, manicured courtyards drinking beer before being gonged in for a sumptuous dinner served with colonial style. We were seated beneath ornate chandeliers amid surroundings of grandeur, chatting, when the storm broke and we had to scurry off to bed. The thunder and lightning crashing all around.

A cool misty morning greeted us, but it had brightened up after breakfast and we were given a guided tour of the grounds. In the gardens were lapwings and peacocks, and these led us past old tanks from a failed trout farm and to a vegetable patch and wheat fields. Then we saw a line of dilapidated garages. Creaking open the doors, we were presented with a cornucopia of vintage vehicles. First there were toy prams and tricycles, then toy pedal cars, and finally the real thing. A Buick and a Rolls Royce, both circa 1930, and both dull, dusty and unloved.

Back out into the sunshine and we came to the working farm of horses and cattle. Avi explained the real reasons cattle are deified and not eaten for their meat. The dung is used to create gas to power generators, dried, it is used for the walls and roofs of buildings. Milk creates a variety of dairy produce; butter becomes ghee for cooking, cream is used in lassi, yoghurt for raita, and cheese in the form of paneer, makes for an excellent curry. But it is the cow's urine that is used as a panacea of all diseases. According to the International Journal of Pharmacy and Pharmaceutical Sciences "her urine is a divine medicine used to treat diabetes, blood pressure, asthma, psoriasis, eczema, heart attack, blockage in arteries, fits, cancer, AIDS, piles, prostate, arthritis, migraine, thyroid, ulcer, acidity, constipation and gynaecological problems". It fertilises the land and can be used as both a pesticide and larvicide. Finally, consumption of cow urine maintains the balance of all substances naturally present in the human body. In this way it "helps cure incurable diseases".

It would appear our western medicine and pharmaceutical practices are falling somewhat short, perhaps missing a trick.

From the farm we walked into the small town of Karauli and behind the main street to a patch of land which housed the camel market. Being tourists we were constantly harassed by child beggars, but enjoyed the hubbub. I had never previously seen pimped camels. Elephants have been painted and decorated for thousands of years, but these camels had areas of their flanks and long necks shaven and blue and red geometric patterns painted on them. These wonderful creatures were personalised, not as beasts of burden, but as pets.

We strolled from the market place into the town. There was one main avenue running downhill, and a couple of streets crossing it. These were all very narrow, and at one cross roads, there was a tiny square which appeared to be the heart of the town. Amongst the crowds of shoppers were pigs, cattle and dogs rummaging for scraps in the water channels cascading down the hill. Wooden hand carts carried mountains of fruit, vegetables and herbs; butchers hung meat covered in flies; there were haberdashers and clothes stores, little workshops where traders were busy at their sewing machine treadles, fabricating metals, heating and stretching resin for jewellery or forming household tools from bamboo and wood. For some shopkeepers their store was a simple sheet of cardboard bearing cigarettes or mobile phones as they squatted adjacent. The smoke of the workshops mingling with the steam from the cooking pots had beams of sunlight arrowing through. The heat, the smells, this was an atmospheric, heady scene, all helped by the cacophony of honking tuk-tuks, mopeds and bicycles. They weaved their way through the people, adding to the general pandemonium.

Eventually we left the bedlam behind and made our way back to the hotel for lunch. Quite a morning.

Avi had arranged a treat for us in the afternoon. Highly embarrassing, he had hired a number of farmers to take us back into town sitting on carts pulled by camels. Lovely to see the pimped camels again, and highly amusing to watch some of the larger ladies heaving themselves up onto the carts with the aid of strategically placed helpful hands. But the ignominy of travelling thus.

We were taken back into the town and up the hill, waving at children and adults alike who happily and innocently returned our waves with not an iota of irony.

Beyond the last shops we came to a small Maharajah's royal palace. This was wonderfully preserved living museum with courtyards, living quarters and dining halls just like its larger cousins. Curators were pleased to see us and in the Maharajah's and Maharani's quarters showed us artefacts and furniture beautifully displayed with ornate pillars and mirrors. Like all palaces there were families of monkeys playing and cavorting throughout the outbuildings. I was able to take myself out onto the roof and had a marvellous panorama of the hills and countryside around, but moreover onto the red tiled rooftops and white marble towers of Karauli. I could see a mosque, a school, a hospital, a Jain temple, and to my right, at the very top of the hill, as the sun lowered in the sky, a Hindu temple. Rising up from the town were the sounds of sitar music.

Avi beckoned us down from the roof and took us to the Madan

Mohanji Temple, dedicated to Krishna, the god of tenderness, compassion and love, an avatar of Vishnu. Karauli is a Krishna town. There was a foreyard where our camels waited patiently chewing cud to our left, and to our right the entrance to the temple, which was quite plain. I have seen many Hindu temples and they always have dancing colourful statuary in amongst decorated pointed archways and gates. This was different, just a doorway into the building beyond.

We entered a dark hall and heard the fast four-peel pattern of the temple bells. We rounded a corner and the temple floor opened out, full of worshippers. The throng were stood facing five doorways, two were open revealing large, blue and gold, seated Krishna statues. There was chanting and clapping, but it is low key. Some people were kneeling, others prone, arms outstretched on the floor. Others on the outskirts chatted, and children were running around oblivious.

Suddenly, as the peel of bells changed, everyone rushed to the right window. Some stretch out their arms, and others clap in time as a brightly dressed priest appeared. He is holding a round tray of candles attached to a chain. He waves it back and forth and the worshippers swayed in time.

Looking around I noticed that most of the men have yellow paint on their foreheads, temples and cheeks. The women were in brightly coloured saris, their heads covered, but all sporting a red bindi above their noses, often extending up into their central parting.

After a few minutes of waving lighted candles the priest moves to the left window statue, and the whole congregation move with him which signals another change in peel pattern. Finally the priest moves to centre stage and as everyone rushes forward, arms outstretched, he dips his hand into what appears to be a bag of sherbet and flings the contents over their heads in several exaggerated gestures. He shakes the dregs onto the people at the front which appears to signal the end of the service, and the congregation began to disperse.

As the crowd thinned I saw a slight man squatting centre floor with a drum and a bag full of bells which he emptied out. Five women join him and he gives one the drum, and the others take up the bells. They begin to play and chant tunefully. More women join to create a circle, and the man gets up and leaves. Soon there are over 100 women sitting, swaying and chanting. Two get up and smile and beckon to Kaz. They hold her arms and lead her to the centre where she sits and joins them smiling happily. The women, including Kaz continued to sway and chant contentedly for some minutes. It was a scene of pure and simple devotion to sisterhood. This was their moment.

Later I asked Kaz how she had joined in, "I just doo-be-dooed," she confessed, also declaring the experience to have been extremely spiritual, "It has to be one of my most special moments ever!" she grinned.

We drove back through the town on the backs of our camel carts. The final indignity was being photographed by German tourists as they revelled in our embarrassment.

That evening over dinner we discussed the nature of Hinduism, a fascinating religion. There are in the region of two million gods and goddesses, give or take the odd deity, which means most people can have pretty much one to themselves covering their own particular needs. In essence there is a triad of main gods; Brahma being the creator and therefore the father figure of all the gods, the Zeus or Apollo. He is often seen with four faces

Vishnu aka Krishna is the preserver of all that Brahma creates and with his wife Lakshmi, who represents wealth and purity, they are two of the most popular of the gods. Shiva is the destroyer, but not seen in an evil context. One of the main tenets of Hinduism is re-birth and reincarnation. Without the power of destruction, that all important re-birth is not possible. Just as grasslands and forests need fire to destroy the old and decaying, giving new growth the chance to keep them healthy, so the grim reaper is seen as the harbinger of creation.

So the world revolves around Brahma, Vishnu and Shiva.

Everyone's favourite god however is Ganesha, the boy with the elephant head. As the patron of arts and sciences; intellect and wisdom, he is revered everywhere, and all towns bear his shrines.

The Mahabharata and Ramayana are two epic sanskrit poems which together make up the Hindu Itihasa, what Christians would call scriptures.

We left Karauli early next morning for Ranthambhore and our chance to spot tigers. I had been here 12 years previously on a specialist five day safari trip from which I learned all tigers are named Roger. Here are my recollections:

Ranthambhore...Number 10

Two hundred and fifty miles south of New Delhi, in the desert state of Rajasthan, lies the town of Sawai Mdhopur, an important town in its own right, with a major rail junction. It is famous however for being the gateway to Ranthambhore National Park, nearly 100,000 acres of hilly, tropical dry deciduous forest, which rises out of the surrounding arable plain like an eruption of Scottish Highland. It is a Narnia of woods and rivers and streams and lakes, of bushland and rocky terrain. At its centre lies the impressive fortress which bears its name, and here roam sambar and chital (spotted dear); Indian gazelle, nilgai and wild boar; hyena, leopard, sloth bear, and the marsh crocodile. But of most importance, and the phenomenon which allows this remarkably beautiful region to remain wild, uncultivated, and protected; the Bengal Tiger.

There are more of these extraordinary big cats kept as pets in the USA than remain to roam wild throughout Asia, where they are still in danger of predation by poachers seeking to sell parts as aphrodisiacs to the sadly impotent Chinese market.

In February 2007 only 25 big cats roamed Ranthambhore where a whole tourist industry has grown up around safari and the vague promise of a glimpse of these magnificent creatures.

I watching televised cricket from my hotel room in the evenings, and lazed around the pool in the midday heat. I visited the fort one lunchtime when a Hindu wedding blew everyone away with their cacophonous drumming and frenzied dancing. The main purpose of the trip however, were the five safari drives; three dusk and two dawn.

Three game drives over two days had been fruitless. Don't get me wrong, the antelope and deer are wonderful; the monkeys, both langur and macaque are active, playful and a joy to watch; the rattling around the terrain in open canters and jeeps, very exciting; and the colourful birdlife a delight, especially the peafowl whose haunting cry will be fixed in my memory of this magical wonderland forever. But it is the tigers people come to see.

It was my final day and game drive number four begins pre-dawn when the canter, an open top 20 seater truck, picks me up from the Raj Palace hotel. Three couples are already seated, and I leap up onto the bus with another two youngsters from my hotel. Our guide, a tall studious young Indian with spectacles and a moustache, introduces himself as Govindra, or just Gov. I nearly touched my forelock and called him Guv'nor, but resisted the temptation. The hotel provides us with blankets as it will be bitter cold before the sunrise. The five mile drive to the entrance in what is effectively a cabriolet, freezes the face and ears as we huddle under the blankets.

This morning we have been allocated a most picturesque zone which takes in an area below and south east of the looming fort, containing three lakes. Dawn is breaking and cockerels crow to mix with the peacocks' shriek, the parakeets' chatter and the babblers' babble, as we pause before entering the stone gate. Gov explains that a leopard can sometimes be seen sprawled along the branches of the trees across the valley. Today, nothing. A few langur, black-faced monkeys, sit and stare as we sit and stare at them.

We entered the stone gate and meandered down the track of a steep sided valley, the sun's rays from behind dappling the foliage ahead and creating long shadows. A long hour passes as the sun rises and we have many spots of sambur, nilgai and gazelle, none of whom appear worried that a predator may be around.

Suddenly we hear the alarm call of a sambar, a low, sharp bark, and the driver heads in that direction.

Rounding a corner and unbelievably there are four canters in a line down the valley in front of us plus a couple of jeeps going up the other side. At the valley bottom, to the right, there is a small copse and word comes back to us that there is a tigress in there with her three cubs. We can see people in the leading vehicles training their long lenses to the right. They have a perfect view and we know they will not relinquish position 'A' for anybody else, even though the park rules state you should not spend more than five minutes with a tiger before moving on.

We stand on our seats, hang on to the roll bars and lean out as far as is safe. Craning out like this with our field glasses, we occasionally glimpse a paw, perhaps a flank, or the back of a head, it is hard to tell.

Eventually, after much complaining, bobbing and weaving, and jockeying for position, a gasp went up, and there she was, sauntering up the track away from us, followed by her cubs, four smudges in the distance, there and then gone, vanished into the undergrowth.

Everyone in our canter seemed elated. All I could feel was desperate disappointment. After all, our vehicle had been the first into the park that morning, how could we have been so far behind.

The traffic cleared and we spent the next hour trying to second guess her movements and listening out for any more warning grunts. Nothing, just the usual sambar and chital. The sight of contented grazing deer sadly means no tiger. We see birdlife galore, wild pigs, crocodile and one magnificent sambar stag, with huge antlers, grazing on a pink lake. But no tigers, and it is now 10am and the drivers are under strict instruction, Gov explains, on pain of a fine and loss of licence, to be out of the park.

We returned and over tea and biscuits on the hotel lawn I contemplated this my tenth safari, and my first big cats, a shadowy glimpse from the end of a traffic jam.

We were back at the stone gate by three, ready for my fifth and final game drive. I was accompanied by the same crew as this morning, except that couple number one had this afternoon brought along their 12 year old daughter, Jemima, who this morning had been too tired to join us. Our allocated route is zone two, where we will mainly follow the ravine of a river valley.

We are in the valley, single track with bushland and a rocky slope to our right, shrub, tall grass and a dried river bed to our left, and a tall grassy far slope on which we can see sambar grazing.

We heard the alarm call. Ahead, no more than 150 yards, and the driver slows to a crawl as we approach the point. All has gone quiet as Gov instructs the driver to kill the engine and we slowed to a halt. We sat, silent and motionless when on the breeze wafts the unmistakable sweet smell of death.

"There is a kill here," whispers Govendra. "It is a recent kill, and my guess is that the tiger has dragged it up the bank into the bush and behind those rocks. Everyone's eyes are trained to the right, where he had pointed, and as we edged forward, the smell and the flies get worse.

"Er, it's here," calls Jemima, pointing down to the left. And there it was. We were right on top of it, a mature sambar stag with its neck broken, the carcass apparently unopened. Gov now assures us the kill has been made in the valley, the tiger has dragged it to the side of the track, and unable to go further was now sleeping.

"He won't be far away. When he awakes at dusk he will go to the waterhole to drink then return to devour his dinner."

We couldn't wait till dusk. It was gone four, and we only had till six o'clock before our driver had to leave.

Other vehicles arrived. Two jeeps stayed beside the increasingly foetid corpse as we departed for the waterhole, a mile or so down the track, to await his appearance.

We arrived at the side of a muddy patch which goes by the title waterhole and sat and watched and waited. The sun was now beating down, and we take on water and reapply sun screen. There was weirdly no sound, no birds, nor insects, nothing. Some dozed, others complained about the inactivity. I was increasingly aware of the time.

"We'll know when he's on the move, by the alarm calls the monkeys make for the deer," whispers Gov. But there was just the continuous silence in the heat.

"Surely there's not enough time for him to get here," I said. "Wouldn't we be better back at the kill?"

After half an hour (it seemed much longer) with no breeze, no sound, and the sun relentlessly beating down on us, Gov agreed our stakeout had been flawed and, frustrated, we creep back to the scene of the crime.

When the vehicle is once again on the move, there is a welcome breeze. Our blankets lie crumpled and forgotten in the foot wells, it now seems impossible this morning can have been so cold.

We relocate the kill and park upwind and a sensible distance from the smell and flies. Minutes passed again and we hear a low guttural bellow. Is it an alarm call, or perhaps a distant roar?

"It is a yawn" confirms Gov. We peer into the gathering gloom to our left. "There, there is a tiger!" he breathes excitedly.

No-one can see anything, and Gov begins that futile exercise of trying to point and explain to where he is pointing. "About three trees in, next to that greenish bush, to the right of the dead branch, above that rock, look."

"By the gap in the fork?" asks a baffled Jemima.

"No, about three metres above that, beneath the arching bough."

People continue to peer through the bush to where they think Gov is pointing. Then they gasped as a paw reaches up, and as quickly disappears, but everyone has seen the movement and are focussed on the correct spot. We are climbing on seats, hanging onto roll bars, dangerously dangling over the side of the vehicle, when a well camouflaged face appears. It is undoubtedly a round head, with fluffy ears, a tiger, and it is looking at us.

The collective sharp intakes of breath and excited shouts prove too much and he goes down again. "Shhhhh!" is the next comment.

Over several minutes we glimpsed him first clean his front, then his rear paws. He gets onto his haunches and finally to his feet. Magnificent. He slopes off behind us back towards the waterhole and is briefly hidden from us again. Then suddenly about 100 yards down the track he jumps down onto the road, saunters three or four steps, to a gap in the long grass, and he is gone, down onto the dried riverbed and out of sight. It had been a marvellous encounter, but with little opportunity to record it.

The rules of safari state that we must not stalk or harass the animals, so we turn around and slowly head back to the waterhole to await his arrival. But it is 5:30 when we arrive and we should be heading for the exit. Reluctantly that is what we begin to do, make our way back towards the Stone Gate. It means retracing our route.

"The tiger we have seen is a three and a half year old male" Govindra explains. "He is very likely a son of Machli, Ranthambhore's most famous Tigress; the Lady of the Lakes."

Govindra continues telling us something of the history of the tiger community here including, rather chillingly of park rangers and villagers who have been attacked and killed. We are progressing slowly up the track, hoping to once again glimpse him, but there are too many blind spots, and deep in the valley, the light is beginning to fade.

Govindra is in full flow when I suddenly bang on the roof of the cab and yell to stop. The driver slams on the brake and everyone lurches forward.

"We can't stop now, Geoff" says Gov. "The tiger is long gone, we must go to the exit."

"But look. There is the gap in the long grass, where he went down. Perhaps he has stayed with his meal". I am pointing into the bush, almost pleading with Gov for one more chance.

Govindra wasn't sure and told the driver to edge forward.

"No," I cried again, insisting. "We must back up. Just give us another few minutes."

All eyes were on our guide as he paused, but his were on the riverbed where our tiger suddenly walked into view.

"Ok, we'll stay" he beamed.

Son of Machli sauntered from the riverbed where we had previously seen him disappear, but he was close to the rear of the canter and we had a good view of him. Then, almost on cue, he sat down and began to groom. He was posing.

"Oh, he's beautiful!" said one, "Do we know his name?"

"How about Raja?" offered another.

Too twee, too Kiplingesque, I thought, and it came to me.

"Roger." I confirmed. "Roger it is then. Roger the Tiger." And it was settled.

The journey back flew by. The driver had only moments to spare. Amongst the crew there were tears of joy, one might also have been me. I was quietly satisfied that I was the one who had made that final encounter happen. Without my insistence and persistence, we would have missed Roger. We all thanked Gov and his driver as we were dropped off at our hotels. The beer that evening tasted particularly sweet.

Why Ranthambhore Number 10? Well this was my tenth safari on two continents spanning twenty years, and the first time I had seen (at close quarters) a big cat.

Shimba Hills, near Mombassa, Tsavo East and Tsavo West, Amboselli, in the shadow of Kilimanjaro; all in Kenya.

Kruger National Park, Hluhluwe Umfolozi and The St Lucia Wetlands of South Africa.

Mlilwane Game Reserve, in Swaziland.

Sariska Tiger Reserve, and now Ranthambhore. Number Ten.

*

Twelve years later and I am driving with my partner, Kaz, our guide, Avi, and six other travellers. We are heading from the town of Karauli, where we had experienced a marvellous spiritual moment, to Ranthambhore where we were hoping to add the Bengal Tiger to our list of wonders. It was a very rural drive as we passed arable flatlands of green wheat fields. Many fields had been flattened by recent storms, and women could be seen attempting an early harvest. Small towns came and went, with their tiny kiosk shops and children always waving. Kaz pointed out the abundance of barber's shops, but no hairdressers.

We did briefly stop at the Indian equivalent of a motorway service station. An awful place, actually named "Midway Tiger Stop", where you could buy from small mountains of tacky souvenirs, or a cup of tea and a packet of biscuits for the price of a slap up meal, or individual sheets of paper before you entered the toilets. I did see a Mars bar, the same size as I remember from my childhood, not the tiny bars they sell now, but generally the place was an anathema to me, just like Watford Gap.

The hills of Ranthambhore gradually hove into view and we were soon checking into the Raj Palace hotel. This was a clean, modern complex with gardens full of birds between the reception and restaurant at the front, and the pleasant two storied residence buildings at the back. Ominously we could see the preparations for a big party being built next door.

At 2:30 a jeep turned up to take us for our tiger safari. Kaz and I sat in the rear with Pip and Paul, the front seats were already occupied by our driver Bari and two ladies from Huddersfield, Sue and Betty. As we drove off, Betty turned and asked, "Have you bought anything interesting?" and Pip and Kaz delightedly joined in. Paul and I gave each other a look which said stick pins in our eyes now, and resigned ourselves to looking at the scenery.

We drove back into town, towards the railway station, then left up the high street full of cows, dogs, pigs and traders, then right off road for about ten minutes until we reached the gate for zone six. A leopard had been spotted here this morning assured Sue. Bari, who had become Baz, told us four tigers were known to frequent this area, with an occasional male. He also mentioned there were now 69 tigers populating the park.

I was back in my dry deciduous forest, and we spotted plenty of food; India gazelle, spotted deer, huge sambar, and bluebulls (nilgai). Also plentiful were peafowl and langur monkeys.

We spent two hours criss-crossing the dirt roads, encountering other vehicles with drivers and guides conversing quickly in Hindi, and much shrugging of shoulders and shaking of heads. We made a toilet stop beside a step well and waterhole which was busy with playful monkeys, rufus treepees, large magpie types with an orange breast and long tale, and various deer. Then it was back into the jeep for more searching. We ended up back at the gate where the leopard had been spotted. It was evident they thought a tiger was here as there were six other jeeps and two canters parked up at possible spots, waiting.

Suddenly engines roared into life and vehicles are off-road, racing up a hill, jockeying for position. At the top of the hill a canter was parked with passengers excitedly pointing down into the scrub and taking photos. We arrived broadside and everyone could see a tail and a striped body down between the shrubs and branches, except me. I searched and searched, being implored to look beyond the fork, by the dead branch, below that greeny bit, but I could see nothing. We moved to a lower pitch and I briefly spotted a torso and tail, but we must go Baz says. He will be suspended and lose his living if he stays off-road any longer.

Result? A most enjoyable afternoon and a successful spot. We drove the 20 miles back to the hotel, at one point passing a twin elephant temple, with a qualified contentment.

Next door's birthday bash was in full swing when we arrived, and after dinner we were urged into the garden to sit in a semi-circle for our own evening's entertainment. It was not easy, coupled with the cacophony coming from over the fence, but a fire was lit, and a drummer and accordionist struck up their gentler melodies. They were joined by the campest dancer I've ever seen, much wide-eyed mincing and flamboyant hand and head movements

"You should be honoured," insisted Avi. "To be in the company of a hermaphrodite eunuch is much revered in India."

Kaz and some of the others got up to shake their stuff bidden by the HE, there is a bit of fire eating, and it is all over, save for the unholy row coming from the party next door. It was now in full swing with drum and base and aggressive rapping.

We drifted off to bed and I found some aircraft issue earplugs.

Magically and unexpectedly, the cacophony comes to a sudden halt on the stroke of ten. But by three Kaz is awake with severe tummy ache. My night najjers kick in with all sorts of worrying thoughts; take the Immodium, or not, let it flush through, what about the missed typhoid booster, was it the eggs, will the insurance cover repatriation, and most importantly, will she be able to safari? In the end, no. Sadly I had to do this on my own. She insisted, honestly!

At 6:30 I made my way down to reception, leaving Kaz sleeping soundly after a difficult night. Coffee and biscuits and our jeeps turn up. I take a back seat, once again with Pip and Paul, there are two southern ladies in the front, very unlike Bet and Sue. It is freezing and the hotel provides us with blankets. You can forget putting it over my knees, in this cold and an open vehicle, I wrap it around head and shoulders. It is a 50 minute drive to gate 10, the terrain is so difficult, Kaz wouldn't have been able to hack it.

As our papers are processed Baz explains that there are two tigers known to roam this area (there are 10 zones and 69 tigers, you do the maths) "But the zones are for humans, not tigers," he explains.

Today's was an unremarkable search compared to the excitement of yesterday. Then, when every sighting of antelope or deer brought photo stops, these were now mostly ignored, and we would speed past. The primary purpose was the tiger. We visited a variety of waterholes and climbed up and down some precipitous slopes being bounced and lurched about like a roller coaster. There was the usual criss crossing of paths and encountering of other jeeps with the drivers shrugging shoulders and shaking heads.

"Why not GP track the tigers?" asked technophile Paul, "How do you communicate any spots?" questions Pip, noting the absence of cell phones and walkie-talkies.

"We give an alarm call" replied Baz (ignoring Paul's point). "You may think this is a random search, but the trackers know their haunts and habits, and we have already seen fresh prints this morning."

As the time draws on we become more resigned to the fruitless inevitable. Inside I felt sorry for my fellow passengers, but pleased for Kaz's sake.

Presently we came up behind three stationary jeeps. The people in the front appear agitated, pointing to their left. No-one moves for several minutes, and I am thinking they should move on to give others a chance to see whatever they've spotted.

Then the tiger gets up and starts walking towards us, "She is a tigress," whispers Baz. It is a marvellous encounter, she is a beautiful beast. She saunters no more than 20 yards from the road between the scrub and trees. Another jeep comes up behind us, and the ones at the front begin to back up. Soon we have the sorry fiasco of five jeeps lurching in reverse as she walks sedately along. But you can see she is becoming increasingly annoyed at our presence, swinging her huge head back and forth, and finally when beyond the rearmost jeep she leapt into the road, and up into the bush and away. She disappeared.

An hour later I'm back in the hotel room and Kaz sheds a tear. She had really wanted this.

On reflection, the tigers will learn from this type of engagement. They'll realise the roadsides can lead to their peace being disturbed. They'll begin to choose areas they know will be free from harassment for their mid-morning siesta. And the trackers will have to work even harder to satisfy the needs of the tourist.

Jaipur

After breakfast we left for Jaipur, four hours until the Pink City where I fell in love with Ruby. I wasn't sure whether she would remember me, it had been many years after all.

During the journey Avi kept us amused and informed by describing the importance of weddings in Indian culture. They are an intense game of one-upmanship. The family takes charge, and mum and dad must do bigger and better than any other members of the family, or neighbours. It begins with the wedding invitations, we had passed a street in Delhi devoted solely to wedding invitation shops. Our invitations have to be more ornate and obviously more expensive than any previous ones in the family, and there have to be more of them. "If you come across a wedding", Avi assured us, "you will be invited", to have British guests somehow increases the kudos for the matriarch, almost like a points system. Only celebrities, Bollywood style, score higher. It can be thought of as one of the legacies of the Raj; maintaining the class system.

After this insight into Indian life the subject returned to the Raj and Avi declared, rather simplistically that the only thing the British had done for India was to give them their language. We begged to differ and in a similar fashion to the Life of Brian sketch (What have the Romans done for us...?), began to reel off a variety of benefits derived from British rule; Democracy, The Legal System, The Railways, Cricket, Unity (then Separation), Schools, Hospitals, the Beatles, Shakespeare, and much more. In truth Avi was won over with Cricket, and strictly speaking the Beatles were post-Raj, but he saw the point.

Jaipur was painted pink, although it's more a terracotta shade, in 1876 to celebrate the visit of Edward VII, when he was still the Prince Of Wales. Contrary to what many believe, the first Empress of India, Queen Victoria, never set foot in the country.

Jaipur, the capital of the desert kingdom of Rajasthan, has a population of four million, and despite that, our first impressions as we entered the city was that it was much cleaner than elsewhere we had visited, and with its wide boulevards, green statued roundabouts and modern clean buildings it seemed a city of which its inhabitants could be proud.

There was some congestion and traffic jams as we approached the centre, but this was because this growing city was building its very own underground railway, so lots of disruption as lines and tunnels and stations are built. Amazing to think that when the London equivalent was built the streets rang to the sound of horseshoes.

We reached the centre and had to become tourists as a cycle rickshaw tour had been organised. It was so embarrassing. The poor little old bloke whose rickshaw we had been allocated struggled immensely just to get the thing moving, standing and pushing down on the pedals. He'd just get it going and the traffic would stop at a red light. I couldn't enjoy the experience, I just wanted to get off and push. But this old chap makes his living doing this, and always has. As soon as he can no longer do it, that is when they have no rice in the pot. So, we stuck with it and gave him a few extra rupees when he finally dropped us off at our hotel, the Traditional Haveli, wonderfully decorated like a Maharajah's palace.

In the meantime we had had two guided tours, first of the Jantar Mantar, an eighteenth century collection of huge observatory instruments. Years previously I had been disappointed at this overgrown crumbling pile of junk used as a monkey playground. Now it had been completely restored and was a gleaming example of man's obsession with the movements of the sun, moon and stars around the sky. There are sun dials with man-sized gnomons giving times all over the world, star plans covering every constellation of the zodiac, and other instruments measuring zeniths, azimuths, declinations, meridians and penumbras, whatever they are. Everything is carefully tilted to allow for the 27 degrees latitude we are north of the equator, with allowances for winter and summer solstices and equinoxes, and both hemispheres. Watching shadows slowly, inexorably recording time disappear at a hand's width a minute was truly absorbing.

Next door was the Royal Palace, astonishingly beautiful, but not as aesthetically natural as that at Karauli. We did enjoy however the museums of clothing and artefacts of years and royal families gone by leading up to relatively modern photographs of polo and cricket matches.

Finally in a square behind the palace we enjoyed a funny musical puppet show before meeting up with our rickshaw buddy to continue his struggling pedal.

At the hotel my Maharini was seeking to restore her strength in bed and I hit the noisy basement bar for happy hour. I watched the Super 10 cricket, saw off six strong Kingfishers and ate two chicken tikka nan wraps. Then I staggered off to bed myself. It had been one long extraordinary day.

Kaz was much improved the next day, but couldn't face breakfast. Our first port of call was the Hawa Mahal, the Palace of the Four Winds. It is the postcard view of Jaipur and very impressive; a five storied building, tapering at the summit with beautiful, symmetrical windows and intricate latticework, totally pink. In truth it is simply a facade at the rear of the palace, formerly rooms for the royal concubines.

We were invaded by hawkers and beggars on the pavement opposite where the best photos are taken, and I took the group through a tiny alcove where we climbed four floors, past several little coffee houses to the top. Here were the most sublime views. I'd been there before.

We drove out of Jaipur, past the Water Palace in the middle of Man Sagar Lake and through a pass in the Aravalli hills to the Maota Lake, above which is built the Amber Palace. There is a marvellous view of the Amber Palace from here, built high above the lake from gleaming yellow sandstone. Beyond it and even higher is the Jaigarh Fort, subterraneanly connected for defensive purposes.

Here at the lake, the elephants begin their journey to carry tourists up to the Sun Gate. The queues were horrendous, at least an hour's wait, and most tour companies now refuse to use the elephants on the grounds of cruelty.

I'll question this. There are 120 elephants, all female who work only mornings, and then only five days a week. After work they go home to their village to join the 25 who at any given time are not working, to graze and be bathed. Every six months they are checked by specialist vets. The work they do is not too strenuous, they might make two trips in a shift, up the winding road to the first courtyard, carrying a mahout and a maximum of two tourists in their howdah. They do this slowly and sedately. These are the largest group of domesticated elephants in the world, and if they didn't pay for their keep I dread to think what might become of them. They are all extravagantly painted, and I am sure being intelligent creatures, feel fulfilled by the work they do.

18 years previously, Ruby, an adolescent at only four tons had carried me. She was beautiful with the most wonderful peaceful demeanour. We had cuddled as I left and I was hoping to meet her again.

Our route up to the palace was via Amer town at the bottom of the valley, using jeeps through the choking narrow streets, it was an arduous route, finally arriving into the first, public courtyard.

Opposite, through the Sun Gate the elephants were arriving and dismounting their loads. As others wandered around the courtyard taking in its magnificent proportions (this was where victorious armies would gather to parade and display their war bounty), I hurried over to the gate. The ladies entering here could easily have crushed me against the pillars but I needed to speak to the mahouts. Such was the size of their mounts I had to shout up to them. "What is your lady's name?" I begged. I met Akana, Bishma, Judy, and Muntala before a soldier insisted I move into the safety of the courtyard. I asked a mahout if he knew Ruby and if she might remember me, "She is at home, resting today. If it was ten years perhaps she would remember, but not so long ago," he took pity on me. I was near to tears, the beauty and dignity and slow sure plodding grace of these enormous ladies. As I walked away to rejoin Kaz, one of the ladies relieved herself. I swear in five seconds she could have filled a bath.

We went up through the Ganesh Gate into the private courtyards and the gardens. There are Mughal water features here, similar to those at the Generalife in Granada, designed to bring cool breezes to the residents. The halls and rooms around the courtyards are wonderfully decorated. There were magnificent views back down into the valley and its lake, and up high to the protective edifices of the Jaigarh Fort. And then east, across the mountains where a wall is built to rival the Great Wall of China. How it hugged the ridges.

One room is full of thousands of tiny mirrors, set into decorated eggshell plaster which reflect you into eternity, infinity. "A glittering jewel box in flickering candlelight!" There were frescoes and mosaics and scintillant ceilings, carved marble relief panels and floral alabaster and magical flower statues.

We wandered the rooms, courtyards, gardens and halls for two hours, always overawed, never underwhelmed, up to the highest most royal apartments. Successive Maharajahs of the Rajput dynasty built, added to and expanded the palace to honour their wives. One Sultan built 13 towers, one for each of his wives. The effect is spectacular with huge proportions. Fittingly it is served by the Empress among beasts.

Eventually we came down from the palace in true tourist style, directed through tearooms and souvenir shops back to the residential town of Amer. Sadly this is overlooked because people clamour up to the palace, even though it is full of temples, mosques and palatial houses built by the dowagers to honour their offspring.

Driving back to Jaipur I asked Avi if we could stop to view the Water Palace, but mainly to admire the birds; cormorants, pelicans and storks, these latter which Avi referred to as flamingoes are famous for flying from China all the way over the Himalayas to winter here.

Along the road, heading for her village plods Lucky, a 25 year old lady whose mahout dismounts so I can talk to her. Sadly her eyes are cloudy with cataracts. She seemed nonplussed to meet me, I must appear diminutive to her, her trunk is higher than me, and I could not even reach around the girth. Despite my insignificance, we cuddled.

We went on to the Green Pigeon for lunch and were entertained by two brothers in scarlet Sikh robes. The magnificently moustachioed elder brother played the ravanahatha, a stringed fore runner of the violin, whilst the younger danced. He whirled like a dervish, winking and blinking faster and faster as he went, revolving with a permanent smile. We ate our curries breathlessly such was his performance.

After lunch Kaz went shopping with the Norfolk ladies whilst I rested back at the hotel. She returned complaining about the constant harassment by beggars. They certainly target white people, and are treated badly by the shopkeepers who know that their activities alienate customers.

I showed Kaz a room I had found whilst wandering (I quite often wander hotels, you never know what you might find. I also seek to find the way onto the roof, which always has the best views). Along the corridor was the Maharajah Room of the Traditional Havelli, a bridal suite. Never had we seen anything so opulent. Everything in the room was gleaming white, from floor to ceiling, all the upholstery was plush white leather, all fixtures and fittings dressed in white, and at the centre of the suite was a stunning silk silver-white four-poster bed.

And so onto our last dinner as a group. It had rained heavily in the afternoon so we ate inside at the Golden Peacock. Unfortunately the entertainment had to be an outdoor affair. It began inside with four traditionally dressed maidens dancing around the tables to sitar music. Never had I seen more bored expressions on girls' faces, totally unlike the brothers of the Green Pigeon. Then they had to dance outside onto the patio where pots of fire were strapped to their heads. Their demeanour didn't change, neither did our appreciation of their efforts.

Just weird.

People all over the world know when you are due to check out of a hotel. They fuss around you trying their best to impress and hopefully influencing your decisions on tipping. It is something I have no truck with.

And so at breakfast an immaculately suited restaurant manager greeted us. He marched to our table and haughtily introduced himself with a loud "Good morning!" None of this namby pamby 'Namaste' supplication for him. He evidently saw himself as a higher caste. "You slept well!", not a question, and "Breakfast is good!" He then proceeded to order the poor waiter who had been doing quite an adequate job anyway, to fetch eggs, pancakes and rice bread. His manner was such that you felt he would slap you on the back of the head should you refuse his poached egg. An Indian Basil.

Pomposity, don't you hate it. I remember a colleague admonishing a child with "Don't you know who I am? I am the acting deputy head of Maths!" I winced, not a head, nor even a deputy, and only acting up. I wouldn't have blamed the lad if he'd muttered "Twat!" under his breath.

It is not something you find a great deal of in Asia, where humility and respect appear to be the principle doctrines.

Then I found myself feeling guilty for being judgemental. Was I being hypocritical? Had I never been rude to people, criticised when I had no right to. My thoughts wandered during the morning.

"Remember that car park in Argelès-sur-Mer?" reminded Kaz of a dark moment in my history. I had thought the woman coming towards us offering a ticket wanted payment. I was so rude, waving her away and declaring that I was English and did not pay parking fees. How was I to know she was leaving the car park and kindly offering us her unspent ticket. Not my best Entente Cordiale moment.

We left Jaipur for Goa. It had always been my quid pro quo with Kaz. Do the Golden Triangle with me, then we can have a week of luxury on a Goan beach. The transfer went like clockwork. Most of the group had left, Avi was going home to Pataliputra and Pip and Paul were flying to Amritsar. Our car turned up at 11am. We were whisked to the airport, fast tracked past the queues of local travellers, flown to Mumbai, and transited onto the Goa flight. We booked a taxi at the airport and for the cost of a packet of biscuits, driven by a mad, rap-loving youngster to the Languinhos Beach Resort Hotel at Colva. Very quiet, unlike the taxi.

I say like clockwork, but the pilot of the second flight aborted the landing. We were almost on the ground when he lifted the nose and we whooshed back up into the sky. He circled and I noted from the roads, river and bridge we passed a second time that we came in at a much shallower angle. There was a huge collective sigh of relief as we eventually landed safely. No explanation was offered. Some weeks later after a disaster in Ethiopia, all Boeing 737 Max aeroplanes like the one we had flown in were grounded.

Goa

The next few days on Colva Beach were idyllic. Goan life is laid back, justifying its reputation as a hippy paradise. The warm ocean crashes constantly onto the perfect golden beach, a lovely playground if perhaps a little too rough for small kiddies. Every 200 yards or so along the beach is a bar/restaurant shack which provides sunbeds and parasols. You can spend a whole day there enjoying the shade and a cool breeze whilst the sand bakes around you, drinking cold beer and eating excellent home made food. For the two of us it cost less than a couple of Big Mac meals, so I'm told. The one we chose was the family run Seahorse, our perfect Marigold moment.

People always complain about hawkers on beaches. It's perfectly understandable. You want to relax and not be bothered by folks trying to relieve you of money, but locals have to make a living. Here was no different to any Mediterranean beach, every so often someone would ask if you wanted a massage, or try to sell you some linen, or handbags or jewellery.

That is how we met Nikita, a lovely, bright young thing with whom we chatted quite extensively, and learned how her business operated.

She bought goods off local manufacturers, small businesses, and distributed them to several colleagues who patrolled the beach for a couple of miles either side of Colva centre. After seeing off her young son to school and cajoling her wastrel husband (arranged, yes!) to seek work on building sites, she would leave their simple one room hut to meet up with her friends. To begin their day's work they would have to pay protection money to the local constabulary and a fee to the mayor's office. Only then would they be allowed onto the beach. Now was nearing the end of the season and she was looking forward to returning home to Karatnika in Gujarat where she would rejoin her extended family and give birth for the second time.

We would also be entertained by local children who would dance or perform acrobatics for a few rupees.

When we left Nikita looked at us quizzically, "You are all the same, you start off like chapatis and go home like tomatoes," she laughed

Every morning after breakfast the local church would ring its bells to summon its worshippers. Goa was once a Portuguese colony hence a quarter of the population are Christian. Nothing exceptional in that, other than the bells sounding more like an ice cream van.

On our fourth morning, after the bells the hotel was invaded. I watched from our balcony with interest as the workers came in with their scaffolding, staging, archways, lighting units, sound systems and pallets full of what I could only describe as pink stuff, and started working on the lawns. There was a very powerful lady in a shining green, yellow, and gold sari ordering people about and directing the various building work. She was formidable indeed, you could see workers quaking in their sandals as she delivered her instructions. As we left for the Seahorse our security guy told us they were preparing for a wedding tomorrow.

When we returned at sunset the sight that greeted us was nothing short of amazing. Every fence, wall, doorway, and tree trunk had been garlanded. Lamps hung everywhere, stages had been set up and walkways were strewn with flowers. Dozens of white chairs were lined up, and everything, everywhere was cloaked in bright pink chiffon and ribbon.

At dinner many guests had arrived to stay overnight and the band booked for the following day performed some practice sets.

I was chatting with Melvyn, the Manager during the evening as cricket played on the TV. The actual wedding will take place in a temple, he told me, then once all the guests have arrived at the hotel the bride and groom will enter from the beach, each on a white charger. The ceremony will be re-enacted, gifts exchanged and the festivities will begin. And you will, he assured me, be invited and expected to take part.

Well, we spent all the next day at the Seahorse waiting for our invitations which never came. After sunset, suitably frazzled we returned from the beach and were startled to see everything being dismantled. What could have happened? We asked the security guy who couldn't enlighten us. He just gave a confused shrug.

Before dinner I found Melvyn. "Sadly there has been a death in the wedding party. The wedding has taken place, but they felt it was not right to continue with the celebrations. More than that I do not know" he confided.

As we ate in a very subdued atmosphere, we noticed that many of the guests were still there, well they had probably booked and paid for two nights we conjectured. Suddenly an elderly man from a table of about ten guests got up and started taking photographs of his companions using a very professional looking, long lensed camera.

"You don't think they've forgotten to cancel the photographer," whispered Kaz with a wicked smile. Then, right on cue the fireworks started. A magnificent display, from the beach right in front of us. This was something they had really forgotten to cancel. There can't be anything else we thought; there's no band or disco or chocolate fountain....then we heard a distant buzzing, which gradually became louder and was undoubtedly the engine of a light aircraft. We looked at each other. No, it can't be. And then it came into view, flying along the shoreline with the banner:

"Congratulations Pritesh and Bhavna"

We checked out at dawn the next morning, our Indian adventures at an end. Taxi to the airport, an hour's flight to Mumbai and ten hours to London. Collect car, drive the M40, M42, and M6 Toll, pick up dog, and home for teatime, or tiffin. Like clockwork.

****

A few afterthoughts:

Many people live in India, approximately three times the population of the United States. This means there are about 20 Indians for every Briton. Mostly they are Hindu, but there is a surprisingly large population of Muslims (16%). History recounts that during the murderous partition of 1947 all Muslims were expelled to either West or East (now Bangladesh) Pakistan, with Hindus displaced to the south. Many atrocities were committed on both sides.

There is a quite small population of Sikhs, only about 6%. I say surprisingly as in my native Wolverhampton, the majority of British Asian families are Sikh. We enjoy orange celebrations and lively Bhangra dancing

Talking of pre-partition India, if that were one country now, the country for which Victoria was Empress, the population would be over 1.7 billion. That is about 300 million more than China, generally accepted to be the most populous country on Earth. Between them they produce about 100,000 more people every day.

The Mughal monuments we visited in the Golden Triangle were built by a dynasty of emperors that lasted only 300 years, and followed Islam. Avi assured us that Indian Muslims are not of the militant Shia or Sunni sects we find in north Africa or the Middle East, but Sufi, which are moderate Sunnis, and would never enter such realms of fatwahs for infidels, or dream of supporting extremist groups like Isis.

Perhaps Avi, like myself oversimplifies matters, we are guilty of generalising. But surely it is better to have a positive outlook on people around the world and their religions, rather than the pessimistic, negative way many folk (and the media) appear to address these issues.

Finally, each evening whilst in Goa, we would wait for the sunset before leaving the beach, and we were invariably slightly disappointed. The sun sinks towards the sea, due west, and a glorious sunset looks assured. Unfortunately Asia is covered in a brown/grey cloud of pollution, which generally you cannot see, until the sun disappears into this smog, just above the horizon.

The Silk Road to Samarkand

Sweet to ride forth at evening from the wells
When shadows pass gigantic on the sand,
And softly through the silence beat the bells
Along the Golden Road to Samarkand.

We travel not for trafficking alone;
By hotter winds our fiery hearts are fanned:
For lust of knowing what should not be known,
We take the Golden Road to Samarkand.

The Master of the Caravan seeks to leave Baghdad through the Gate of the Moon in James Elroy Flecker's verse play.

I can't recall when this became a goal, an ambition; but surely it must have been in my schooldays that I came across the magical name of Samarkand. It sounds like it should come from Kipling or Coleridge, but Jimmy Flecker has to get the credit.

The Silk Road has been the trade route used since before the Roman Empire to link North Africa, Europe and India to China. It has not only been the source of trading goods, but also ideas, philosophies, religions and, unfortunately, plague. There are magical personalities associated with it, Alexander the Great, Marco Polo, Genghis Khan, Sheherazade, Tamerlane, and place names, Venice, Constantinople, Arabia, Mesopotamia, Babylonia, Persia. So important was the route the Chinese even lengthened their Great Wall to protect it.

Caravans of camels would be continuous in both directions, the land route from the Levant skirting south of the Black, Caspian and Aral seas, then north of the Himalayas into Tibet, and across the Gobi desert. They would typically carry dates, saffron, frankincense and myrrh; ivory, rhino horn and turtle shell; carpets, tapestries, precious and semi-precious metals, and of course, slaves. They returned with bolts of silk, porcelain, paper and medicines.

Caravanserai, ancient motels, sprang up every 30 miles or so, the limits of a camel's trek for a day, and towns and cities were developed at natural crossroads, mountain passes, river fords and oases.

A significant part of the journey traverses modern Uzbekistan, in Central Asia, one of only two double land-locked countries in the world (Liechtenstein's the other). It is bordered by five other 'stans (tribes); Turkmenistan, Kazakhstan, Tajikistan, Kyrgyzstan and Afghanistan.

I flew via Istanbul to the Uzbek capital, Tashkent, from where I took an internal flight west to Urganch and began my land journey via Khiva, Bokhara, Nurata and Samarkand, back to Tashkent, a distance of over 600 miles. Or 20 days by camel.

Tashkent

I had 48 hours in Tashkent where I checked in to the 17 floor Uzbekistan Hotel on Amir Timur Square at 7am. My overnight journey had left me tired and emotional so I was overjoyed to learn I wouldn't be able to access my room until 2pm ("You can try again at one, Meester Geoff, housekeeping may have your room ready by then").

There was nothing for it but to engage my get-up-and-go adventure gear and begin my exploration of the first ex-Soviet city I had ever visited.

I strode out into bright sunshine under a clear blue sky on a cool mid-autumn morning. I had already learned on my journey from the airport that nine out of ten cars were white Chevrolets, and the city had wide, tree-lined boulevards. I crossed under one now, via the subway next to the hotel and was in a circular park. Bright-eyed myna birds chattered and hopped, shawled women were sweeping up leaves, blue-overalled men fly-mowed the grass, and students were having their photograph taken with a huge statue of the 14ᵗʰ century ruler Amir Temur. He was riding a horse atop a plinth proclaiming "Strength in Justice". A very Soviet principle, I thought.

The statue was a memorial to the legendary Tamerlane, who extended a Timurid empire from here to the Levant, through Persia to the Gulf, and south east to northern India. He died of pneumonia in 1405 aged 71 before he could take on China. During his expansionist wars he is estimated to have murdered 17 million people, which probably makes him the most evil person who ever lived. So why is he revered by the Uzbek people, and looked upon as a benevolent dictator by the west?

He also proclaimed himself supernatural and ordained by God. His hobby was building pyramids of skulls and he had his soldiers decapitated should they fail to reach their quota of slaughters. It was indeed a different time.

I left Tamerlane and entered a pedestrian area full of fairground stalls, fast food and drinks kiosks. There were people playing table tennis, children in toy cars and cycles, and folk just enjoying the sunshine. It all appeared happy and carefree, and there was a marked lack of alcohol outlets, usually an essential to oil the wheels of leisure. But to me the people looked disinterested, rather solemn, and unsmiling. Or was it just me still miserable about not having a room?

I returned to claim my room. "Ready in half an hour, sir" So I slumped into a reception sofa and waited. I had seen a Hop on Hop off bus outside the hotel for only 75,000 Sum (about £6.50) and resolved to see the city in the afternoon.

The room ready I took the lift to the eleventh floor, lay on the bed and slept solidly for five hours.

Oh no! I awoke to see the city in lights. I've broken my rules, forgotten lunch and missed the bus. It is already night time. How will I sleep tonight? My mood darkened even more as I prepared to return to the streets.

It was really cold now. Central Asian weather, unaffected by any oceanic influence can have hot days and freezing nights. But the city was lit up like a Christmas tree. Even the hotel frontage, a huge expanse had dancing lights as the colours changed from blues to reds to greens to announce their advertisements.

On Sayilgoh Co'Chasi Road, you would expect to find Santa on each corner, such was the festive atmosphere. I wandered into some of the fashion shops (of which I know nothing) and was impressed at the quality of the clothes, jewellery and perfumes on sale. I did have one criticism though. As I have noted previously, advertisers use white, round eyed models for their mannequins, billboards and posters. Do Asian people really hate their Tartar, Cossack, Mongol, Kazakh origins, and aspire to be western? We are all Caucasian, after all.

Outside on the streets I was aware that all the men wore tatty jeans, dark coats, and remained unshaven, women were wrapped in dowdy clothes, and fully scarfed. Many people still smoke.

The Arga family restaurant looked welcoming and I ordered a beer and beef in a creamy mushroom sauce. The meal arrived and filled a corner of the plate. "Where are the vegetables?" I asked. The waitress shrugged and pointed to a sprig of dill. The meat and sauce were delicious if leaving a hole. Mental note to order sides in the future.

Returning to the hotel I ordered a bottle of wine from the bar for my room, the Uzbekis are proud of their vineyards. There was a wedding party in the ballroom, karaoke in full swing, and the bride and her bridesmaids were posing for photos.

The barman delivered my bottle.

ME "Thank you. Rahsmat."

HIM "You German?"

ME "No, English"

·HIM "French?"

ME "No, I am English, from England"

HIM "American?"

ME "No, I am from the United Kingdom, Great Britain, I am from England, therefore I am English" I said slowly and patiently

HIM "Aah, you're from Anglia!"

ME "Yes, Anglia, English" I grinned and nodded.

HIM "Not American?"

Interesting bouquet I thought. I was getting cucumber and broccoli (overcooked). I must have been still hankering after veggies.

Following a good night's sleep, I would like to say I awoke refreshed. But as I lay there playing the game "wonder what time it is, can I go down for breakfast yet?", I was aware of the clues. There's traffic outside, chinks of light through the curtains, voices on the corridor. I turned to my phone; 1:45! The voices I'd heard were people coming to bed from the wedding party, the chinks of light, my bathroom with a permanent on switch. I visited said bathroom. There were bare wires sticking out above the loo, a mirror hanging off the wall, as was the shower head, no sink plug (Muslims have to wash in flowing water?), and an empty but noisy fridge. I switch it off. It was 2 o'clock for goodness sake, not even bedtime at home.

Breakfast eventually came around and I was delighted to find chana and dahl, my favourites, but the fruit juice was watery and the coffee instant. I didn't care, I spread lashings of honey onto dark brown dry bread and wondered at what time this ballroom had ceased to be full of party goers and been magically converted into a breakfast buffet.

A second day in Tashkent and I needed to get my head together, I was in a negative place. I can do that at home. Here I had to switch on my adventure mode. It was time to go gallivanting.

I readied myself and stepped out once again into the sunshine, armed with a street map. Crossing the Amir Timur gardens I began my exploration and had soon seen all four M's of Mosques, Minarets, Mausoleums and Madrasas. 85% of Uzbekis are Sunni Muslim, but their religion was suppressed during the Soviet era, 1921 to 1991.

Mausoleums, tombs, were allowed to remain, minarets fell into disuse, mosques became barracks, and madrasas (Islamic schools) evolved into bazaars. Since Perestroika, mosques have come back into use, and a liberalised form of Islam worshipped. Some minarets issue a courtesy call to prayer, if you want. There are four services a day which you might like to attend, there's no need for a prayer mat, nor to pray to Mecca all the time. You don't need to kneel; save your knees and be seated to pray. With religious freedom has come the freedom to interpret your worship. Madrasas had courtyards with learning workshops set into the cloisters. These are now used to display skilled crafts and artisans, and their wares. Perfect arcade markets.

What has not changed is the beauty of the architecture and Majolica tile colours and patterns. Soaring arches and porticos, reaching to Heaven; wooden doorways intricately carved without a starting or finishing point, a continuous, contiguous pattern; marble floors and silk carpets, domes within domes, tiny cupolas combining to create towering recesses. And the colours, iridescent blues, cobalts, turquoises, and indigos, laced or crowned with gold.

The guides give information overload of course. When it was built, who by, who sacked it, who recommissioned it, what's it for, how much is original, it's a palace, a tomb, a school, a mosque, or is it all those things?

I also went into the famous Chorsu circular bazaar, and had sample nuts and dried fruit foisted on me at every stall. At the butcher's stalls, meat hung as normal, but not a single fly could be seen. The cleanliness and orderliness and friendliness of the people was paramount everywhere, Suddenly there were lots of smiles, which is infectious and I began to feel better about life, still very tired though.

I bought a ticket for the underground, 13 pence and I could travel all day. The stations were stunning with mosaics, murals and chandeliers celebrating artistic and scientific achievement. There was one dedicated to the Soviet space programme to which the Uzbeks still contribute. All of the stations are 102 metres long, divided into three sections of 34 metres each separated by a 2 cm seismic seam in case of earthquake.

Back above ground I read about the earthquake of April 1966 which flattened the city. (I don't recall it in the news, but maybe we were too preoccupied with the terrible Aberfan disaster, or the World Cup. Also Soviet Russia had always had a habit of suppressing bad news, as in nothing bad can happen with Communism). The Monument of Courage is a 30 foot black statue featuring a woman holding a child and a bare chested man protecting them from the force of nature. Tashkent was subsequently rebuilt to a Soviet model, hence its wonderfully wide boulevards, hosts of green spaces, but homogenous housing blocks.

Finally I made it to Independence Square, a huge open space skirted by marble columns crowned with storks, and flanked by the Finance Ministry and the Treasury. But most powerfully evocative, after a short walk through the tree-lined avenues, was to come across the Eternal Flame, watched over by the a statue of a kneeling Weeping Mother. Her significance is to await her sons' return.

Just beyond were two verandahs housing brass pages of the names of the fallen in World War Two, 400,000 Uzbeks, a quarter of the population.

I took dinner on the 17th floor of my hotel, overlooking Tashkent, lit up like Blackpool 'luminations, as my father would have said, and I understood more. Marvellous what a day's gallivanting can do for the soul.

Khiva

Aaaargh, I still awoke at two. It didn't matter so much as I had a 5am alarm call to get me to the airport. At breakfast I felt sorry for the waiter who had also to be awake at this ungodly hour. The poor lad kept slumping and burying his head in his hands after serving coffee, juice, porridge, cereal or whatever.

After checkout it was the same driver who drove me to the airport that had transferred me two days previously.

On the flight in from Istanbul, the passengers appeared overwhelmingly Turkish or Uzbek, and I'd had a long chat with an engineer from Ankara employed to help with dam work in the north. He had complained he would miss his children. On the internal flight to Urgench however the passengers were nearly all tourists, mainly French.

I was seated on a row with Richard and Judy (honest), retired teachers from Sussex. They were also headed for Khiva, but were taking a detour to the northern forts and asked if I'd like to join them, share the price of a taxi. Didn't mind if I did, I'd not heard of this destination.

After an hour's flight west over mostly featureless desert, we organised a taxi for the day. Mansoor was our driver, a local with little English, but a remarkably large head, and at well over 6 feet, quite a presence on a rugby field, I reckoned.

We drove first through the town of Urgench, a pretty unimpressive grey sort of city with low-rise uniform shops and businesses, not many people wandering around, nor vehicles. At home you would say it was shut. However we passed alongside a meandering river, full of sand bars and oxbows, a very muddy, sedate affair. This was the Amu Darya, a major historical river known in classical times by the Latin, Oxus, and seen as the major border between Persia and the east. Beyond here is Transoxiana.

The Oxus rises from glaciers of the Pamir mountains to the south, which border the Hindu Kush. This is the sole source of water as there is so little rain in this lowland basin. Although it was a raging torrent regularly overflowing its banks 700 years ago, now due to irrigation and summer evaporation it rarely manages to discharge into the Aral Sea, which itself is now called the ex-Aral Sea, or even the Aralkum desert.

It took over an hour to reach our destination. The journey was quite disconcerting as although the road was perfectly straight, it was in urgent need of pothole maintenance. The result was that you would be approaching a lorry say on the other side of the carriageway, which would suddenly swerve head-on to avoid one of said potholes, or Mansoor would do the same. Either manoeuvre would be accompanied by sudden lurches, both left and right, and fearful sharp intakes of breath. Mansoor laughed heartily at our anxieties.

We were driving through the Kyzyl Kum (red sands) desert into the semi-autonomous republic of Karakalpakistan to find the abandoned forts and settlements of Topraq Kala and Ayaz Qala.

The first rose up to our left, and if you didn't know you would simply think it a natural desert hill. There was a small community of Yurt tents at the base, and simple shower and toilet shacks indicating the desire to turn these archaeological finds into a tourist attraction.

We parked and clambered over the sandstone to the summit. We could now see the partially restored mud and straw battlements, and below the outline of living quarters, and in the distance a rise which indicated a sister settlement. In fact in recent years 50 of these settlements have been found which apparently made up a defensive line of citadels which UNESCO are intending to market as the Golden Circle of Khorezim.

Little is known of the people who lived here between 800 BC and 800 AD, a civilization span of 1600 years. It is fairly certain they settled and built on the banks of the Amu Darya, a perfect defence to the south, and we could see a line of black mountains to the north, which were on the Aral Sea. These citadels would have housed nobles and garrisons, and protected the farming peasants from the nomadic raiders from the north.

The Amu Darya carries a huge amount of silt from the mountains, this is what causes the sandbars and oxbows, and it is thought caused a major diversion in the Middle Ages. Losing not only their defence, but also their irrigation source would have been a major blow to these people and the citadels would have been abandoned. Those left were quite probably swept aside by Genghis Khan and Tamerlane.

(There is a legend that when first attacked these forts were protected by the fast flowing Amu Darya, so the attackers killed sheep, and used their inflated bladders to buoy their horses across and successfully continue the assault)

I had climbed this first, Ayaz Qala, beneath a pure blue sky, marvelling at the silence and the views over a low scrub desert in every direction. We were accompanied solely by a zephyr breeze and scarab beetles scurrying into the shadows.

The second, perhaps ten miles distant was a much higher and harder scramble, with quite improbably, even more spectacular 360 views. We all three worried at the erosion of these gems once hordes of tourists discover the Golden Circle.

We also discussed the demise of the Aral Sea. As recently as 1960 it was the fourth largest body of inland water in the world, the size of Sicily. Now, due to damning and the diversion of rivers for irrigation by the Russians, it is merely a collection of small lakes in the Aralkum Desert. The climate for neighbouring countries has changed; hotter days, colder nights, less rainfall, harsher seasons. Its towns have been devastated, industries destroyed, populations unemployed. But worst of all, a whole ecosystem laid waste, wiped out, exterminated, extinct. Rusting hulks lying at crazy angles on the dried sea bed stand testament to our stupidity.

Mansoor drove us back south with the occasional violent lurch to Urgench and an hour out the other side to the ancient city of Khiva, on the Khorezm Oasis. Perfectly preserved behind high golden walls the city is packed with the four M's. Domes and minarets all decorated in shining blues, indigos and greens. Cobalt and cyan geometric patterns shimmering in the late afternoon sun.

We were dropped off at the western Ata Darvaza Gate, Mansoor indicated we should walk past the unfinished or short minaret to the Hotel Arkanchi where by chance we are all billeted.

Feeling invigorated I set off to explore. The main street has three minarets, headed by the short but stout Kalta Minor which is about 100 feet high, only a third of its projected height before funds ran out (hence unfinished), with a girth of 50 yards. From here downhill there were souvenir sellers galore, also selling gloves, huge woolly hats, thick socks and camel skin tunics, evidently preparing for a cold snap. The old women sat and smiled sweetly, showing their gold teeth, as I browsed. No-one hassles you, except fr some children begging. One pretty little girl asked for bonbons with her left hand whilst picking her nose with the right.

There was only one place to head for for a beer, the rooftop terrace of "Terrassa Bar". With the sun sinking into a purple horizon, I met up again with Richard and Judy, and they introduced me to Pauline, a GP from Runcorn, Two Pints of Lager and a Packet of Crisps country, who was also staying at the Arkanchi.

Birds were flocking to roost, and pipistrelle bats announced their appearance with acrobatic swoops, when Venus appeared in the early evening light-blue sky. With domes and minarets now floodlit, another beer was in order before the cold and the need to dine drove us indoors.

We decided on the national dish, Plov, which has many regional varieties. Here it was beef with onions and mushrooms on a bed of rice and carrots. "It's just like Scouse!" announced Pauline in an almost scouse accent.

Our waiter was a short, dapper young man in white jacket and shirt, with a black tie. He had a shock of black hair and the large, round face with high cheekbones of the Tatar community. He was efficient and pleasant, but it was evidently in his job description not to smile.

"What's this called?" asked the GP, pointing at her meal, anxious to hear how Plov is pronounced.

Our waiter looked confused, he had little English, "Erm, rice?" he hesitatingly replied in a deep voice.

"Nor!" said Pauline, "This" she encompassed the plate with her hands.

The waiter shifted uncomfortably "This is meat" he stuttered, beginning to look perplexed.

"Nor, the whole thing, what is it called, this dish, what is it?" implored Pauline, smiling.

Still confused he ventured "This is not what you ordered?" wondering (as most men do) what he had done wrong.

"No" I intercepted, trying to bring harmony to the increasing confusion. "There is nothing wrong. We just want to know the name of this, your national dish"

"Ah", he nodded. The penny appeared to have dropped. He drew himself up to his full height, straightened his back, fully at attention, and took a deep breath. Then, with his right hand outstretched, he announced from the deepest part of his being the word, "Pulurv!" It was so profound, the crockery rattled and the resonance caused cutlery to shake. He paused for victorious effect, turned on his heel, and strode away back to the kitchens.

"Oh" said Pauline evidently feeling the vibrations, "Rahsmat" she giggled. It had made her evening.

The next morning we were met in the hotel reception by Tangina from Poltergeist. You will remember the tiny yet fiesty actress Zelda Rubinstein. This was her doppelgänger.

Rosina had been commissioned by the hotel to be our guide for the day in Khiva.

We began at the Khan's palace. There were the usual three courtyards used for public and private audiences, and then the inner family and concubines' area. I was interested to learn a new take on the role of concubines. Here, girls as young as eight were taken into the palace, but it is not as sinister as it sounds. It appears they were educated and used as ladies-in-waiting for the four favourite wives, and as they grew, added to the entertainment at court, singing and dancing. In their late teens they would be returned to their families as well-educated young ladies of court who could now be married off to the most eligible of bachelors, raising the status of their families. Much better

123

than the sex-slaves Victorian propaganda wrote into our history books. I wonder!

Rosina was much more interested in the use of the outer courtyard. Yes, there were plays and pageants and musical events; bazaars and audiences and other celebrations, even a thriving slave market until outlawed in 1873. But the most interesting was it's role for corporal punishment and executions every ten days. We were shown the prison cells into which criminals and other felons were incarcerated. When it came to meting out punishment, Sharia Law was used.

Thieves and pickpockets had their offending limbs removed, more serious criminals lost their heads, and a variety of interesting punishments awaited people like adulterers. Of course these events were public, and families would be forced to watch their loved ones' demise. The guilty men were hung, whilst their lovers watched. The women were then stoned to death. Their fathers were made to cast the first stone. Rosina was relishing her telling of these macabre tales, and showed us pictures (thankfully paintings, not photos) of these punishments taking place. As I so often have to remind myself, different times.

She was positively cackling when she recalled the events of 1923, when the Bolsheviks took over and outlawed religion. The women finally were able to enjoy freedom, and there was a big celebration to burn their veils. When the Russians moved on to the next town, the elders took back control and had the women stoned.

Once she'd settled down and composed herself Rosina explained how Zoroastrianism had featured in the development and especially the architecture of Khiva. Everywhere were the ankh looking twin stones representing the twin elements of good and evil, truth and deceit, heaven and hell, even yin and yang that underpinned the ancient religion.

She also described the traditional dress, Chapan robes and tyubiteika hats, round caps, squared at the top with ornamental designs to describe your status; wives, children, grandchildren. There were

Purdah veils which covered women totally until banned by the Russians, and the rather comical huge woollen hats called Karakuls which protected from the bitter cold of winter and are the favourite posing accessory for tourists.

Rosina left us after lunch and I spent the afternoon wandering the narrow streets, revisiting the Royal Palace where musicians, puppeteers, acrobats and dancers entertained all day. There were some rather sparse museums and galleries housed in the Madrasas, but there was always something happening in the streets which made for a lively atmosphere. Khiva is wonderfully small, everything of interest within the city walls. Climbing the watchtower showed a sprawl outside that the tourists never visit

As I entered the main Mosque, gazing as always at the ornate, decorative tiling, a family arrived. Mum, dad, aunts and uncles, and grandparents, all in western dress. At their centre was a young lad, maybe eight or nine years old, and he was dressed as a prince, all gleaming white and silver suit, and a magnificent bejewelled golden turban. He looked magnificent, especially in the midst of his rather drab looking family. He was flanked by two elder brothers struggling to suppress smiles as he was led solemnly into the inner chamber of the mosque. An Imam followed behind, pocketing his mobile phone as he prepared for the ceremony.

"Circonsision" a French woman whispered. No need for translation as there were muted giggles all around. No wonder his brothers looked smug.

I wandered the back streets. There was bread being kneaded and baked in tandoors, wood being carved and shaped, gloves and socks being knitted, canaries sang from hung cages, men chatted and smoked, children skipped to and from school. I decided I liked Khiva.

Sunset, another beautiful experience was once again taken with beer on the Terrassa, and to end the day I dined on French Onion Soup. Unfortunately the entertainment ended there. In Uzbekistan, when darkness falls, people dine then go to bed. There was little in the way of nightlife, and it does get cold, so I sourced a bottle of wine from a supermarket outside the walls and repaired to my room to read and consider the days events.

I'd learned about concubines and Zoroastrianism, stonings and hats, Sharia Law and baking bread, but what stayed with me was Rosina's laughter and the serene look on the lad's face as he prepared for the unkindest cut of all. Why do people find it so amusing?

Bokhara

I managed to sleep through to six, hurrah! An early breakfast of pancakes and sweet croissant cakes before we hit the road, the Silk Road, from Khiva to Bokhara. Richard and Judy and Pauline had persuaded me to share a minibus with them and two more tourists we'd found, Jayne, a tall, slim semi-retired nurse from Essex and Joan, ex-teacher, ex-tennis player, Paralympic coach and landowner from north of Norwich. It was a near 300 mile journey and took up most of the day.

We followed the Oxus for much of the early journey where it formed the border with Turkmenistan, then we were in the featureless Kyzil Kum desert. The road, although quite poor was dead straight, and we continued to experience sickening lurches to avoid potholes whilst narrowly avoiding head-on collisions.

Sometimes, either side of industrial communities there were stretches of good road, for which tolls had to be paid. Once the driver stopped to show us cotton fields, a strange juxtaposition, cotton fields on the Silk Road.

We rolled into Bukhara just before sundown, and saw camel caravan statues, a disused water tower reborn as a restaurant and viewing point, and the imposing walls of a citadel or fortress. First impressions were that this was a much larger place than Khiva, and getting to know it would take a little longer. Well we had three nights here, a little too long for my taste, but I couldn't arrange transport away before then.

The minibus took us onto a wide ring road, past an impressive football stadium then dropped us off in a residential area south of the city at the family run Hotel Mosque Baland. The map helpfully calls this type of residential area "People's Houses". It's not helpful, as I was to find to my cost.

Mama, who does all the cooking, Papa, who only did eating, and their two daughters greeted us warmly. Sofia, the elder girl had the best English. She was training, as she proudly announced, to be a tour guide. She was due to be married the following year when she would have to move out of her parent's house into his, Pieter's, who was also there to greet us. Papa's papa had built this place and the dining hall was a gem, every inch from floor to ceiling beautifully decorated in Zoroastrian and Muslim geometric patterns. Niches galore contained dozens of Chinese and Japanese vases, but it was evident his main collecting joy had been chiming pendulum clocks. They adorned every wall, none working, so every single one of them was correct twice a day.

Sofia took us for a walk into the town to ensure we wouldn't get lost. We had to take head torches because the roads weren't made up and there were ankle breaking pot holes everywhere. Occasionally holes had been dug to repair pipes and just left, simply a pile of earth next to a potential grave. It was a good twenty minutes into the centre, along some very dodgy, unlit alleyways.

That evening we dined at the first restaurant we saw in the town, but recommended by Sofia, the Minzafi. We arrived at ten to seven and it was empty, by seven it was full. Tourists, all given the same time to turn up.

I was happily into my second beer before we ordered, and I plumped for a dish called Jiz al Urgua (don't google it!). It turned out to be strips of fillet steak with fried onions, tomatoes and cabbage in a soy sauce and was absolutely delicious. I'm afraid I made a spectacle of myself assuring everyone within earshot, on several occasions so that the joke would fully sink in, that this was the best Jiz I had ever had.

We found our way back; past an art gallery then fork left, fork right after the Hammam baths, then after a rusting classic car there is a wall with a number 2 up high, turn right and follow the alleyway until it opens up into the road along which is the Mosque Baland hotel

The next day after a beautiful breakfast served in that gorgeous dining room, Sofia introduced us to Munisa. Muni was young for a tour guide, and very pretty, with long black hair tied back and wearing the uniform of the youngster, jeans and trainers, a tee shirt and denim jacket. It was clear this was the life for which Sofia yearned, and she hung on Muni's every word. Whether it would be allowed once she was married with children, who knows? Maybe she would return to it as a mature tour guide. For now we were in the hands of Muni, with a full day's stories ahead of us.

We began by clambering into the minibus and driving out beyond the ring road to the four minaret Madrasa called Chor Minor. On top of one minaret there was quite clearly a stork's nest but Muni told us storks hadn't been seen in Bukhara for 70 years, possibly to do with the constantly shifting River Oxia, or the demise of the Aral Sea, but their nests certainly had staying power. The Madrasa had been bombed by the Bolshevics in 1923, and now only the four Minarets were left.

Next, to the north of the city Muni took us to the Khan's summer palace called Sitorai Mohi Hosa. This was a welcome diversion from the 4 M's, as it was relatively modern, late 19th early 20th century.

Everything was designed for coolness; white airy buildings with water gardens. The attractive rooms, reminiscent of our hotel's dining room, were set off with period furniture, works of art and Chinese and Japanese porcelain. The gardens were sadly a little worse for wear, and not well maintained, but there were artists and craftsmen displaying their wares in the avenues, and there was an atmosphere of calm tranquillity.

We walked through the Samanid park and museum before returning to the bustle of the city and Muni showed us the Bolo Khauz Mosque which had a courtyard with many wooden pillars. Here we were next to the water tower and opposite the fortress known as the Arc, but all that was scheduled for after lunch. We ate at an outdoor restaurant full of worshippers from the Mosque. Interestingly the women sat separately from their menfolk, and there was a definite atmosphere of Ladies That Lunch. This was their quality time with friends. We dined on excellent Plov.

The Arc is a fortress with huge battlement walls. We entered through a narrow gateway, and there were several rooms up to our left. The most important being the courtyard where the Emir took audience. This was a wide and long open space, near the rear of which stood a significant wall. When your audience with the Emir was over, you bowed and walked backwards to this wall, only when you had backed into the wall and moved around it out of sight, could you stand up and leave. Here I learned of the plight of two British officers, Stoddart and Conolly.

During what Captain Arthur Conolly termed the Great Game, Colonel Charles Stoddart visited the Emir of Bukhara, Nasrullah Khan in 1838. British forces were keen to keep these emirates on board as they feared Russian advances through Afghanistan might threaten their hold on India. Unfortunately Stoddart used British army protocol, riding into the courtyard and remaining on his horse to salute the Emir. This was not received well, and when the Emir became tired of his bleating on behalf of Her Majesty, Queen Victoria, he had him thrown into the dungeons, and wrote to the Queen for clarification of Stoddart's position.

Experiencing appalling conditions Stoddart converted to Islam and was given a house in the city.

Three years later Conolly, an evangelical Christian, dispatched himself in an attempt to free Stoddart. Dismayed that he brought no reply from Victoria the Emir also placed Conolly on house arrest where he was appalled over Stoddart's conversion.

When the British army suffered a defeat in Khabul the Emir realised he had no need for these spies and had them thrown back into prison. On the 24th June 1842 both men now severely emaciated were brought out into the sunshine and executed in front of the fortress. It was said that after Stoddart's beheading, Conolly was offered conversion to save his life, however he refused and met the same fate.

When news of this atrocity reached England there was a furore and the population insisted on reprisals. However, as history has continued to show, Afghanistan proved too great an obstacle, and we turned our backs on this part of Central Asia. The Tsarist Russian Empire ceded these Emirates, which found themselves part of the revolution of 1917, and they were plunged into the misery of communism which consumed them until the late twentieth century. It might have been so different had Stoddart bowed respectfully.

I felt subdued leaving the Arc, we hear of so much barbarity, but when it's close to home, even if so long ago, it can hit hard.

We walked from the Arc to the Poi Kalyan complex, a beautiful square flanked by two magnificent Madrasas but dominated by the Kalyan Minaret. This had been a beacon signalling to so many Silk Road caravans since before Genghis Khan.

There is a legend that when he was sweeping across Asia, destroying everything in his path, the Great Khan came to The Kalyan, which under normal circumstances he would have destroyed. Standing at its base he looked up at its great height and his hat fell to the floor. Genghis knelt to retrieve it and when he turned he saw his whole army following what they thought to be his lead, and kneeling in worship. He saw this as a sign and spared the Kalyan.

It was a little sad to see the marvellous Madrasas, once the seats of great learning, reduced to souvenir stalls. Some of them at least, housed worthy museums and art exhibitions.

We walked on to two more, the Ulugbek and Abdulaziz Khan, stunningly beautiful, but we have reached saturation, the oft-quoted tourist plea of "Not another Temple". But these entertained an interesting aside. A Bollywood film crew were set up and a young actor armed with a rifle had to stand, feign fear then run off down the road. It was fascinating seeing the poor lad being directed to do this at least a dozen times, whilst continuity people adjusted the lighting and other props, and one poor bloke had to continually beg people not to walk behind the action.

There was a another short walk through two souks called Trading Domes and into the Lyabi Khauz, the centre of the city where cafes surrounded a duck pond. This is a favourite place to promenade, and I saw four wedding parties (yet not one funeral) strolling and being filmed and photographed. Stunningly beautiful brides in their white flowing dresses which sadly kept being caught up in the cobbles, bridesmaids falling over themselves to pick up the tresses. Proud and haughty grooms but so few smiles.

I saw the Minzafi restaurant and knew my way back to the hotel from here. Muni had done such a grand job showing us the sights of Bukhara and weaving its tales and we said a very grateful farewell as it was approaching dusk. It had been a long day.

Back at the hotel Mama showed us how to prepare Manti dumplings, an Uzbeki favourite which looked like samosas filled with mashed pumpkin or minced meat. These were to be the highlight of our meal that evening. We had opted for the home cooked option, twice the price of a city centre restaurant, but home cooked must mean top quality.

Well, the soup was good, and I enjoyed the honey cake dessert, and Sofia did a grand job of explaining the decorations of her grandfather's dining room, while her sister modelled traditional wedding dresses, but the dumplings were awful. Steamed, they were like soggy suet pies containing lumps of grey gristle.

And then it was only 8:30 and everyone took to their beds complaining of a tiring day. With no company, feeling disappointed and bored I decided to go for a walk. "Thank God" I was to write later, "for Odil Beq!"

I left the hotel and turned right, at the end of the road I went right again, turned left, realised there was nothing to do or see and tried to make my way back to the hotel. I didn't try to retrace my steps, but trusted to my sense of direction and quickly became lost. The streets were dark and empty, the alleyways looked very foreboding, and I soon started to feel quite alone and a little worried. What a foolish thing to do, coming out at night in a strange city into a maze of streets. And in my predicament I realised I had forgotten the name of the hotel, didn't know what street it was on, had no paperwork on me, and was very vulnerable. I shrank away into the shadows when the occasional motorcyclist passed by, and began to look for lights which might offer me some succour.

I kept blundering on, not knowing if I was any nearer, or drifting further away. I saw through a window a group of women working at the treadles of their sewing machines and knocked on the door. "Do you know where the Hotel Mosque is?" I asked pathetically, but they had no English. I showed them my room key which had a fob with a Zoroastrian design, but again they shrugged. I thanked them and moved on, beginning to feel a little distressed.

I came upon a small shop and asked the elderly man behind the counter, and showed him the key. He just got up and went into the back. Presently he came out with, I presumed, his grandson, a thick set teenager who I guessed wasn't in the top sets in school. "Do you know a hotel, hotel mosque?" I realised this was fruitless. He came out onto the street with me and looked around. He beckoned me to follow him down a side street and pointed between two buildings. There, I could see it glowing in the distance, the top of the Kalyan Minaret, lit up brilliantly. If I could find my way there I could reach the town centre and find my way back. I thanked the boy and moved off. The task was harder than it seemed, some alleyways I went down in the direction of the Kalyan turned out to be dead ends and I had to back out to start again. Again occasional cyclists would spook me, and I imagined all kinds of danger lurking in the shadows.

I found a lit street which seemed promising, turned a corner and came out in the gleaming Poi Kalyan complex. It was deserted. I saw a hotel, the Hotel Minoroi-Kalon and went in, immediately feeling relief at its modern reception area. There was a boy behind the counter and I showed him my room key which he didn't recognise.

"Do you want to check my computer?" He asked in perfect English, and I immediately relaxed and told him the whole story.

"We can check on Bookings.com" and I spent the next half hour looking at all the hotels in Bukhara, all 186, but there must have been at least one unlisted, mine.

"If I can get to the city centre, I think I can find it from there" I told him.

"Wait there, I will see my boss" he said, and went upstairs.

If all else fails, I thought to myself, I'll stay here and find my way back in the morning, then realised I only had about £10 worth of Som on me.

The young man returned. "My boss said I can take you" he smiled, "Let's go"

"Thank you" I said, feeling very relieved. "What is your name?"

"Odil" he said, "Odil Beq"

We left the hotel, turned right, up some steps, along a bridge, then down more steps into an alleyway. At the end of the alley was a shopping dome, on the other side of that across a courtyard we saw the restaurant Minzafi.

"I know where we are" I said, "Up here, past the art gallery"

Once out of the town centre in the dark, things didn't look quite so familiar, but we found the rusted classic car, and then the wall with the number 2, and turned right, and then we were there. I remembered a hole which had been dug and an old ladder rested on it as a barrier, and 100 yards further on, the Hotel Mosque BALAND!

Odil came into reception with me, making sure it was still open. "Thank you, Odil, I don't know what I would have done without you", and I shook his hand, not sure whether a grateful hug was the manly thing to do.

"No problem,"he smiled, "I am happy to help", and he turned on his heels and ran back up the street.

I entered my room, now looking very welcoming indeed, and checked the time, nearly one o'clock. I got into bed and fell fast asleep thinking "Where else in the world would I have got away with that unscathed?"

The next morning I told my travelling companions what had happened (neglecting to add it was their lack of social skills that forced me out in the first place!) and they all agreed I had left myself very vulnerable indeed. Another plus for Uzbekistan, not only the cleanest but probably one of the safest countries in the world, with people who just generally want to help. Sometimes generalizing just through one experience can be a good thing.

I'd not been looking forward to this day, in my mind I'd done Bukhara thanks to Muni's excellent guide, and I wasn't due to leave till tomorrow, so all I could do was revisit some of the highlights from yesterday. Well, the sun was still shining and it was a clear blue sky, so after breakfast I set off for the centre. There were now familiar sights, an unprotected hole in the road, rusting classic car, hammam and art gallery. I visited the art gallery.

It wasn't an art gallery, it was an exhibition of photographs depicting Bukhara then and now (Then, was monochrome and sepia and peasants. Now, was colour and smiles and modern clothes). It was very atmospheric with mood lighting and music. I particularly enjoyed the juxtaposition of old and young people and was put in mind of the expression, "As you are now, so once was I; as I am now, so will you be"

As I left the curator turned off the music. I wasn't surprised. Mood music for a short while sets the scene, all day it becomes music to slit your wrists by.

I visited the synagogue. There have been Jews here since the Romans persecuted the Palestinians, and I realised this was the first I'd ever visited. I don't know why. There were the objects I recalled from Religious Education lessons; the Torah, the lectern from which it is read, the eternal light, the ten commandments written in Hebrew, the Ark, and the Menorah, the multi-branched candelabra. The holy place resembled more a classroom, with its lines of ancient wooden desks, possibly all facing Jerusalem.

From the duckpond I went into the Devon Begi Madrasa, and browsed the shops tucked into the cloisters while a string quartet played to an audience of empty white chairs. I was sure it would fill up later.

I was amused (at first) to see a woman in full black burka, with only a slit for what were dark, pretty, young eyes. She was going all around the courtyard enthusiastically taking selfies. I sidled away when I mischievously thought she might be 'casing the joint'.

Outside the Devon Begi was a reminder of home.

In Wolverhampton, pride of place in the middle of Queen's Square stands a statue of Prince Albert astride his horse. Wolverhampton was the first place Victoria visited after her period of mourning, to unveil the statue. The square is a favourite meeting place, especially for young folk who arrange their liaisons by agreeing to meet at "The Man On The Os". As a teacher, how ashamed I was of their ignorance.

Here was also a favourite meeting place and indeed, a man on an 'os, well in fact, an ass. This was a black metal sculpture of Nasreddin Afandi a jolly Sufi storyteller who features in fables throughout Central Asia, but the Uzbeks like to call him their own.

Lunchtime and I sat by the duckpond complex for a hot dog and beer and watched the world go by. Later I wandered through the shopping domes and onto the Poi Kalyan complex. I found the hotel, saviour of the previous evening and popped in to see Odil. Unfortunately it was his day off. Onto the Arc and I treated myself to an ice cream (being the family business, it is my duty to sample ice cream in every place I visit; a chore, I know, but someone has to do it). I sat eating ice cream on the very spot those two brave soldiers were beheaded. Strange world.

I decided to find my way back to the hotel from here and once again became hopelessly lost. I'd been too long in Bukhara, time to move on. Tomorrow Samarkand (following a brief sojourn in a yurt).

Nur

I once again hitched a lift with R and J, the Doc, and Joyce, to Samarkand, or so I thought. We came upon the city of Navoi, which I was impressed to see had not only a huge coal-fired power station,, with electricity pylons stretching far out into the desert, but also a large passenger and cargo airport. This was a major industrial city, and there were also the hotels based around the airports which no doubt had international businesspeople as their clients. After visiting a preserved step-well which serviced a now ruined caravanserai, we stopped for lunch which was a really authentic dish of Plov. There was a pile of brown rice with carrots and onions and whole bulbs of roasted garlic. The meat, proudly sitting atop the dish was a section from a cow's backbone, the spine below the ribcage. Here was where Richard informed me we were diverting from our Samarkand destination to spend a night in a yurt, a traditional nomadic tent. So we turned left at Navoi and headed north for the ancient city of Nur, now known as Nurata.

The town itself was pleasant enough. There were residential areas with the very same rows of uniform bungalows we'd seen everywhere; schools, office buildings, statues to mark the fallen, the 'weeping mother', and shops. It was Friday, so there were lively markets in fresh goods. The usual children playing in the gutters, some stopped, open-mouthed as we passed, and waved, unsure. The women, busying themselves buying and selling, men sitting around chatting and smoking. Some men or indeed children were leading the family goat or sheep for what would be a one way journey. We parked up near the Djuma mosque, next to a cemetery containing the graves of holy people, where a spring ran deep, full of trout. This is a place for Hajj, holy pilgrimage, visit here three times, said our driver and it counts for one Mecca.

Dominating this scene was the hill fort that Alexander the Great had built in 327 BC. This place provided a link between the agricultural areas to the south and the mighty steppe north-east for Russia and China. He also engineered the spring that brought lifeblood for the town. Unfortunately the trout contain minerals that cause intestinal upsets and cannot be eaten.

There is only one thing to do. Climb to the top of the fort, and it was a steep and treacherous ascent, but totally worth it for the views over the town and across the steppe. There was also graffiti on the opposite hillside, white stones set out ancient messages. I imagined I saw "Cleo hearts Antony".

With a silence disturbed only by the crunch of rock underfoot, standing at the summit, we all felt a sense of wonder realising we were on the very spot Alexander had stood and surveyed his army in ancient history. It was strange how you felt some sort of kinship. He was, after all like us, European, and had worked and fought his way a long way from home to this eastern outpost. For us it had been a lot easier. There was a brooding greyness about the sky as the biting desert wind sent a shiver through me.

North of Nurata the road was dead straight as we passed the occasional herd of goats or camels in a dark green undulating landscape. Eventually, where the steppe had become more sand dune than scrub we came upon our hotel for the evening, a camp of ten yurts surrounding a campfire, nearby a communal building which was our restaurant and bar.

A yurt is a round tent with a conical roof, but these were on concrete foundations, and each contained six beds. Sixty people could have stayed here, and there were tales of drunken antics of western tourists which made me feel slightly ashamed. Thankfully, this evening there were only the five of us plus the driver, and Ahmed our hotelier, camel driver, cook and entertainer.

Behind a sand dune five camels had been saddled up and were tied to posts ready to take us for a walk. None of us wanted the Uzbeki equivalent of a Blackpool donkey ride, so we just fed them from the woody scrub and admired them. They were indeed admirable. These were Bactrian, the double humped variety, and seemed much more handsome in their thick fur coats and pretty features than their Saharan Dromedary cousins. Their long eyelashes made them almost sultry. They also appeared more even tempered, even friendly.

There were a couple of things I was unhappy with. They were tethered to their posts via massive metal studs pierced in their noses. Also, when it was apparent they wouldn't be earning money today, they were unsaddled and untethered, but their front legs were tied together with short ropes (one had a chain) so that they couldn't walk properly.

"We have to do this," I was assured "or they could easily be 25 kilometres away in the morning."

Be that as it may, I was concerned to see that all they could manage now were tiny, mincing steps, or ungainly hops to move up and down the dunes. This was clearly uncomfortable, but my snowflake western sensibilities cut no ice out in the middle of the Kyzil Kum desert.

We enjoyed a spectacular sunset across the wasteland as the sun finally appeared briefly below the cloud cover we'd endured most of the day.

Dinner was.....Plov, with beer, and the campfire was lit so we could enjoy the cold evening. Ahmed gave us a bottle of local vodka to help with the warming and played his tanbur, a three stringed guitar, and sang folk songs. It was very atmospheric, almost haunting in the dancing flames of the campfire. The vodka enabled us to join in with Carpenters, Joni Mitchell and Carole King.

Everyone went to bed leaving me with the dying embers and a quarter bottle of vodka. Well, it would have been rude not to finish it.

When I finally went to bed I had to cannibalise the four remaining beds in my yurt to find enough depth of mattress to enable a decent night's sleep.

Samarkand

Awake at dawn, visit the shower block and porridge for breakfast. Back on the road, south through the desert into Nurata, another look at Alexander's fort then we hit the road, the Golden Road for Samarkand. "For the lust of knowing what should not be known"

Samarkand is probably 3,000 years old, but evidence has been unearthed to show human activity here for over 12,000 years. It has always been important in the area, UNESCO calls it the Crossroads of Culture. Alexander introduced Hellenic culture, and at the birth of Islam it quickly became a centre for learning, for which it proudly remains. Genghis Khan took it, sacked it then restored it to a garden of Eden before Amir Timur, Tamerlane made it his capital and set about creating the artistic centre of his empire. His patronage of the arts was matched only by his cruelty in battle.

Timbuktu, Marrakesh, Kathmandu, Machu Picchu, Mandalay, Tipperary. Some place names are alluring, magical, mysterious. Immortalised in verse, they conjure up mystical pictures in the mind of the adventurer, images that say I must go there, discover the source of the mystery, understand the hype. Samarkand falls into that category.

Once we left Nurata, it was another hour to Navoi before we rejoined the Silk Route. Out of the city the steppe quickly reappeared, scrubland desert, occasional waterholes, the only life the occasional farm cottage with goats and goatherd. There were mountains to our right, to the south, and you could see villages built into the cols where the water run off could be managed.

When we hit Samarkand it was a disappointment, a vast urban sprawl with impatient, choked traffic jams. This was unlike anything we had seen elsewhere in the country. It was getting late, so we quickly lunched to ensure it wouldn't impose on dinner. We stopped at a modern cafe, the owner, Jez, had lived five years in New York before returning to open this business. He catered for the young and middle classes of Samarkand. If anything, this is a university city, and there are faculty schools on every block of the new town. I celebrated this modern cafe with a pizza.

Prior to checking in we visited the city's ancient necropolis, on a hill to the north east with wonderful views over a city we had yet to discover. The cemetery contained many beautiful mausoleums with excellent acoustics. (I challenge anyone who is told of a building with this sound quality to resist uttering a low "Oooh" at the entrance) Some of the tombs here were probably part of the oldest unspoilt area of the city.

Next door was the famous Ulugbek Observatory. I was expecting something similar to the Jantar Mantar of Jaipur, which Ulugbek may have influenced, but all that remained here was the trench for the lower part of the meridian arc of the sextant. The attached museum however, was very informative.

Of its time it must have been wonderful, and the ruler Ulugbek, a grandson of Tamerlane summoned scientists and mathematicians from all over the empire to design its construction. It could calculate the time and the length of the year, distances to the sun, stars and planets, and the timings of eclipses. As a tribute to his work, the Ulugbek Madrasa, having been restored, was reopened to coincide with a total eclipse of the sun. Voila!

Unfortunately the enlightened Ulugbek kept his scientists busy but not his generals, and he was assassinated in a coup led by his son in 1449 at the age of 55.

It was time to to check-in and the minibus eventually dropped us off at the Malika Prime Hotel. This happened to be next door to Tamerlane's tomb, opposite a park with fountains leading to Registan Square, and adjacent to the main road with a superb regal statue of Tamerlane seated on his throne. No chance of getting lost from this location.

There was barely time to unpack before we hit the sights (just as I like it). From the lobby six of us crossed the road and in the twilight walked past two beautiful fountains to the other side of the park which was flanked by a pair of huge seated tigers. As we approached Registan Square we were hit by a wall of sound. To celebrate tomorrow's half marathon there were rock groups playing music, the like of which which would have graced Eurovision, to crowds of youngsters on the steps of the square.

Then we came upon it, saw it, over the road to our left, and it is jaw-droppingly beautiful. Three Madrasas flank the Registan which is probably 100 yards square, and they are three of the most beautiful buildings imaginable. One on its own would be awesome, but to have three together surely this should be one of the seven wonders of the modern world.

Everything was lit up in the early evening, each portico more ornate than the next; minarets and domes, archways and arcades, cloisters and corridors with lights dancing and gleaming. But there was more, behind each fascinating, glittering facade were courtyards equally colourful and impressive. Each niche contained tasteful shops of art and craftwork. Behind the north Madrasa, a jade dome atop a mosque. Inside, the golden ceiling is unsurpassed. But my favourites were the tiled decorations above the entrance opposite Ulugbek's science school; tigers and gazelles and the faces of the sun. I was struck by the whole place and wandered for hours desperately drinking in every tiny aspect of my new favourite square (previously St. Mark's, Venice).

Dragging ourselves away from Registan Square we eventually dined opposite. The pizza had done its job, I could only stomach a bowl of soup, plus beer, of course.

A much better night's sleep in a hotel which was certainly a cut above the rest. After a breakfast with lovely sweet cakes and croissants I could dip into my hot chocolate, our guide Shukrat, arrived. He's going to spend a very long day with us. The first good news was that because of the half marathon, most of the roads were closed, so no traffic. Secondly, today would be continuing warm, a comfortable 23 degrees. Tomorrow heralds Winter, and it will be a numbing six degrees. That is how quickly temperatures can change in Central Asia.

(I am hoping to drive out to Shahrisabz to visit Tamerlane's birthplace tomorrow, but Shukrat tells me the mountain passes could be closed because of recent heavy rains)

I warmed to Shukrat, a family man in his late thirties. He was as happy talking English football and rugby, as discussing the ancient and modern history of Central Asia. He was especially passionate about his home town of Samarkand, and the flora and fauna it supports. And he liked a beer.

We began by walking the 100 yards to Tamerlane's tomb, the Gurl Amir. Before we can enter the runners come by and we spend ten minutes cheering them on as they wave their gratitude. Then into the mausoleum, an imposing building as beautiful as any we have seen. I was a little disappointed by some noisy tourists, mainly French, who appear to have forgotten that this was a family's tomb.

In hushed tones, Shukrat explained Tamerlane's role in the defeat of Hitler. A Russian scientist had unearthed his bones two days before Hitler launched his invasion of Russia through Operation Barbarossa. The remains were flown to Moscow where Stalin ordered that the pilot circle 200 kilometres around the city, thereby creating a barrier Hitler couldn't cross. He was re-interred the day the Nazis were defeated at Stalingrad. That, at least was the Uzbek interpretation of events. The Russians reckoned Tamerlane's curse pre-empted Hitler's invasion, which was only halted once the curse was put to rest.

In life, Tamerlane, or Timur the Lame was the son of a Mongolian tribal leader, who came to prominence as a military tactician in the mid 14th century. He was injured whilst poaching in his youth and always carried a withered right leg and hand missing two fingers. He married a granddaughter of Genghis Khan, allowing himself to use the title Khan, and founded the Timuric Empire. He amassed a huge army which caused worldwide havoc, killing over 17 million people. He devastated the Hindus of North India, slaughtered the armies and massacred the cities of Muslim Persia, destroyed the Christians of the Levant and finally butchered the Sultans of the Ottoman Empire. Historians believe his ruthless destruction of the Turks saved Europe from Ottoman domination. Christian Europe, it is said, was saved from Islamic annihilation by the most brutal Muslim warlord of all time (and that is probably why he has been depicted favourably in European literature).

His trademark hobby was to build pyramids of skulls. If ever a city displeased him in any way, he would wreak terrible revenge, first trampling children to death, raping and slaughtering the women, and burning and mutilating the men. He once promised not to shed any blood if a population surrendered, only to have them all buried alive. He did have one saving grace, marching off any skilled artisans back to Samarkand to enrich his home city.

He died in his seventies, in the north east of his empire, planning an invasion of China. His Empire didn't long outlive him, it broke up after the death of Ulugbek, but his legacy in art and architecture and a free Europe certainly survived his tyrannical evil.

(So what was happening in Europe whilst Tamerlane was rampaging through Central Asia? England and France were embroiled in their Hundred Years War, the Renaissance was beginning in Italy where the Papacy was moved to Avignon, the Spanish were busying themselves in pushing the Moors back to Africa. Oh, and the Black Death killed a quarter of the European population)

Leaving the mausoleum Shukrat took us across the park, past the fountains and tigers to Registan Square. This was the first time we'd seen it in the sunshine, and Shukrat spent some time telling us about how the buildings had been restored, how the Minarets had been saved from toppling over (they still seem to lean at angles), and about the origins of the remarkable artistic representation of tigers, gazelles and sunshine faces.

"Look at the sun" ordered Shukrat, and foolishly everyone did and flinched "You cannot see a face, therefore you cannot say it is a representation."

"The tigers are symbols of Samarkand, the gazelles their food."

There were no crowds, just a few runners having finished their worthy efforts with their smiling families taking selfies, and at least five wedding parties strutting their stuff. Brides and grooms certainly enjoy this walkabout tradition, especially in the warm sunshine.

Again I wandered the little shops and galleries which lined the cloisters of the Madrasas, delighting at one display of large oils showing the major shrines of the cities of Islam, from Casablanca to Cairo, Istanbul to Jerusalem, Damascus to Palmyra, Najaf, Mecca and Medina, and on to Samarkand and Tashkent.

I lunched on lagnam, a very tasty vegetarian noodle soup, not unlike minestrone, and in the afternoon we left Registan Square, and walked the pedestrianised road down to The Bibi Khanum Mosque. Again this is a restored building, the original, built towards the end of Tamerlane's life having suffered for being too big. Its structural integrity could not stand the test of time and it gradually fell into disrepair. It was virtually rebuilt during the Soviet era, but there are still areas where tiles and brickwork can suddenly fall and brain the unlucky tourist.

Bibi (sweetheart) was Tamerlane's wife, the granddaughter of Genghis Khan. She commissioned the architects, whilst her husband campaigned in India, one of whom fell in love with her. The young man resisted his feelings fully realising the consequences of succumbing to her beauty, but eventually the young couple consummated their desires. Legend has it that once the Mosque was completed he grew wings and flew away leaving Bibi distraught.

In all probability the phrase "grew wings and flew away" is a euphemism for had his head chopped off, who knows, but the legend is in contrast to another story.

This tells that when Tamerlane returned from India he was angered that the Mosque was lower than the mausoleum of Bibi, built opposite, indicating she was more important than Allah. Therefore he had his generals executed. Any excuse! This tale assumes Bibi was already dead, which we know she could not have been because of her liaison with the young architect.

Or maybe I am beginning to suffer from Islam overload. Just too many Mosques, Minarets, Madrasas and Mausoleums.

As we were leaving I noticed that the magnificent blue domes of the mosque looked covered in plants, and asked Shukrat if they were ever cleaned. He explained that sand from the desert blows in and coats the tops of these domes. The desert sands carry seeds which germinate and grow, their roots creating havoc with this garden effect. There are attempts to clean them every ten years, he assured me.

We returned to the hotel for a brief rest before meeting up for our last meal together which Shukrat had arranged and which was to include entertainment. The meal was an uninspiring four courses; a bowl of salad, followed by noodle soup (including a quail's egg which I lifted out), some of those greasy samosa shaped dumplings, and honey cake. Musicians arrived and played in another room, out of sight, and made a couple of French tourists dress up traditionally as bride and groom and jig around to the amusement of their fellow travellers.

The main course however was still to come. Leaving the restaurant we walked to Regimen Square where the Madrasas were lit up as the previous evening, but there were no groups playing loud music.

We found a position on the steps to watch the sound and light show which Shukrat told us would begin at nine.

Gradually, solemn classical music began to play and the lights began to dance. It was very similar to the previous evening but more in time with the mood music. For half an hour we stood and watched as the different elements of the square glowed and gleamed in turn making for a kaleidoscope of shapes and colours, and when the show was over the gathered crowd applauded politely.

I say gathered crowd, there were perhaps 50 or 60 people, and one or two began to drift away. The temperature had really fallen from the 24 degrees of the day, and we were shivering, our teeth chattering. But Shukrat wouldn't let us leave.

There was a row of ten chairs set up beside us and the guards now asked everyone to line up behind them. Some VIP's were expected.

A very ordinary looking family turned up and took these seats, and the signal was made to begin the second show of the evening, the 3D show.

Suddenly every light went off and we were plunged into a cold, black, moonless night.

When all was quiet a fanfare began, (similar to the Fanfare for the Common Man by Aaron Copland, but more Soviet style) and the lights gradually phased in on the cloisters, porticos, minarets and arches, blends of oranges and blues. As the crescendo arrived all went black but for a glowing dot which expanded into an event horizon. Then it came, an explosion of sound and light to indicate The Big Bang (Oohs and Aahs all around). Stars appeared then a distant planet which grew larger in its approach until clearly Central Asia could be seen. There was commentary to the holographic scenes but not in English.

Fire appeared in a cave, then a torch indicated cave drawings of bison and mammoth. The music had moved from strident horns to gentle strings. Horsemen appeared but then there was an all encompassing light of the Egyptian civilisation with pyramids and temples. Obelisks reached to the sky as the face of Queen Nefertiti revolved into view. The desert evolved into jungle and images of Mayan and Incan architecture.

The music changed to feature a sitar as Hindu temples, gods and goddesses danced seductively into view. Then a change again with a Chinese dragon swooping and flying into the crowd. An armoured warrior with spear and shield ran and leapt, Achilles style above our heads.

The imagery and music continued until we reached the present day and the message was clear that education and science are the keywords for our modern civilisation.

The conclusion met with great applause and even greater nodding of heads as people chatted, appreciating the work and artistry that must have gone into the creation of this pageant.

We made our way in the now bitter cold, back to the hotel and drinks, especially Shukrat's warming vodka. The show was complete, I thought, and now so was my emerging knowledge of this part of Central Asia. I've learned of a route linking east and west with ideas and culture, of the rise and fall of ancient civilisations, the foolish man-made changing of landscapes, heroism, despotism, and spiritualism. There has been the futility of wars, the revolting carnage of empire building and, as everywhere man's insatiable appetite for both cruelty and beauty. I've been touched by a society working its way out of the communist dirge and embracing the twenty first century. And none of this could have been accomplished without beer and plov, and the help and guidance of people like Shukrat, Ahmed, Munisa and Rosina, and especially Odil Beq.

Tomorrow it's back to Tashkent by evening train as the weather has put the kibosh on my trip to Shahrisabz, and I'll learn the remarkable origin of the Vok-Zal rail network.

My final morning in Samarkand, and the cold had enveloped the city. I had nothing planned so began by revisiting Tamerlane's tomb and the shops set up in the cloister now doing a roaring trade in those big furry hats, mittens and heavy woollen socks. I walked back passed the hotel and turned left down the wide University Boulevard. I found a Chinese monument signifying the end of the Silk Road (precious close to mine), with Confucius, dragons, artificial trees and a water garden. Beyond I discovered the Russian Orthodox Cathedral to Saint Alexis, as you might expect, festooned with biblical icons.

As the morning grew I strolled, a little briskly in the weak sunshine back through the park and the twin tigers, to Registan Square and saw another five weddings, some of the poor brides were shivering in their low cut shoulderless ensembles. Through the square and down the hill to the Bibi Khanum Mosque and what I had missed yesterday, Bibi's Mausoleum where she lay with her mother and three nieces. As I left I realised these were the first steps in my journey home.

Outside in the bazaar there were stalls selling nuts and dried fruit, and the doves were gorging on them. It seemed too cold even for the

147

stallholders to shoo them away.

I lunched on Shorma, another thick vegetable soup and walked back through the Square onto the park where the women continued sweeping their leaves, keeping the country spotless.

At the hotel I had to check out, and could only sit in reception awaiting my taxi to the railway station. I had no wish for any more exploring. I had finished with the lust of knowing what should not be known. I knew it now, I thought, naively. I sipped on a warming bottle of vodka, purely medicinal.

The torpor was broken with my ride to the station, declaring itself in huge letters on the roof, the VOK-ZAL. Shukrat told me that a group of Uzbeki engineers visited England in the late nineteenth century to learn how to build and run the railway. They were shown the engines, rolling stock, sidings and lines, and the LSWR station at Vauxhall (VOK-ZAL). This was possibly apocryphal, as other stories have Tzar Nicholas II as the visitor, and the railways of Russia have a similar etymology, something to do with pleasure gardens. Still, why let facts get in the way of a good story.

The station itself was beautiful, with stained glass windows and chandeliers. My train when it arrived was of a new era, a bullet train. Sadly it was now dark and I would not be able to enjoy views of the countryside, so I spent a few more pennies and secured a first class aisle berth. A mistake, as I shared six plush seats with five huge businessmen. They each had two telephones (which is always dodgy) which they consulted on a regular basis, and the bear seated opposite kept kicking my shins. Mercifully the speed averaged 120 MPH so we were together for only 90 minutes. The meal I was served was inedible but for a small cake, but the coffee was good.

In Tashkent I checked into the same hotel and this time had a suite on the twelfth floor overlooking Amir Timur Square and the Christmas tree city. I dined on the 17th floor on river fish with cheese and potatoes and stole myself to walk into the town. It was freezing, and although the streets were lit up as mentioned, everything was shut tight, closed, dead. So I returned to the hotel spent my last twenty thousand Sum on large brandies and fell into bed.

I had an early morning flight and therefore a dawn wake-up call. My familiar driver (does Tashkent only have one driver) took me to the airport and I flew to Istanbul. Awaiting my connection to Birmingham I saw Dr Pauline striding towards her Manchester connection, and banged on the window to wave. She saw me, smiled and waved back. She said something which might have been "Two pints of lager and a packet of crisps, please?" or "Pluuurv!", I couldn't be sure.

Walking the Great Wall

No greater icon for a bucket list could you consider. The Taj Mahal, perhaps or the Great Pyramids, or even Stonehenge. But as far as bucket list icons go this is the one. There are some myths surrounding the Great Wall of China; "the only man made object you can see from space" for example, but that is a fallacy, not that I've ever been able to disprove it, of course. Along with photographic evidence of the moon landings, strangely there doesn't appear to have been any of those either. One for the conspiracy theorists.

I set off to walk the Great Wall via Schipol Airport. The combination of the transfer from Birmingham, the eleven hour flight and Beijing being eight hours ahead meant I arrived one day into the future without having had a proper night's sleep. In short, I was shattered and disoriented. I recall seeing the impressive Bird's Nest Olympic stadium as I was driven through a very modern city to my hotel, but little else.

I arrived mid-afternoon at the undistinguished Xiuo Xiang hotel and rested before walking the few streets into Tiananmen Square. Seeing this historic place by artificial light when most of the crowds had disappeared was surreal. A huge empty space in this city of 13 million souls. Much of it was cordoned off, especially around Mao Tse Tung's Mausoleum in the southern centre. This was to prepare for a parade the following day. There were pairs of armed soldiers around most corners, but mostly smoking and chatting amiably and affecting a rather relaxed air.

Pictures of Mao (now renamed Mao Zedong) loomed down from every building, especially at the northern end where beyond the Gate of Heavenly Peace lay the Forbidden City. The sky was clear, but starless due to the ever present smog, and everyone hawks. You hear the great clearing of the throat like some rising pneumatic hammer behind you, then the pause, the spit and the splat. As you move aside in disgust a petite and pleasant young business lady will walk by. Hawking is a sadly ubiquitous national habit which the authorities tried to ban during the Olympics, but has sadly stayed with the whole population. I suppose the smog doesn't help.

I wandered the square and visited the place where tanks entered in 1989 and the student stood in their way. That episode didn't end well. With images of one young man blocking the advance of a column of tanks in mind, I headed for bed. A brave man indeed.

I had a full day in Beijing before I was to head off to the eastern end of the Great Wall to begin my trek. So I decided to explore the Forbidden City and then take in an opera. "You must visit the opera when in Beijing" I had been told. "It is unbelievable". I thought they meant unbelievably good. I was to be enlightened.

I left early to mingle with the crowds in the great square. Experiencing Tiananmen in daylight made me appreciate how lucky I had been to visit the previous dusk. The crowds were enormous and there were hundreds of groups of Chinese tourists, all distinguishable by their uniform coloured caps and following, sheep-like one person with a raised umbrella.

I headed across the square to the entrance to the Forbidden City and to join a jostling throng. I'm not overly tall by western standards, but to be in such a crowd, towering over most, felt like I was stood on a box on an old football terrace. The whole time in the queue, the 100 foot visage of Mao smiled contentedly down at me.

Once inside the crowds dissipated and I was left to wander this magnificent structure. There was square upon square, each flanked by cooling cloisters and the most beautiful and ornate pagoda temples of state. Lion statues guard every entrance and topiaried trees and shrubs lend a green hue to the hushed ambiance. Eventually at the far end of these squares I arrived at the private quarters for officials, concubines, dowagers, and finally the Emperor himself. Built around 1420 during the Ming dynasty, no-one from this vast country was allowed to see this walled city for nearly 500 years, save the Emperor and his entourage.

To illustrate how the royal house operated there is the example of a Ming Dynasty dowager (the Emperor's widowed mother). A typical lunch for this regal lady would consist of the total production from five farmers' annual toil. The feast would be spread before her, and she would just pick at it and dismiss it. It is no wonder that such corrupt imperial waste would lead to peasant revolt and communism. And similarly little wonder why these palatial grounds and buildings are the top tourist attraction for 1.3 billion Chinese. There are reputedly 980 surviving buildings, mostly wooden and wonderfully colourful, and superstition has it, 9,999 rooms. But that is another myth.

I hailed a rickshaw to take me to the Huntun district, an ancient suburb of narrow alleyways, and Drum and Bell towers. I took lunch at the restaurant house of Mr Leung who not only fed me but also showed how traditional peasant households lived. Not dissimilar to our own dark ages; small, sparsely adorned rooms where tea and rice and bringing up children were the daily chores. Similar, except for the tea and rice.

Less than 24 hours in China and two things have struck me. One, the absence of children; the well-documented one child per family law applies only to the Han ethnic group (over 90%), and doesn't apply if you are that "one child" when you marry. Secondly, the food, which is wonderfully delicious, and I've only had three meals. What happens between here and Blighty that makes the food from Chinese takeaways so bland?

Back home (it's a faceless hotel where I've spent one night, and I'm already treating it as home!) I readied myself for the opera. The theatre was only a short walk away and as an auditorium very similar to those in Britain. Front of house box office, stall, circle and wings, simple seating and stage below.

And the performance began. I have never in my life (except in school music lessons) heard a more cacophonous caterwauling and discordant jarring instrumentation. It is an assault on the ears, even if the costumes, props and actors seem pleasant enough. In fact the "singers" seemed to almost take on board the ridiculous nature of their performances to add a blend of humour. The final scene of juggling sword fighting saved the whole evening and the finale which saw the diva playing keepy-uppy with the weapons was almost surreal.

I had learned my first Mandarin words; bin pijo means cold beer, and a couple of bin pijos led to an early night. Tomorrow leave the smog, the crowds and the traffic behind. I'm going to see the Great Wall of China.

In the morning I met the group with which I would be sharing the next few days. Led by Peter, a 25 year old local lad, bespectacled and studious, there were two Brummie ladies, Jo and Cassie on a sabbatical from their businessmen husbands, a quiet northern lass, Karen, and two married couples. Terry and Joanne were a retired couple from Leicester, and Raymond and Lynn, travel agents from Dorset.

We caught the 7:30am train to the coast from Beijing's West station; a clean, spacious, bright complex. We were led onto the train and to our reserved seats by the most beautiful and attentive, uniformed stewardesses. It took over half an hour to clear the city, then there were three hours of rural flatness and strip agriculture. Suddenly the countryside relented and the train passed oceans of huge industrial complexes, mostly steelworks, on the outskirts of which were built featureless cities of five storey apartment blocks to house the workers. The rural landscape returned as we arrived at the coast. We took a street pancake for lunch at Shanhaiguan where a minibus awaited to take us to the "Entering Sea Stone Wall"

Here was the ocean; the Pacific Ocean and the Old Dragon's Head of Laolongtou. This was the beginning of the Great Wall, although not the first part to be built, it is at least a natural start point, where the wall emerges from the ocean. To imagine the Dragon, you have the sea, then a section of square stone wall (the snout), then a raised square watchtower (the head and eyes). All of this is restored with a rather new, grey and dull appearance. But at least there was the sea, the beach, and a beautiful golden Sea God temple. It housed huge statues of fiercely bearded and wild eyed warriors (fighting or appeasing the Sea God, I wasn't sure). There was also a shop on the beach, the equivalent of our Poundland. This "Two Yuan" shop housed all sorts of valueless curios, but I bought a couple of lion statues; 20 pence apiece.

I spent some time on the beach, a magical moment, about as far from home as I had ever been. We live on the very western edge of the huge land mass that comprises Europe and Asia. Our shores are washed by the warm Atlantic brought by the gulf stream. Here, on the very eastern point, lapped by the cold Pacific, I was at least half a world away.

There was a sea mist and hazy sunshine and I gazed across the water towards the home of the greatest enemy ever known to the Chinese, worse even than the Mongol hordes protection from whose attacks this wall was built. The Chinese nemesis has always been the people from the islands of Japan.

Daydreaming done for the moment I walked along the refurbished ramparts before our minibus took us to the garrison town of Shenhaiguan and the Shanhai Pass Fort, the First Pass Under Heaven.

We checked into a cold, soulless hotel and set off to experience the First Gate Garrison. Here again, the wall and fort is totally rebuilt, almost like new, and as such is a grey and barren edifice, thoughtlessly sterile. There appears to be no sense of originality or history here, very much in keeping with an emotion free, lifeless regime. From the battlements there is a misty horizon, but the only vista was of slums, high rise apartments, wastelands and factories.

Returning to the hotel we were made to feel like strangers in a strange land, lots of staring and pointing. Oddities indeed. Tonight's meal included donkey. I had to try it, and it was nothing like chicken, more gristly tapioca. And we ate in the most cold, deathly white-tiled restaurant with bleak formica furniture and buzzing, bare, bleaching fluorescent tubes. It felt and smelt like a 1950's urinal. Tomorrow has to be better.

The Great Wall of China is over 5,000 miles long, and runs mostly east to west. It was built to protect the civilised Chinese in the south from the Mongol, or barbarian horsemen who raided from the north. It had to be garrisoned constantly so there were watchtowers with living quarters built at every high point, and often at the lower levels towns rose up to provide legitimate border crossings. We're not intending to walk the whole thing, but to visit recommended trekking areas and places of interest. For this purpose I had joined this small expedition which had the benefit of a guide and transport taking luggage to pre-booked hotels.

The group checked out of Hotel Cold, not an auspicious start. It was already a depressing town, now the weather was grey and misty and cold and wet. We appeared to begin the trek from an industrial estate where we climbed a mound and could suddenly see a paved wall disappearing upwards into the distance. "Don't worry," said Peter, smiling, "as we climb we rise above the cloud and will see Jiaoshan, the first mountain of the Great Wall".

He wasn't wrong. This first section was renovated, but only in a repairing way. Much of the original wall was left intact. It was like walking on a street with large cobbles. Rarely was it wider than 10 feet, and mostly there were small walls either side protecting us from a sheer drop. The wall is rarely too high off the ground, maybe 20 or 30 feet, after all its purpose was mainly to stop horses, and the battlement was always steepest on the northern side.

The trek began, inexorably upwards, and the spirits lifted with the mist. Soon we were beyond the rain and cloud and in bright sunshine. For the first time I could see that iconic view of the wall snaking before and behind me, hugging the contours of the landscape. After three watchtowers and at the top of this section was the Jiaoshan Pass, and as others rested I climbed the to a high point which had magnificent views back to Shanhaiguan, Laolongtou and the Bohai Sea, and forward to Yangsai Lake and Changshou Mountain.

We picnicked at this point then trekked down a more wild section of the wall to meet our transport. We were driven three hours to the town of Panjiakou, beside a great man made reservoir. Here the wall disappears into the water only to miraculously reappear the other side. Of course, the wall was built long before this reservoir was created to drown this section.

Now, having seen a fair portion of Chinese landscape, I can make a few observations. No piece of land is natural or very little wild. There are sprawls of towns and colossal industrial complexes. Occasionally you see huge swathes of land being given over to new highways or building projects. That which is not built on is given over to agriculture. Even the mountains are terraced as far up to the peaks as possible. All furrows hug the contours and seem to go on forever. Where trees are allowed they are similarly only planted in straight lines. Only where the land is unusable, next to a road or rail line, or in corners of fields where rocks have been dumped, have families used these areas for burial sites. Although this is strictly illegal, the practice is allowed.

Sadly, in such a vast country with such overwhelming vistas, and where at this time of year the blossom is stunningly beautiful, litter is a huge problem. It features everywhere, all sorts of litter, not just the usual plastic bags. It gathers in holes and corners, choking waterways and sticking to buildings and trees. I'm afraid the Chinese people seem to have the same attitude to litter as to hawking. If they continue to aspire to being western (and looking at their billboard advertising which feature attractive round eyed models in western clothes, it appears they do) then they very much need to bring themselves into the 21st century.

On second thoughts our record on litter is nothing to aspire to, looking at our parks and beaches after a warm spell. I blame the teachers.

With four hours of strenuous walking behind us I felt we had earned the beers we shared before dinner at a very pleasant provincial hotel.

I love a lazy susan on a round table. The only problem is that we are used to being given a plate of food and on completion of that plate we generally know that we are full. With lots of plates of food being whizzed around so that you fill a little bowl, then again and again, you don't know when you've had your fill, or too much, or, God forbid, not enough. Still, amongst all this confusion the chat and the laughter were sustenance aplenty.

After breakfast (I loved the flavoured tofu) it was time for day two of our great trek. A speedboat was waiting to take us the 30 minutes at exhilarating speeds to where the wall emerged from the reservoir. As we climbed we passed what looked like an abandoned village, but Peter told us its origin was much more sinister. It was the set for a film entitled, rather humorously "The Japanese Devils are Coming". Somewhat racist, in these days of political correctness. But the Japanese Devils or "Riben Guizi" was the term used for the invading Japanese armies from 1931 to the end of the Second World War. The atrocities committed by these soldiers included rape, torture, massacres, cannibalism, and horrific medical experimentation. Truly inhumanity to rival the European Holocaust.

When we try to understand the attitudes of the peoples of these lands of the Orient to each other, we must delve into very black histories indeed.

The climb was invigorating. The wall here had been mostly left to return to the wild, so it was fairly difficult terrain, but much more authentic than the sterile rebuilt wall around Shenhaiguan. The trees, shrubs, flowers, insects and birds appeared much more natural and abundant. With the sun shining in a clear sky we climbed up from the blue waters of the lake towards the summit, and upon reaching it the vista around was incredible. Mountains in all directions, the wall snaking out to the East; and turning to look at the direction we had come, the wall plummeting into the lake below only to reappear and snake off into the mountains to the North West, towards Mongolia.

We descended to the boat which took us across the lake to the opposite bank where we could engage in another ascent at Xifengkou. These were quite strenuous walks, but the boat still managed to return us to the hotel for lunch after which we were bussed to our next port of call at Luowenyou where we undertook another strenuous but breathtakingly beautiful six mile trek overlooking two valleys.

Our final port of call for the day was the Eastern Qing Imperial tombs near Zunhua. We entered along chestnut groves onto the Sacred Way flanked by marble obelisks, and statues of elephant, lion and mandarins. It had been a long day so hotel, beer, dinner and bed beckoned.

There was an overnight storm which cleared the air leaving it sunny but with a bitingly cold wind. I took a walk between dawn and breakfast along the Sacred Way which acts as entrance to the tomb complex. It was wide, flat and very peaceful. And with Chinese architecture all around, flanked by distant mountains I felt a long way from home, albeit harmonious. It was a Feng Shui moment.

Breakfast was rice in dishwater, not my favourite, and afterwards the group assembled for the tour of the tombs. We visited three Qing tombs, all of which were marvellously endowed with riches and decorations and opulence which would have been long since plundered elsewhere in the world. The biggest and most impressive tomb was that for the Emperor Shunzhi whose huge burial hall was richly decorated with bas-relief Buddhas and Sanskrit. This tomb is called Xiaoling, and all the other tombs were aligned with it.

I fell in love with CiXi. Peter informed us she began life as a concubine, rose to become Empress (though never officially crowned), but then as Empress Dowager effectively ruled "from behind the curtain" for 47 years until her death in 1908. Her dynasty came to an end three years later. This magnificent woman was a contemporary of Queen Victoria. This means that for the second half of the nineteenth century these two grand ladies, who would have never met, ruled empires which governed more than half the people on Earth. Mind you, CiXi was a plotter, poisoner and murderer of rivals and political enemies. I doubt Victoria will ever be accused of any such shenanigans.

Her tomb is called Dindongling (I'm sure a Chuck Berry or Goons ditty may come to mind) and it displays the most exquisite architecture. The refined decorations and carvings are in gold, the symbol of royalty. There are phoenixes and dragons, drifting water and flowing clouds, and on white marble balustrades they perfectly illustrate the philosophy of Yin and Yang.

Following lunch we were taken to a section of the wall called the Yellow Cliff or Huangya Pass. We walked up the Huangya Sky Ladder, a series of steeply ascending broken stairways to a prominent watchtower, and then down past several collapsed watchtowers to the garrison town of Huangyaguan set in a river valley. Here we entered a pleasant grey stone courtyard for our hotel, dined on beef, chicken, pork, and pineapple, and then devoured divine banana fritters in toffee. We would have socialised more, but the bitter cold drove everyone off to bed. Had they not heard of patio heaters?

Everywhere in China you see carved or drawn or painted or stickers of the symbol for Yin and Yang. It is a circle divided into two apostrophes which perfectly spoon. The circle is black and white and it represents the philosophy that everything has its complementary opposite; from fire and water to mountains and valleys; from male and female to sun and moon. Yin is old and cold and can be represented by a tiger whereas Yang is warm and young and features the dragon.

In this philosophy the universe has perfect synonymity and harmonisation, with the most powerful concepts being good and evil. We might talk about good and bad karma, or simply assert that what goes around comes around. Yin Yang complements Buddhism, as acceptance and adherence to this philosophy can bring you to a higher plain of peace and contentment. In Chinese religion Taoists favour Yin whilst followers of Confucius tend to Yang. It is believed that when there is too much of an imbalance, natural disasters occur; floods wild fires and earthquakes, typhoons and tsunamis, droughts and plagues.

I felt, as I tucked into a breakfast of pancakes and spicy tofu, that I could feel Yin and Yang in the town of Huangyaguan; a symmetry of river and hills, urban surrounded by wilderness, order in the new town's architecture complementing the run down wall to its either side. Even the sun and clear skies contrasted the cold and damp.

With this feeling of wellness surging through my spirit I climbed onto the bus for the long journey to the mountain resort of Chengde, the summer retreat for the royal Qing dynasty.

Over four hours we discussed many things. Western hypocrisy (investing on other cultures our own sensitivities), was a favourite of the Brummie girls, both vegetarian. "We eat cattle, sheep, pigs, and all sorts of birds and fish life", they stated. "We cannot condemn others for using horses or dogs, or whatever in their food". Provided we can eradicate cruelty and ensure sustained stocks, surely, they argued, we must respect each to their own. A fair point, well made.

The subject turned to poaching. A hundred years ago we were still lording it over Africa and India and shooting elephant and rhino, leopard and lion, tiger and bear, and even fellow primates for sport. The Great White Hunter was a hero and a figure to be admired and emulated and the success of a day's hunting for members of the nobility was measured sometimes in the thousands of creatures destroyed. I even remember as a child reading of Prince Philip proudly shooting a tiger measuring some 15 feet from nose to tail. How times and our sensitivities have changed. We used to be proud if we owned ivory ornaments and fur coats.

Now we are enlightened we chastise the Chinese using powdered rhino horn for an aphrodisiac. Fur coat wearers are demonised. Owning ivory is now illegal. And we argue poachers should be shot on sight by game wardens.

We wholeheartedly agreed there is a need to nurture our wonderful planet's fantastic diversity of life. But not everybody can be as enlightened as we think we are. Maybe we need to be spending millions on education rather than enforcement, looking after those who live alongside our endangered species.

Just as one man's terrorist is another's freedom fighter, what we see as a poacher, could simply be a father trying to feed and keep his family safe.

Karen, the quiet northerner was quite outspoken over this. "Look at us obsessed with our Xboxes and Iphones, feeding our obese kids on McDonald's, and draining the world of fossil fuels, when the vast majority of people in the world exist on one bowl of rice a day"

Terry, a retired binman from Leicester added that "Our Meedja" campaigned against low wages being paid to children making our clothes for Primark. "If they succeeded in closing down these sweat shops" he argued, "We'd be depriving those families of their only income."

Funny thing this Yin and Yang.

I tried to lighten the mood by recounting a story told to me by a colleague, Frankie, who had lived with her forces husband and their two little children in Hong Kong. The kiddies, like little ones everywhere wanted pets and the family decided on guinea pigs or hamsters. One Saturday morning they took a trip to the livestock market where you could buy everything from pigs to pangolins. Finding a stallholder with a cage full of hamsters, the little ones deliberated over their favourites. After much excited debate, the two chose their favourites, Hammy and Sammy, and happily pointed them out to their owner. He carefully lifted them from the cage and quick as a flash, "Squik, Squik" wrung their necks and handed them with a toothless grin to the mortified children.

Arriving late into Chengde, we visited two temples. The first, Puning Temple is known as the Big Buddha temple as it contains the world's highest wooden sculpture. The next, the Putuo Zongcheng is an appeasement to Tibetans, an almost perfect copy of the Dalai Lama's temple in Lhasa, the temple to the "Living Buddha". This was not only impressive in itself, but the views back down to the city and mountains beyond were indeed sumptuous.

Back down in the city we undertook a tour of the Summer Palace where latterly CiXi had ruled as Dowager Empress, but where more famously the McCartney Mission had come to grief.

In 1793, George McCartney was Great Britain's first envoy to China and his delegation set out to meet the Emperor Qianlong at his summer residence to establish links between the two great empires. Although much was learned and many agreements reached, the meeting fell short of achieving its main goals, and will be remembered in history as the time we "refused to kowtow" to the emperor. In truth McCartney executed an agreed genuflection, and all was amicable, but China remained virtually closed to the western world for the next 100 years and our language acquired a cliche to the effect of not allowing ourselves to be browbeaten into submission.

We finished the day taking in the lovely gardens and parkland surrounding the Cheng Lakes. Here locals flew kites sky high, courting couples floated on their swan pedalos, and careless dog owners allowed their mutts to harass the stags which were trying to protect their herds of does and fawns. Very cruel, although as I've said before, we should not invest on other cultures the sensitivities we hold fast in our own. It was pretty wonderful, however, to see huge stags with great antlers roaming a public space. It was almost like being back on Cannock Chase.

That night, in Chengde centre I was stuck in a restaurant, the others having left. I was beckoned over and invited to join a local family to share their meal; two brothers, their wives, and a child each. Conversation was naturally difficult, they had no English, neither me Mandarin, but they did manage to convey that the two men worked as HGV drivers and they were very proud to be able to welcome tourists into their country. I had already dined on sizzling beef and a delicious aubergine dish, so we shared beers and some divine cherries. My hosts ate ribs and poultry and assorted noodles. It was interesting to observe their casual attitude to waste. Whilst laughing and joking and smoking, bones and stones and any other unwanted fare were nonchalantly thrown under the table. I imagined this was traditionally for dogs to devour, but with no dogs allowed in the restaurant, the mess on the floor just piled higher and higher.

I retired to my rather soulless hotel quite pleased with the day's excursions, discussions, and rest from strenuous trekking.

I like exploring hotels; you never know what you may find. To demonstrate this I will often accompany sceptical friends to the roof (there's always a way) by taking the stairs beyond the lift and there will be a door, sometimes perhaps, quite stiff, and, hey presto! Up here, there will be cabling and air conditioning units, lift winding mechanisms, flues and vents, and usually assorted rubbish as housekeeping dump broken furniture. Whatever view you have from your room or balcony, the roof view is ten times better and 360 degrees, with full sky.

I had been to the roof of our Chengde hotel at sunset and enjoyed the views especially of the false Llasa temple and the mountains beyond. The next morning I decided to explore further as I had woken well before breakfast. Somehow I managed to take a wrong turning and found myself on a staircase leading down to the rear of the hotel. It was signed as an official fire exit so I knew I wasn't heading for any private quarters, so I continued. At the bottom of the stairs was an unlit and windowless room, but I saw a door which I tried. The door opened and I was bathed in the light of dawn coming from another opening across the floor. There was a pungent smell of kitchens which I would have expected and the room I was about to step into looked a little dilapidated, but it was an unused rear entrance, no problem there. There were shelves piled high with boxes to my right and left, and the floor was black.

I stepped down onto the floor which abruptly erupted and exploded around me and I was instantly engulfed in a huge swarm of bluebottle flies. This was hugely unexpected and a great shock as the whole room became a black swarm of buzzing insanity. For a moment I was completely confused, confounded and bedazzled; but my instinct was to carry on walking towards the light. The floor was slippery but I knew I couldn't fall, and in six or seven hurried steps which seemed to take forever, I stumbled out into the sunshine and away from the flyblown room. Having cleared it by several yards I stopped and put my hands on my knees, breathing heavily. As it struck me what had happened, I began to rub my hair, face, eyes, skin and clothes to make sure none of the evil little creatures were still attached to me, in much the same way you see someone appearing to fight the invisible man when bothered by a solitary wasp.

Having gathered my senses I walked back to the open doorway and looked inside. The boxes on either side were full of eggs, it was an egg depository. The floor was covered in egg, and the air eruption was beginning to subside as the inhabitants went back to settling and feeding on the broken contents. It was beginning to return to black.

I walked around the block to the front of the hotel, wiped my feet, entered and smiled at reception. The receptionist had her glasses perched on the end of a tiny nose, and she watched, open mouthed as this dishevelled guest shuffled by. I made my way back up to my room, showered and changed clothes, and went down for breakfast. No eggs!

Today was to be my final day walking the wall and we were heading for what is purportedly the most beautiful section of the whole 13,170 miles (it would reach half way around the world), from Jinshanling to Simatai. Much of the wall is restored, but only sufficiently to make hiking relatively safe. The views from back and forth and around were just stereotypical of every picture you've ever seen of the Great Wall.

The earth dragon, snaking (sorry about the mixed metaphors) up and down the green hillsides, mountains all around, but not another soul to be seen. The sun shone, the air was clean with a light zephyr breeze, and the vegetation green and lush. The fragrant flowering shrubs heavy with the low buzz of flitting bees. Butterflies hunted nectar with the humming-bird moth, and tiny birds joined them as storks and cranes whirled high above. This was 360 degree wonder. There were 32 watchtowers in all, some only about 150 yards apart, this must have been logistically a most important defensive section, guarding the approaches to Beijing.

All those watchtowers. That's 32 ups and 32 downs, and some of these were precariously crumbling, near vertical stairways. It was a five hour hike, quite strenuous at times, but well worthwhile. At the end of it were the Fairy Maiden and Wangjing towers, both built over a sheer precipice looking down into the valley and the town of Simatai. We rested and took our packed lunch at the highest point, the Wangjing tower and expected a long, winding trek down into the town. But no, our descent was to be far more spectacular.

Below us was a gorge through which ran the Xiaotang river. We were each fitted with harnesses, and one at a time attached to a zip wire and hurtled down over the river to a small jetty. Here we boarded a speedboat which, a mile or so downstream deposited us at the village of Simatai and our final hotel of the walk. In the courtyard beers were gratefully received and consumed with gusto. That evening we dined as usual around a well laden lazy susan and said our goodbyes. Peter had been a remarkable and well informed guide, if a little confused by Jo and Cassie's constant teasing and flirting.

Tomorrow it's back to Beijing, the only capital city in the world with three consecutive dots.

I had left the city by train, and previously entered when tired and jet lagged. This final arrival into the huge metropolis was a real eye opener. Officially with a population of 13 million people but actually closer to 18 million, Beijing is mighty indeed, and looking to become mightier yet. Massive office blocks, apartment blocks, hotels, shopping malls, factories, and where you can't see any of the above, then they are being built. Extensive construction is everywhere. The roads are choked with both traffic and pedestrians, and it takes two hours to get from the suburbs to the teeming centre and Tiananmen Square.

Harassed commuters in the UK may say "So what!?!", but after the peace and tranquillity of all of our sections of the Great Wall, the Eastern Qing tombs, and even Chengde, this was a shock to the senses.

My only regret this trip is that I haven't had the time to see the Terracotta Army at Xian. Typical, I always leave a country with reasons to return.

My final ambition was to make an excursion to the main park for Beijingers, the Gardens of Heavenly Peace (Tian'anMen), which were indeed, just a short walk from the Square. They are a tranquil setting in the midst of the city. But there was so much going on. First thing in the morning thousands gather for Tai Chi. However, it was lunchtime and there were still pockets of people everywhere, young and old, practising synchronised Tai Chi. Kite flying seemed to be the main active pastime, and flyers were all around, although it was almost impossible to see what they were flying. Their kites were so high they virtually vanished into the smog. Many couples idly strolled the tree lined avenues, arm in arm. Office workers sat on the grass or at benches frantically dipping their chopsticks into their take away boxes, and groups of tourists or schoolchildren still wearing their colour co-ordinated hats were being ushered hither and thither.

As I walked on I came across a man practising whip cracking. Several folk stopped to see him unfurl his giant leather whip and fling it till the very end snapped back on itself creating the clap so familiar but so impressive as it came with his own special flourish. He of course wore black, with a Zorro style mask. Just around the corner and a male voice choir were rehearsing. I didn't recognise the tune, but it was miles better than the opera. Not far away, but to their own piped music were ballroom dancers, their pace only slightly above that of the Tai Chi, extraordinary indeed. And finally, line dancers, stepping out to country and western. I wandered then just sat and admired. People from the most populous country on earth unselfconsciously emulating cultures so alien as to having been banned during these people's lifetimes, right up to the end of the Cultural Revolution.

Rapid economic development and social changes have created a desire to emulate the freedom of the west. This led to the student protests of 1989 and the "Tankman" incident witnessed by the world. The violent suppression which followed sent China back into darkness just as the rest of the communist world was coming into the light. Subsequently China has seen the error of its ways and entered the 21st century as an enlightened society, albeit with a long way to go. The catalyst for this has been industry and trade, and not only is China no longer a closed country, its tendrils can now be seen all over the world. It is especially prominent in developing countries, aiding with their advancement. There is, of course, no such thing as a free lunch. We shall see.

On the subject of lunch, it was time for my own lunch box, and to make my way to the airport. Amazingly I had a 20 hour journey ahead, but when I eventually reach home, it will still be today.

Sri Lanka Serendip

Serendip is the ancient Arab mariner's word for Ceylon now Sri Lanka, possibly derived from the sanskrit for dwelling place of the lion's head. Horace Walpole adapted tales of three Princes who chanced upon lucky adventures and the term Serendipity was born, a quite beautiful description of happen-stance, unplanned fortunate discovery. And this is the perfect description of the pearl of the Indian Ocean, the teardrop off the southern shores of India, the paradise which is Sri Lanka.

Roughly the size of Ireland, but with a much greater population, Sri Lanka has featured on the world stage in modern times as a holiday destination, the home of a wonderful cricket team, and sadly because of civil strife, terrorism attacks and suffering at the might of the 2002 tsunami.

The vast majority of Sri Lankans are Sinhalese and practice Theravada Buddhism. There is Hinduism alongside, of course, and a good deal of Christianity, brought here by the Dutch, then Portuguese who developed most of the large coastal cities and provided many of the family names.

In my travels around Sri Lanka I met probably the friendliest people I have ever encountered. This is partly due to their happy, relaxed religious views, but the genuine smiles you see on every face matches their idyllic climate, fortunate geography and simple economy. The sun shines, they eat fish, and are surrounded by beauty. Serendipity indeed.

Negombo

We arrived in the early hours via a Sri Lankan Airways direct flight from Heathrow (yes, we, for this was an adventure I shared with my partner, Kaz) and quickly secured a taxi for the transfer. Sometimes it is nice to have a non-English speaking driver, it allows you to relax and take in the scenery without having to small talk.

"Welcome to Sri Lanka. Where you from?" began the driver.

"England" I replied unenthusiastically.

"London?" he ventured confidently.

"No, 200 kilometres north of London" I sought out my stock reply.

"You like football, Manchester United?" he ventured again.

"Yes, but not Manchester, Wolverhampton Wanderers."

"Oh"

There was the insistent ring of his phone. He answered and spoke in Sinhalese. It was the first time I had heard this language, and I was shocked at the speed and tempo. It was all up and down with D's and B's and rolling R's, and completely incomprehensible. It was then I was impressed with his, albeit limited, English.

We had travelled about half an hour from Columbo's airport, Bandarinaike, north past Negombo on the mid-western coast when our driver turned left off the main road and followed a track about a mile to the Dolphin Hotel, at the mouth of the Maha Oya river, near the village of Waikal.

We were tired and grumpy but even at this late hour people fussed around to welcome us and we were led to our little bungalow at the edge of the beach. Our final thought before sinking into our beds was how huge the complex was. I had chosen the Dolphin so that Kaz could have a few days relaxing around the pool before I could uproot her to begin our gallivanting.

We rose late but refreshed and hurried along to the restaurant for breakfast. Ah, my favourite, dahl with chapatis. I prepared for my diet of three curries a day. We loved the restaurant, set in a garden sheltered by trees, it was a cool shady retreat from the searing sunshine. With a stream running through, and the main area accessed by decorative bridges we particularly enjoyed the frog chorus which always greeted our evening meal.

Kaz settled on a sunbed around the pool which advertised itself as the largest on the island (the pool, not the bed), and I set off to explore.

Next to the pool, approaching the ocean was a huge lawn, dotted with palm trees which had chipmunks scurrying between. At the edge of the lawn, the beach of beautiful golden sand was quite steep, and crashing against it huge white foaming breakers which rolled in from the blue horizon. This was the Indian Ocean whipped up by the winds which normally brought the monsoon. I had been assured by the hotel manager over breakfast that this was delayed by a phenomenon he called El Niño.

I turned right along a line of bungalows which led to ours at the end. A small fence indicated the boundary of our hotel, and behind it was a shop in a beach shack with a wooden sign proclaiming itself AZDA. Beyond Azda I could see the straw conical roofs of a village, and men were climbing the palm trees to harvest the coconut flowers with which they made the local drink, Arak. There were double rope systems hung between the trees to save having to go down and back up the next tree. I resolved we would visit the village later.

I turned back towards the lawn where a game of croquet was beginning. A gardener had also ascended one of the king palms with a machete to hack down the coconuts which are a genuine guest hazard (they kill 150 people each year, but hopefully not here).

I came to the southern boundary of the complex and here was a similar shack with a wooden sign, this time proclaiming TESKO. Beyond the little shop was a sandbar, and I could see where the river ended. Here was a huge flock, a murder, of grey headed, hooded crows. They were startled by my arrival and amid a chorus of cawing, flapped into the air. The river that ended here was choked with attractive water hyacinths and their purply-pink, lily like flowers. There was considerable litter also, which I imagined attracted the crows.

I rejoined Kaz and we spent most of the rest of the day playing croquet and sipping gin 'n' tonics. I don't think I have ever felt more colonial and decadent. The breeze from the ocean was very welcome, the heat well advanced of 30 degrees.

Later, with the sun descending and the heat dissipating I took Kaz to visit Azda and the village beyond. As we approached we were surrounded by children asking for Bon-bons. Kaz had a bag of Fox's glacier fruits which she happily distributed. She was delighted. She beamed.

Personally I'm not at all comfortable with this tourism ritual. The sweets aren't good for the children, it encourages them to beg, and it reinforces the image of tourists as white elitists. But on this occasion I happily went along with it.

I have often thought we should adopt Starfleet's Prime Directive which prevents tourists and visitors from interfering with other societies for fear of affecting them adversely. Especially introducing technology or wealth, and therefore not allowing the indigenous people to develop and evolve naturally. I have seen villages throughout the developing world where do-gooder tourists add kudos to their self-esteem by providing their money and labour to build schools. Meanwhile the young men (and children) of the villages hang around the hotels to be used (and abused) by sex tourists. Am I being too straight-laced, or even naïve? After all, the Prime Directive of which I speak comes from the sci-fi Star Trek series. It's fiction.

As we left, one of the little girls detached herself from the others and began to play with Kaz. She was really very pretty, a dark round face with big black eyes and shining white teeth. Her hair was jet black with oceans of curls. She danced and frolicked in the surf, doing cartwheels along the beach, laughing and chattering away.

We eventually had to tear ourselves away, and as we left she held out her hand and in a low almost menacing tone said "Give money!"

We were flabbergasted and returned to the complex a little saddened and chastened.

There was excellent fare at dinner, a veritable continental feast, as advertised by the hotel, and afterwards we took part in a pub quiz where I learned that the actual capital of Sri Lanka is Sri Jayawardenepura Kotte (one to bank for back home) before taking an early night. The short walk along the beach with a black night full of

170

stars and the waves crashing their white luminescence, was very romantic. Outside the door of our little bungalow a mosquito repellent coil burned its incense, and we were soon asleep.

Awake at dawn I watched in awe the fleet of hundreds of Oruvas, small single hulled fishing boats with their white square sails, leaving Negombo lagoon heading out into the ocean for their daily trawl. This and the production of Arak are the main industries around here. Oh, and tourism, of course.

Over the next few days we embarked on a number of adventures. We took a tuk-tuk into Negombo town centre. A mistake. Eight miles on a main road with lorries and buses treating you like you should be in a cycle lane is not much fun in what is essentially a bubble car. We enjoyed Negombo though; the harbour, the fishermen's huts, the smelly fish market, the impressive ceiling of the pink St. Mary's church. There was however too much evidence of poverty, and in places the litter and flies were just awful.

The hotel provided cycles and canoes, so one day we cycled around the little local villages. Off the main road was delightful, and there was always a cheery wave from the locals. The main problem was that inland from the sea without the breeze, and in the middle of the hot, steamy rain forest, it made any physical work really difficult. And the antiquated cycles weren't the easiest to handle.

Then we canoed the canals which had been dug by the Portuguese for ease of travel and irrigation. We realised the villages we'd seen from our bikes centred around the waterways, so children bathing and women washing were common sights. The aromas of the wood fires and cooking were intoxicating and several times we would stop to take tea with local families. Our little trips were delightful except when we got stuck in the water hyacinths, but the wildlife we saw more than made up for any small difficulties. Jacana birds would stride the lily pads, colourful kingfishers, with large beaks perched on each wire we crossed beneath, and water monitors stalked the banks. Occasionally they would swim alongside as we paddled, easily six foot long as they wriggled effortlessly along.

171

We had met John and Jacquie at the quiz, and John suggested I join him for a one day international taking place in Columbo between Sri Lanka and South Africa. Kaz gave all the usual positive female replies; "It's Fine. It's your decision, I'll be OK on my own. You go if that's what you want to do" which all actually mean"Don't you dare!" So I had to let John down.

The match ended in a tie, Sri Lanka having scored something like 320 in their 50 overs, and South Africa nearly overhauling them in a tense and exciting finish. John was ecstatic over the day out, the quality of the cricket and the joyous, carnival atmosphere at the ground. Kaz said I must have been pleased I hadn't gone. "Who wants to come all this way to go and watch a boring draw" was the way she saw it.

On our last morning at the Dolphin, whilst walking near the river mouth Kaz was attacked by the hooded crows who probably saw her blond hair as nesting material. I suppose I wasn't totally committed to shooing them away, after all, as they say in Yorkshire, cricket is God's own game.

Kandy

Chicken George arrived to take us away from all this. This was how he wished to be addressed, and I had employed him to take us to Hikkaduwa in the south of the island, but with some excursions on the way. George was a tall, slender middle aged man with tightly curled white hair and a broad grin. His English was excellent and his car a very comfortable Toyota.

We were sad to leave the Dolphin. The staff had been wonderfully friendly, as had been the other guests, some of whom never left the complex during their holiday. We were gallivanting inland, into hill country.

The driving was interesting, up through the rain forest, very verdant despite the drought, and past several road blocks manned by rifle wielding young soldiers. This was a security feature left over from the civil war fought against the Tamils of the north, who had wanted independence.

Our first stop was the elephant orphanage at Pinnuwela, firmly on the well trodden tourist trail. Twice daily, calves and adolescent elephants are taken to drink and bathe in the local river and people watch them from the balconies of local restaurants. Whilst Kaz watched from above I actually broke free from the tourist shackles and went down to the river to be amongst them. However I was advised to keep my distance by their minders; for my own safety you understand.

The elephants here are orphaned because tragically too many adults get in the way of farmers. We both thought the place was a little exploitative, albeit important to raise money for its upkeep. George had the answer for us, however. Completely unbidden he took us a little way down the road to the elephant retirement home. This is ignored by the coachloads of tourists, a bonus for us and it is a truly magical place.

You will recall I fell in love with Ruby from the Amber Palace of Jaipur in India. Here, where these noble and beautiful creatures come when they reach the end of their working lives, I encountered an even greater love.

We parked up and George led us first into the elephant museum where I learned that elephants only ever have four teeth, two up and two down, and they're each as big as a cobble stone. Out of the back door and we were introduced to 60 year old Lakshmi. She had worked as a painted guard to the Temple of the Tooth in the centre of Kandy, a hugely important holy place for Buddhists as it contains one of his, well you guessed it. The relic is symbolically bathed every Wednesday and the waters, which are said to contain healing powers, distributed amongst the pilgrims. Lakshmi had officiated at this ceremony most of her working life and now continued to entertain the odd pilgrim in her dotage.

She was standing in the river up to her (four) knees and her mahout helped us up onto her back. We were miniscule. The first thing she did was to bathe us. She filled her huge trunk and fired the substantial contents over her back, drenching us in a gigantic wave. It was like water cannon and very nearly bowled us over where we could have tumbled a great distance down into the river. This grand lady seemed to stand at least ten feet high.

Later we became better acquainted when she lay down in the river and allowed us to bathe her. Kaz grew tired and left the river for a cup of tea whilst I used the husk of a coconut to rub Lakshmi's head, neck and shoulders, every so often splashing her with water, which she seemed to enjoy. As our relationship progressed I sat in the river myself and chatted away to her. She occasionally blinked her eyes with the most wonderful four inch lashes, and gently flapped her ears in contentment after I had scrubbed behind them. On her head age had given her a paler pink skin for the top of her trunk, with elephant style freckles and considerable wizened lines.

I can't recall what we discussed, after all what subjects can you engage a mature lady with for over an hour. Whilst the conversation might be forgotten, the time I spent sharing Lakshmi's bath, the meaningful looks we shared, the touch of her soft, leathery skin and the very real warmth I felt existed between us, will remain with me for always. Pure serendipity.

We bade Lakshmi farewell and George drove us to the Royal Botanical Gardens of Peradeniya where we spent a couple of hours wandering the manicured lawns and enjoying the fantastic colourful flora. Some of the trees, especially the kapoks with their flying buttresses, and the giant Java willows were truly spectacular. And there were copses of bamboo, grasses with huge girths.

"You know," explained George seriously, "Bamboo is the fastest growing plant in the world." He paused then continued with a grin, pointing at a veritable forest of the stuff, "This morning that wasn't there!" We groaned.

There were also many forest animals; bats, monkeys, lizards, chipmunks. Behind one bush a local holding a fruit bat extended the poor creature's massive wings. He smiled (not the bat) and indicated we could have our photo taken with the bat, for a small fee. We ignored him.

We had lunched on boxes provided by the Dolphin, but now it was time for a more substantial meal and we chose a small restaurant on the outskirts of Kandy evidently unfamiliar with non-locals. We ordered a green curry expecting something similar to a Thai Green Chicken Curry which is a fairly universal staple. We were each presented a plate of boiled savoy cabbage leaves.

We were still laughing at this culinary cock-up when George delivered us to our overnight guest house. Our room overlooked the verdantly walled city of Kandy, and as I sat there on our fan-cooled bed admiring the drizzle falling, I could here a band playing somewhere, the almost constant hooting of passing vehicles, and the clunk of some poorly oiled machine drifting up from the kitchen. A large bird of prey perched on a vine covered tree less than 30 feet away. Lakshmi was in my thoughts. Her's would be a glorious eternal memory. Nirvana.

That evening we braved the rain and walked into the city and around the artificial lake to see the Temple of the Tooth. This is one of the most holy of Buddhist pilgrimages and houses the eponymous relic in a casket protected by numerous other caskets as in the layers of a Russian doll. There was much golden decoration but my favourite part of the temple complex was the stuffed Temple Tusker known as Raja who had died in 1988 aged 75 years. During the Perahera processions, which we had missed, the Tusker leads and is painted and clothed in wonderful golden vestments. Raja would have known Lakshmi. She never said.

Although we had missed the Perahera, there were traditionally attired dancers and drummers to entertain us and a demonstration of fire walking, performers hurrying barefoot over a 10 yard line of red hot coals. Thankfully, volunteers to join in weren't demanded, so we could watch and enjoy the show in peace.

The next morning we travelled two hours north to Sigirya. It was very slow progress out of Kandy, with lines of trucks struggling uphill.

Once clear, however, up onto the central plateau, the journey became enjoyable. There were tea plantations and bustling villages. All of the schoolchildren absolutely immaculate in their blazers, white shirts and blouses, and grey trousers or skirts. And then we came upon what Chicken George assured us was the eighth Wonder of the World.

We were crossing a flat plateau, and mountain ranges could be seen distantly on the horizon. Suddenly this rock looms up before us. It is an almost sheer 660 foot high monolith. Not unlike Uluru, but mostly green, and on the top of this one was built a fortress.

In the 5th century AD the usurper King Kashyapa chose Sigirya for his capital. It took seven years to build, including an entrance into the mouth of a huge lion. It was only used for 18 years, and was abandoned after his death at the hands of the rightful heir, Mogallanna. It became a Buddhist monastery for nearly 1,000 years and had been virtually forgotten for 500 years before a project to restore it began in the late nineteenth century.

George parked and we approached the rock via water and then boulder gardens up to terraced gardens. The staircase climb began between two huge lion's paws, the original entrance having collapsed, and was rather arduous, especially as the sunshine and heat had returned. As we wound our way upwards we were delighted by the many coloured frescoes of semi clad maidens which adorned the walls and overhangs. There were once over 500 of them and they had religious significance, although one theory has them as Kashyapa's harem which has led to the belief this may have been his Palace of Pleasure.

We eventually reached the summit upon which the city had been built. Now it showed only the footings of the buildings, but the views from every angle beyond the gardens and lake across the green plateau to the distant hazy mountains were without equal. One of the most stunningly beautiful places I have ever visited, and to think, this morning neither of us knew anything like this even existed. When people ask me why I travel, I could sum up all of the myriad reasons in just two words; Lakshmi and Sigirya.

Eventually we descended and George took us just a few miles away to the caves of Dambulla. Lunch before we entered the cave system was a predominately carrot chop suey.

Climbing up to the caves we first encountered a Golden Temple with a seated Buddha and a dragon mouth entrance, all teeth. There was also a golden pagoda. On entering the Buddhist shrine caves, we came across a 50 foot reclining Buddha. Did they want to sculpt a reclining Buddha, or was it just that there was only a low ceiling? Impressive, nonetheless. There were another four caves to visit with Buddhas seated and standing, frescoes of kings and gods, ceiling paintings and stupas. There are 160 statues to admire here, and I even found my old friend Ganesha.

When we had finished Dambulla, feeling a little Buddha fatigue, George put the front seat of his Toyota down so that we could recline fully and advised us to sleep, with evening approaching.

He drove us back to Kandy, turned right towards Columbo then turned onto the Southern Expressway, a toll road. "This new road will save us nearly three hours" he proclaimed proudly to no-one in particular as we both dozed in the rear seats. At Baddegama we left the motorway and travelled the last ten miles of our journey to the seaside resort of Hikkaduwa.

We bade a grateful goodbye to Chicken George as he dropped us off at the Chaaya Tranz hotel. It was 9pm and the staff greeted us with friendly bows, hands clasped together and the beautiful phrase Ayubowan, a general greeting. There was a garden in the middle of reception and a green lizard, just like Harry from Death In Paradise, was scampering about. This one was certainly not CGI.

Our room was on the fourth floor and had its own garden on the wide balcony which overlooked the gardens, the ocean, and islands beyond. A stunning view. We were only just in time for dinner, and had to hurry to the restaurant. We had been here less than half an hour, but could tell the place oozed quality.

The restaurant also impressed. Where the Dolphin's food was served in a forest, here was a modern, sumptuously furnished luxury eating house. Greeted by genuinely friendly Ayubowans we were shown to our table and explained how the buffet system worked. Great starters, superb mains and heavenly desserts washed down with an Australian Shiraz Cabernet took us to bed. Tomorrow we had different types of adventures to discover.

Hikkaduwa

We awoke and in the daylight able to take in our surroundings. The balcony overlooked beautiful gardens surrounding the pool. Ahead and to the right was a palm fringed beach and beyond we could see the sweep of a wide bay moving north. To our left, and west was the open ocean, and about half a mile off-shore two rocky outcrops. It was a gorgeous view.

I had come to "Hikka" as I had heard turtles came here to feed. I was keen to find out how this could be. We are told turtles only come ashore at night to lay eggs, and then only once a year. After breakfast we made our way downstairs, set up a couple of sunbeds and I set off to explore.

I discovered that the south western beach was rocky and shallow and stretched away from the shore. Here boys from the hotel were cutting and gathering green seaweed from the rocks, mainly dead coral. The offshore islands split the tide therefore sheltering the bay, and there were coral outcrops at the head of the bay, also acting to deflect the ocean swell. Where the bay met the western shore was a shallow channel, and it was here the boys stood twice a day with their buckets of turtle food. And it was here, attracted like Pavlov's bell, the adult turtles came to feed.

We were present for their first feed that day. Five or six swam up to the boys who fed them by hand. We sat in the shallows and were able to stroke them gently as their heads bobbed out to chew. They were huge, beautiful Green Sea Turtles. I had swum with Loggerheads in the Mediterranean, and snorkelled in the tropics occasionally sighting small Hawksbills, but I had never experienced anything like this.

Turtles have been predated by humans for thousands of years, hunted for their delicious flesh and valuable leather carapace, and their nests raided for their yolk rich abundant eggs. They understandably have developed a real fear of humans. Their natural habitat has been polluted, industrialised and over-fished.

In the enlightened 21st century their relationship with mankind has totally turned about and quite properly we now protect them, conserve them and even enjoy each others' company.

Kaz was captivated by the experience. She christened one Tina, and was convinced she came there every day just to see her. Kaz would sit in the shallows stroking Tina whilst I splashed about trying to capture the visitors with underwater photography. The turtles seemed to genuinely enjoy the company of people who half a century earlier would have been eating them.

The beach next to this channel was a genuine laying beach. Females which had been born here would return after 40 or 50 years roaming, growing and then mating in the open oceans. They came ashore during the full moon to dig a hole, deposit their eggs and cover them up. As tourists also enjoyed the beach, a turtle watch had been set up to protect the nests.

Our interest in these reptiles had been whetted and on our third day we visited a turtle hatchery. Here we saw tanks of baby turtles we could handle. I could pick up about a dozen with my bare hands. I was a little concerned that this was a tourist encouraging venture which exploited the turtles, but my fears were allayed by Vikram, the curator who assured me the eggs were carefully lifted, incubated and hatched. The hatchlings were released into the sea after four days. This protected them from immediate predation, giving them a much better chance of long term survival.

This visit and our encounters with Tina and her mates were wonderful, but remarkably eclipsed that same evening.

After dinner we decided to take a stroll near the shore to marvel at the star-filled clear night sky and listen to and watch the crashing white foam of the waves. A man approached us with a torch and insisted, "You come. You come now!" He was the superfluous hotel security guard, and thinking he might be wanting to sell us souvenirs, we followed cautiously to where he beckoned. He led us through the palm trees onto the quiet beach and to the floodlit enclosure which housed the turtle nests. There to our great surprise and delight were scuttling around hundreds of tiny turtles. They must have hatched and emerged only minutes previously.

Encyclopaedias and conservationists and natural history TV presenters assure us that turtle hatchlings instinctively head to the ocean. Well, it may have been the effect of the floodlights, or that the eggs had been removed from their original nest, but these particular tiny turtles were quite clearly heading in every direction except the sea.

Left to their own devices, these tiny creatures would have been picked off by predators as the dawn approached. So, aided by the guard we began to coax the little fellers to the sea. We didn't want to touch them for fear of adversely affecting their natural compass which should ultimately lead them back here to continue their life cycle. Therefore we tried to herd each one gradually to the sea where once they encountered the water, their tiny whirling flippers would do the rest.

But while we were carefully trying to entice each little turtle to the sea, their brothers and sisters were whirling their flippers in any and every other direction. It was becoming an impossible task so, against our better judgement we began picking them up and placing them on the tide line where the next wave could activate their natural instinct. This was beginning to work, but was still taking too long. We both started taking them to the water, wading in a few steps and gently releasing them. This went on for an hour or so and we appeared to be winning when every so often I could hear a splash as I waded with my tiny dependents into the sea. I looked around and there was the security guard, who had finally lost patience and was carefully lobbing the babies into the surf. It didn't seem to do them any harm, so the last fifty or so found themselves being thrown gently into the water until the beach was clear of all save the three of us. There was nothing left but to congratulate ourselves on a job well done.

What happens to the hatchlings? Mostly predated, I'm afraid. But of the ones who do make it to maturity nobody knows for sure of their progress through the ocean. We only know that one day they will return to this beach to mate and spawn, and hopefully be won over by a new generation of people frolicking in the surf. And that might not be for another 50 years.

Hikkaduwa was not just a turtle town. We also visited the shops and small industries and the residential areas up the hill behind the main street and over the railway tracks where there was still jungle. We love tuk-tuks; little three wheelers which are often pimped like the old Lambrettas, to have myriad mirrors, chrome, nodding Jesus's, rosaries, sitting Buddhas and sparkling lights. Our favourite was the tuk-tuk bread van with ice cream chimes. And everyone was so cheerful all the time. Rarely do you see a long face, even as you leave their shops empty handed.

One morning we crossed the rail tracks and walked up the hill into the jungle. There were residences on either side with open plan, outdoor kitchens. Mums were preparing meals and waved, grandmas smiled in their rocking chairs, knitting, and naked toddlers played in the gardens. The men were at work, older children in school. Dogs lazed in the sunshine as chickens clucked and pecked around them. We could hear and occasionally see exotic birds flit by, monkeys also played in the trees, and we saw a huge water monitor lazily waddle across the road in front of us.

Presently we turned left along a small track and came across a clearing, in the centre of which stood a gleaming Hindu Temple. It glittered gold in the sunshine and its statue gods were wearing colourful clothes, extreme make-up and adopting a variety of dancing poses, and stood on every ledge. The door was locked so we walked around it then prepared to leave, walking back down towards the ocean.

Suddenly two children, shouted and ran towards us. A boy and girl, who had evidently been playing in a garden when they saw us. They were grinning shyly and held out a large golden key with which they insisted we open the huge ornamental door. Inside it was just beautiful. Drapes and paintings and statues were all around. In pride of place at what we might call the altar was seated a huge imperial Ganesha, his elephant head highly decorated and with sixteen blue arms emanating synonymity from his back.

After a few minutes we left and the children were waiting as we locked up and gave them back their key. They simply smiled and ran back into the jungle. What had happened there?

The next day we took a tuk-tuk to Hikkaduwa Lagoon. On the way we stopped at the Tsunami Remembrance Memorial and the driver explained over 34,000 people from Sri Lanka alone perished on that awful Boxing Day for South East Asia in 2004. We were on the Galle Road, and it was here at Peraliya that the Columbo to Galle train was engulfed, crushing and drowning thousands who saw the locomotive as a safe refuge. The World's worst ever rail disaster.

When we reached the lagoon, a young man, Lahiru greeted us and enthusiastically beckoned us onboard his catamaran. He sailed us around the lake, and we saw monitors, fruit bats, cormorants, and flying fish as we wandered the little mangrove inlets. Presently we moored at a small village and he introduced us to his elderly parents and we shared a simple meal of fish and rice flavoured with cinnamon which is farmed here. Mum, Deepani, had cooked for us as we dangled our feet off the jetty for the numerous tiny fishes to nibble and clean our toes. This was, as Lahiru described, a tiny paradise, and in our two journeys across the lagoon he had waxed lyrical about its unique plants and animals.

The tuk-tuk driver had waited for us and drove us back to the hotel where we spent a final two days enjoying the sun, pool, sea, and general bonhomie. We snorkelled the coral reef, fed the turtles and ate, ourselves, well and copiously. Entertainment indeed.

We left Hikkaduwa and the Chaaya Tranz with heavy hearts and many heartfelt "Ayubowans".

We weren't travelling far, just a short taxi ride down the coast to Galle, a fortified city built by the Portuguese, and expanded by the Dutch. En route, Angelo parked on a river bridge and suggested we might like to stretch our legs. We looked down at the shallow, wide clay-coloured waters with its sandbars and grassy banks. "Here is where they made the film Bridge Over The River Kwai" he proudly announced. I could see it.

Later at the village of Ambalangoda we visited the wooden mask factory with walls full of anthropomorphised, colourful, fierce dragon heads. Finally we stopped at a huge, hollow stupa, or in Sinhalese a Dagoba with impressive acoustics. (You have to shout "Ooh!"). There was also a marvellous storyboard representation of the life of Siddhartha Gautama, the Buddha.

Eventually reaching Galle, we passed the cricket ground, little more than a picturesque village green, but which has hosted every major test country. It had been more a guided tour than a taxi journey.

Galle

We entered through the fortified gate and paid Angelo outside the Villa Aurora guest house where we dropped our bags and set off to explore.

It was immediately mesmerising. Galle is a small city built on a promontory, therefore is pentagon shaped with five walls protecting a small red-roofed town and natural harbour. It features a white lighthouse, the twin towered Jesuit cathedral of St Mary, and a white church-looking Mosque which wouldn't look out of place in South America.

We started at the lighthouse at the south eastern extreme bastion (there are three bastions called Sun, Moon and Sky), and walked east along a raised grassy avenue atop the granite walls. There were palm trees and baobabs, but the majority of welcome shade came from the hugely spreading ancient banyan trees. The beauty of these trees delighted us, their root entanglements, trunk size and shapes, leaves, flowers, fruit, and the gravity defying branches spreading endlessly.

Circling the town via these raised lawns, with the Indian Ocean crashing onto the rocks below and the sun sinking towards a curved horizon is surely one of the most breathtaking short treks in Asia. We were strolling on the very edge of the teardrop.

Our second night was curtailed as I had booked a safari to Yala National Park, and in order to make a dawn game drive we would have to leave the Aurora at two in the morning.

"Take your pillows with you" advised our host, Sami, generously,"You can sleep in the car."

The journey wasn't so bad and we awoke to find ourselves at the entrance to the park with dawn's pink light struggling through the windows. After a small breakfast of coffee and cake we were allocated a jeep and entered via the Palatupana gate.

The terrain was rather flat with large areas of green savannah hedged in with woodland and scrub. There were rocky outcrops and we were very excited early on to spot a sloth bear, Baloo himself, enjoying the sunshine splayed out on a large, flat rock.

You hope to see leopard so keep one eye on the shadows, another up in the trees, but expectation in the full light of day is low. We soon came across the real stars of the park, elephant. We saw several herds, and one family group decided to push past us on the road. We could have reached out and stroked them, they were that close.

Amazing to think that during the Raj in the 19th Century, less than 200 years ago, killing wildlife was a sport, and British soldiers in Sri Lanka were commended for killing over 250 elephants. At least three officers gloried in their having killed over 1500 elephant each. Some people would go on a shoot and kill thousands of birds in just one day.

Prior to the Second World War, in the age of Ernest Hemingway, shooting big game was still a legitimate pastime. Even post war, trophy hunting was still a sport. Today we like to think we are an enlightened society, and the occasional hunter and guide are vilified as inhuman monsters in the press and on social media. Now the biggest threat to wildlife are poachers and to elephant, farmers.

Perhaps today we have gone too far the other way. Some believe that thoughtful culling is needed to curb over population or ageing immobility (in animals!). I am of the school that argues Mother Nature will intervene when numbers exceed food supplies. And don't we all wish the gazelle could outrun the cheetah when in reality this would mean starvation for her and her cubs.

Then again meaningless slaughter still legitimately takes place even in modern times. In some areas of the world and among the upper classes, "huntin' shootin' and fishin'" is still an acceptable hobby.

Thankfully here in Yala, and in National Parks across Asia and Africa, the thought of destroying any of these wonderful animals is a complete anathema.

Our four hour game drive was a complete joy and we arrived back at the gate for a proper breakfast at ten in the morning, it felt more like lunchtime. Apart from Baloo and the pachyderms we also saw plenty of deer, monkeys and mongooses, water buffalo, warthogs and crocodiles, storks, herons and peacocks, and a jackal, which Kipling wonderfully described as "Tabaqui", the dish-licking dog.

Our car, complete with soft pillows awaited and returned us to Galle, only stopping as I had requested at the seaside village of Matara which is famous for its stilt fishermen. We walked through the palm trees to the beach, and sure enough, there they were. We could see about a dozen of them out in the shallows, the skinniest of men perched on perpendicular branches with their trademark wide brimmed straw hats and a fishing rod.

I've often wondered how the conversation would go, within a simple hut somewhere in their fishing village, as one old man comes to a momentous decision and gathers the family around. He addresses his eldest. "Son, I'm retiring, it's time I slowed down and enjoyed my dotage. I'm leaving you the family business, no questions asked, it's all yours, apart from the hat, I'll need that, and the rod, a man must have a hobby. But the rest of it, all of it, the whole stilt, is yours."

We were back at the Aurora for 2pm, an amazing 12 hours. We spent the rest of the day relaxing in the warm sunshine, dozing and reading in Sami's shaded courtyard. For that night we were beginning our journey home.

It is two hours and a $50 taxi ride back to the airport, and as we had a 5am flight to Dubai to join our connection to Birmingham, we had paid Angelo to pick us up from the Villa Aurora at 1am. Sami our superb patron had no guests expected so allowed us to keep our room on until we left.

Thus after having taken an excellent meal with Sami and his wife earlier that evening and enjoyed a final stroll around the ramparts to say goodbye to some of our favourite trees and definitely my favourite ocean, we were seated in the cool of the courtyard at 12:50am awaiting Angelo's arrival.

But he wasn't there at 1am. In fact he kept on not arriving, and Kaz was becoming rather worried by ten past. I had not taken Angelo's number, and I had no more dollars, although I could have withdrawn sufficient rupees if we had had time to find an ATM and book another taxi. By 1:15 we were panicking and Kaz persuaded me to knock on Sami's door for help.

"I will sort you," said a sleepy Sami when I had explained our predicament.

He was wearing light blue Sri Lanka cricket pyjamas as he shuffled into reception and picked up his phone. The sleepy demeanour had left him as he punched a number into the device, waited a moment, then gabbled excitedly, waggling his head vigorously and gesturing with his free hand.

"Brrrrdrrrgrrrr taxi brrrrgrrrrtrrrr airport prrrrtrrrrdrrrgrrr barstad idiot brrrrgrrrr"

"He is coming," he said smiling, as he pocketed his phone, put his hands together, yawned and added "Ayubowan" then shuffled off back to bed.

Just then a car screeched to a halt outside and I saw Angelo rushing to put our bags in the boot. He apologised profusely as we got into the back of his taxi, "I put in my phone one o'clock in the afternoon. I will get you there," and we sped away. I noticed Angelo was wearing the same pyjamas as Sami. He hadn't had time to change.

Thus we said goodbye to Sri Lanka. What serendipity.

A South East Asian Odyssey

The South East Asian peninsular includes five countries; the previous French Indonesia comprising Vietnam, Laos and Cambodia; Thailand which used to be Siam, the provenance of all those lovely cats; and Burma now Myanmar, part of the old British Empire. These are magical, mystical countries with wonderful people, fabulous flora and fauna, marvellous rivers and forests, legendary cities and some tragic if fascinating recent histories. (The Malay Peninsular is on the end of Thailand, but that's another chapter)

I had flown to Bangkok via Dubai, and because I had a layover with a subsequent flight on Thai Airways, I had free access to their lounge. What a great idea. Free access to really comfortable chairs, buffet and drinks. How civilised. Bangkok airport immediately went to the top of my list of favourite airports.

Now there is an oxymoron. Surely airports are places to detest with their queues and crowds, endless security measures, extortionate shops, uncomfortable seating (if you can find one), stuffy bureaucracy and seemingly interminable delays. Top of my hate lists are all British and American airports, where customer comfort and service have always had low priority. However, places like Dubai, Schiphol and Istanbul are modern hubs with many interesting characteristics designed to alleviate both departure fatigue and arrival bottlenecks.

There are others with intelligent features. Kuala Lumpur has its own rain forest, Tocumen had free rum flowing both sides of its concourse, and New Delhi has Ayurvedic relaxation points. But my favourite of all is the small airport on the island of Lesbos. After a family Greek holiday we rolled up to the airport to check in to fly home. "I am sorry" said the young Nana Mouskouri on the desk, "We do not have a departure lounge. Please, if you could sit at the taverna on the beach until you see your flight arrive." Bliss. I do hope it hasn't changed, but fear it might have.

Siem Reap

Back to Bangkok, and my flight to Siem Reap. It was a little different, from the China Airways (Taiwanese) Jumbo. I boarded a twin propeller 30 seater for the 35 minute trip over an Everglades like jungle. It is almost as if the whole country is an extension of its central lake, the Ton Le Sap, all underwater albeit shallow. I stepped down from the aircraft for the briefest customs check then a mini bus transfer to the hotel. Each side of the street from the airport into the small town of Siem Reap were hotel constructions. This was Thai investment aimed at American and Japanese tourists.

I had arrived in Cambodia, a poor, Khmer and French speaking country populated by young people since the older generation was virtually wiped out in the killing fields of the Khmer Rouge. Their insurgency had been precipitated by America's mistaken belief that Cambodia was aiding the Vietcong's invasion of South Vietnam. President Richard Nixon unleashed the B52's to bomb the alleged route, pouring agent orange onto their forests and ultimately paving the way for the evil Pol Pot to oust Prince Sihanouk's peaceful regime.

During this holocaust in the 1970's the country was briefly known as Kampuchea. All knowledge was assassinated, with teachers, students, scientists, business people of all kind slaughtered as the country was reduced to year dot. There are still a huge number of amputees as previously deployed landmines continue to be discovered the hard way as the killing fields remain.

With overnight flights from the UK, my body clock was as usual shot to pieces, but I checked into the Angkor Boutique Hotel and briefly napped before an early lunch of noodle soup. I then briefly met up with the group with whom I would be sharing this adventure, and we were whisked off to see the temples.

Angkor is an ancient city with the largest array of temples (Wats) in the world. Scattered over an area of 60 square miles it is actually a series of cities built by Khmer kings between the 9th and 13th centuries. It is believed nearly a million people lived here in its heyday.

At the entrance I was photographed for my three day passport and allocated a seat on a bus with the other seven. Our guide was a young slim man, academic looking (He wore glasses and would have been shot for such a heinous crime 30 years ago)

Mao briefed us on our itinerary. "We will begin with the oldest temples, in Roluos. There are three in the north of the complex." He announced as we were driven about half an hour past temples, green fields, rice paddies and woodland, and the occasional cycling peasant to our first temple, and the exploration began.

Lolei Wat had four pagoda style towers carved in red and grey sandstone. The vegetation had climbed up one side, and there were doorways and columns and bas-relief statues, all tapering and reaching to the sky. They remain on what used to be an island.

We moved from here to Preah Ko, dedicated to the sacred ox, which had unsurprisingly, carved bulls. Then there was the Eastern Mabon the one with the elephants, and finally Phnom Bakong.

All of these temples were wonderful, warranting fuller individual descriptions, each one a stand alone delight. But when you are constantly bombarded with who built it, how, what for, when and why, and you realise most of that is supposition, you simply turn off from the drone of the guide. You need sometimes, to allow yourself just to get lost in the wonder of the architecture and the beauty of its juxtaposition. It was sad to see the bored expressions on the faces of people trying to keep up with their guide's description instead of just enjoying the moment.

But then there was the clambering and climbing. These fantastic edifices aren't kept behind barriers and ropes. I spent hours discovering and ascending to survey the views of the Cambodian jungle, as far as the eye could see in every direction.

Unfortunately it had rained, and the sunset when it came was lost behind cloud, but what an experience.

Cambodia is one of those dark countries. Such is the quality of the light bulbs, or the electricity grid, that with the night and the switching on of the lights, everything remained gloomy. The jungle, and the humidity, and the biting insects that come out in the evening don't help; neither that I hadn't slept in a bed for over 48 hours.

Thus I wearily consumed beer and a plate of frog's legs, cuisses de grenouilles, which was a first, and yes, they are just like skinny chicken wings. We were in a restaurant on the upper floor of a wooden stilted house, and the little girl who had served me asked if I wanted more, "Voudriez-vous un peu plus, monsieur?"

Not too keen on the delicacy I smiled, shook my head and patted my overlarge belly, "Merci, non. Je suis pleine," and the girl suppressed a little giggle and left.

I looked over at Mao slightly puzzled. "What's so funny?" I asked, "I told her I was full."

He grinned rather smugly, paused and explained, "You told her you were pregnant."

The next morning I was up at six to enjoy the Cambodian rush hour, which consisted of dozens of cyclists, all wearing a 'coolie' conical hat, known as a *do'un* . No-one over 25. Still wet, but hot; steamy.

Mao collected the group at eight and we drove alongside a river past a village of stilted huts. Underneath children played, stopping to wave and shout and run after us as we drove by. They shared their play areas with ducks, pigs and cattle. Women beavered away with their household chores and the men were already lazing in their hammocks.

Presently we came to a landing stage and took a boat to see the famous floating village of Chong Kneas. It was fascinating to see a community living in this transient way, the village moves dependant on the water levels. It was a bit touristy, but the shop keepers and children in the schools seemed genuine enough. On the water, dragon boats with 16 oars were practising their racing techniques as more sedate fishing canoes cast their nets closer to shore.

We re-boarded our boat for a trip around the sunken forest and various fish farms until we made the open water of Ton Le Sap, the largest fresh water lake in South East Asia which is 15 feet deep now, but will be largely dried up in less than six months.

We were back in time for lunch, an excellent excursion. This afternoon Mao promised us more Angkor Wat.

Being too tired last night, the group had had time to gel this morning. It was half term so there were two other teachers, Sue and Gill (in this event I always avoid pedagogical issues which bore other people); a German couple, Kev and Ken who were enigmatically, "something in IT"; Simon who worked in the city in advertising; Fred, a Cuban-American "traveller" and Tessa, a pharmaceutical nurse.

On Meeting People.

It's always lovely to meet new people, like visiting new places, you know you will learn something different, and may even develop a friendship.

After the initial introduction, there will be opening gambits about the weather, perhaps, and where you live, how you got here, etc. Then, strangely, and almost inevitably, you will be asked what you do. It is as if your profession defines you.

I've found there are some people who are a little reluctant to divulge this information; those of us who practice the dark art of teaching young people, for example. That is why I have my stock answer to the inescapable "Oh, what do you teach?" of "Little bastards". After the laugh (hopefully), they always add "No, but really" and "I couldn't do your job"

Others I've known to be disinclined to discuss their day jobs are those in law enforcement. They appear to be ashamed of their profession, as if they know it has become a toothless, impotent one.

Then there are doctors and nurses. It is impossible, once they declare what they do, not to think "What's wrong with me?", so you can touch them up for a diagnosis and some free advice."

It's not always that simple though. I recall taking my parents to France for a gite holiday, south of the Dordogne. Across the field in the village of Tortoirac lived the owners, from Stourbridge. On our first evening the couple came over to introduce themselves.

"Hello, I'm David Jones" smiled the middle aged husband.

"Nice to meet you, Mr Jones," said my father, shaking his hand.

"Actually it's Doctor Jones." he replied emphasising the title.

"Oh, I'm glad to hear that, My colitis has really been playing up no end on the drive down," said dad.

"Actually I'm a Doctor of Geography," he added smugly.

Well, that was embarrassing! Except; who goes around announcing they're a doctor of geography. Snob!

*

We met up after lunch for the minibus back to Angkor and its most famous temple. It is huge, the largest religious monument in the world. There are lovely aspects from all directions and we began with a group photo on a grassy approach. The main driveway however, splits a huge lake, actually a moat, and we walked over this causeway to enter the complex. A number of features struck me on this walk. First, the length of the walls, over a quarter of a mile either side of the entrance, then the intricacies of the wall's architecture and the symmetry of the main towers, five of them, tapering up to the sky. and most striking the perfect image of the complex captured in the lake making Angkor Wat appear twice its size. There were even two huge, bolt upright king palms also mirrored, adding to the whole majesty

It was built by the Khmer king Suryavarman II, around the same time William the Conqueror was compiling the Domesday Book of England. This temple was dedicated to the god Vishnu, and looks

193

perfectly preserved. Unlike the temples we saw yesterday which have had to be reclaimed from the jungle, Angkor Wat has remained intact as a religious centre throughout the centuries. It soon became adopted by Buddhists, survived centuries of what Henri Mouhot described as "the barbarism into which the nation (was) plunged", and surprisingly even the Khmer Rouge occupation. The worst damage it has seen in all this time has been the plundering of its statuary by modern Thai art thieves.

Once inside Mao introduced us to the myriad cloisters with walls decorated painstakingly and beautifully with bas-relief carvings of scenes from the Ramayana and the Mahabharata. These are two Sanskrit epics of ancient India. The former follows Prince Rama's quest to rescue his wife Sita from the clutches of Ravana, helped by an army of monkeys. The latter, possibly written by my favourite, Ganesha, is purportedly the longest poem ever composed, and details the struggles of the Kuru clan in the kingdom of Hastinapura. It culminates in the battle between the Kaurava and Pandava families at Kurukshetra, and the death of Krishna, heralding the beginning of the fourth and final age of humanity. That, in a nutshell, is the Hindu Itihasa.

These complicated but fascinating murals of warriors and battles, dancing princes and celestial maidens, horse drawn chariots and armoured elephant, gods and goddesses, surround all of the walls and you could happily spend a lifetime in their interpretation.

We moved up through the levels of the galleries of bas-reliefs and reached the stairs to the top of the towers. There are five towers, shaped as lotus flowers, one on each corner and a central one depicting the mythical Mount Meru at the centre of the universe. This effect is called a quincunx.

The lessons of the origins and meaning of the complex now over, the cultural bit behind us, it was time for a spot of fun. The steps up to the highest level looked almost impossible. On one side a rope hung to help haul yourself up, and on another a rail had been positioned to help you down. The steps were no more than three inches wide with irregular risers of between nine inches and a foot. Centuries of use had left then worn and rounded. Very few places in the world would have Health and Safety rules allowing people to attempt them, but here was not a nanny state, "Volenti non fit injuria" or even Caveat Emptor, let the buyer (climber) beware. On your own head be it.

People went up forwards, backwards, sideways, rarely having less than three limbs attached, and came down similarly if even more gingerly. The rewards were worth it. Not only did you have views across the Angkor Wat complex, the 360 degree horizons were distant beyond the moat and green. And then the sun came out bathing everything and everyone in a golden early evening glow. The sun even glinted off the moat, and I recalled the words of John Denver., "Sunshine on the water looks so lovely". It surely does. A heavenly moment to be cherished.

Later at dinner, Kev and Ken announced they were from Hamburg, the home of The Beatles. That raised the level of the conversation especially as Tessa was from the Wirral and therefore a closet Scouser. Fred made the conversation even more surreal when he unashamedly asked, "Who?" (of The Beatles, not Tessa) and the evening progressed with us all giving the American a lesson in 60's music. It ended with a fair sing along of Sergeant Pepper's Lonely Hearts Club Band. We did quite well, from the opening "It was 20 years ago today..."; onto With a little help from my friends; Lucy in the sky, Fixing a hole; It's getting better; She's leaving home; When I'm 64; For the benefit of Mr Kite; Lovely Rita metre maid. We couldn't do Within you without you, nor Good morning, but hit A Day In The Life and the Reprise. Mao and the restaurant staff, who had rarely met people this old, were well impressed. I can't say the same for the other guests.

But then Kev started on Blackbirds and I had to slur "Nein, Kev. Es ist die Weiss Album. Morgen." and we all laughed and staggered off to bed.

Our third day saw us at the south entrance to Angkor Thom. Described as the Atlantis of Plato, this was the last great city of the Khmer dynasty. There was once again a causeway over a moat, to steps and terraces and a myriad of towers. The walls were covered in bas-relief sculptures telling stories of wars and battles and magical creatures.

Every temple tells a story. This one concerned demons and gods battling by pulling a giant serpent around Mount Meru. Their objective was to stir up the Sea of Milk to create an elixir of immortality.

At the centre of Angkor Thom is the Bayon Wat. In itself a beautiful temple, but the most striking features are the multitude of four faced statues of serene smiling heads thought to be of both Brahma and King Jayavarman VII.

We enjoyed a little light clambering up and down a small temple before strolling around the royal residence and the elephant terrace.

Finally on this bright sunny morning we were driven to the temple of Ta Prohm. It has been untouched to illustrate the ruined state of the majority of over 6,000 temples before restoration. The walls and towers and pillars recline at crazy angles as they have been taken over by the jungle. Centuries of neglect saw the growth of huge banyan and kapok trees, their root systems and buttresses pulling and tearing the temple apart. One particular cavernous entrance has been created which seems to lead down into the bowels of the earth, and it was this feature which was used in the Lara Croft, Tomb Raider film.

We headed back to the hotel, heads full of stories and adventures, both ancient and modern, for a brief lunch before being driven back up the avenue of building site hotels to the small airport. Our twin prop took off into the teeth of a tropical storm but circled over Angkor Wat to give us one final aerial view of this wonderful place. We then headed over Ton Le Sap, a mere 35 minutes across a flooded basin, to Cambodia's capital, Phnom Pen. Such had been the extent of the rainy season that the Mekong river which meets the Ton Lé here was over two miles wide.

Phnom Pen

By the time we had checked into the Queen's Hotel, a rather tired and dated single width, ten storey building, it was early evening and still raining. This isn't the best way to be introduced to a major metropolis, but all I could see here was desperate poverty. Cambodia has a long way to go to catch up with its Vietnamese and Thai neighbours. I can't speak for Laos, in the north. Mao, who hadn't joined us had advised us not to go out at night. There was a restaurant next door but most of my companions were still hungover from the night before so I dined quietly with Fred, Sue and Gill. We ate well, on something enigmatically called River Fish.

We had to laugh. Sue and Gill had paid a little extra for a room with a bath rather than just a shower. It turned out there was no bath plug, making it worse than the "avec douche". I had noticed a tiny games room in the basement, snook in and stole the cue ball off the pool table. "Stick it in the hole," I said, "Works every time".

The next morning the rain had relented and we went down to the riverside to the National Museum. Beautiful pink pagoda style buildings and gardens, and many interesting artefacts, but the guide we'd hired was almost indecipherable with poor pronunciation and unending explanations which served only to put us to sleep. A shame as I am sure it would have been a worthwhile visit.

He insisted he join us for the Royal Palace, virtually next door. We thanked him and suggested he didn't. Subsequently the golden complex was a joy to wander with birds and chipmunks in the gardens. Next door was the Silver Pagoda, a temple with an emerald crystal Buddha and an unbelievable six foot pure gold Buddha inset with nearly 10,000 diamonds. Its only security appeared to be a small padlock. We then climbed the hill to see the statue dedicated to the city's founder, Madame Penh.

Finally it was time to ready ourselves for the real purpose of our visit here; to be taken to the Choeung Ek Killing Fields. I suppose it must be difficult to celebrate the joys of a city when the whole mindset is directed towards seeing the evidence of a holocaust. As it happened this journey to a site of mass graves was not possible due to flooding so we had to make do with the Tuol Sleng Genocide Museum.

This was harrowing. Tuol Sleng was a secondary school which during the reign of Pol Pot was used as a concentration camp, interrogation centre and torture chamber. It became "Security Prison 21", S-21 and processed 20,000 people in its four years of operation from 1975 to 1979. All, bar about a dozen died. It was one of probably 200 similar establishments.

Prisoners from all walks of life were held in appalling conditions, beaten mercilessly and tortured horribly to confess and name family members and friends. They were then taken to the Killing Fields where a variety of implements were used to hack them to death. Ammunition was too expensive. Towards the end of the insurgence Pol Pot's paranoia meant many of his former comrades suffered the same atrocities, such was the bloodlust of the Khmer Rouge.

Our guide began by explaining how Phnom Penh had eventually fallen to the Khmer Rouge after a long bitter siege, and how the emaciated people had been force marched out of the city to take up an agrarian existence. This became a death march thus decimating the population.

We were then led through the four three-storied buildings. This former high school had been acquired and the classrooms converted into cells and torture chambers. It was discovered by the Vietnamese liberators in 1979 when they followed the stench of rotting bodies. Inmates had been hurriedly murdered as their gaolers fled.

We saw corridors of chequered linoleum off which led cells with barred windows. Some cells had iron beds and above a picture of what had been found on the bed, the walls were of dirty, light-brown stucco, on which you could imagine blood spattering. Other cell walls were covered in black and white photos of just some of the victims. We were drawn to these pictures of the innocents, they looked just like the people we had met in villages, in shops, on the water, amongst the ruins, ordinary Cambodian men, women and children.

We moved on. There were torture instruments like leg irons, shackles, water boarding instruments and electric whips. There was a gallery of paintings by former inmate, Vann Nath, showing people being tortured. It is known that inhuman experiments were carried out on people, alongside the vilest torture methods.

Lastly there were cupboards full of skulls, and a map of Cambodia composed solely of skulls. It was a sobering, if necessary experience.

Cambodia was finally released from this nightmare by the Vietnamese army who, post liberation, restored Prince Sihanouk to the throne. This was a bittersweet result for Cambodians whose history is full of conflicts with their neighbours and, in this case, benefactors.

Tuol Sleng has been kept as a museum to reinforce the important "Lest We Forget" maxim.

After this harrowing and eye-opening experience I needed some air. I took a boat trip across the swollen Mekong to a stilted village with its young and smiling families and happy and waving children. I remember little of this excursion other than I needed it to purge the evil to which I had been witness.

Thanks to thoughtful foreign aid and sensible, stable government Cambodia is now a young emerging country, with growing industries. A true phoenix rising out of the most horrendous conflagration.

I bade goodbye to my companions who were all travelling on to Vietnam. I was returning to Bangkok. It was a pretty miserable evening back at the Queen's Hotel, if an opportunity to gather my thoughts. I had a dawn flight out of Pochentung airport and a reservation at The Royal Hotel in the centre of Bangkok.

Bangkok

Unfortunately because of the efficiency of my flight, baggage and passport control, and transfer, I rocked up at the Royal at 7:30am.

"Hello, Mr Leo, yes I have your reservation, unfortunately your room will not be ready until 12 o'clock. I can contact housekeeping and ask if it can be prepared earlier."

Even during the ride from the airport to my hotel, I could see Bangkok was a different world from Phnom Penh. Gleaming skyscrapers, busy motorways, private cars, modern shopping centres, western style advertising billboards, parks and gardens.

Thailand is one of those countries which has managed to develop its own history and culture. Sandwiched between the empires of French Indonesia and the British Raj, you have to applaud how the country has managed to resist becoming part of a larger empire. Only during those years of the Second World War when it was overrun by the Japanese has it ever had to kowtow to invaders.

Previously Siam, westerners tend to have certain images of Thailand.

- My parents' generation loved Yul Bryner as King Mongkut with Deborah Kerr as the English governess, Anna Leonowens in Rodgers and Hammerstein's The King And I. This was (loosely) based on a true story, and shows how the Royal family came to love all things British. They educated their heirs at Sandhurst, partly adopted the language, and became a relatively peaceful, tolerant society, admiring western values (education, legal system, health service, welfare state, etc.).

- We all know and love Siamese cats, those rather haughty, proud felines with smooth, cream coats and pointed chocolate faces and blue eyes.

- There is Thai boxing, a mixture of western pugilism and eastern martial arts.

- Ladyboys; those young hermaphrodites which frequent bars and nightclubs with the sole purpose of confusing western men.

- Talking of western men, there is a huge market for so-called Thai brides, pretty girls who will marry to move abroad and who promise to literally "love and obey".

- Finally there is the capital, Bangkok, the subject of giggling schoolboys everywhere.

I was sure there must be much more to Thai society than these simplistic observations, and I now had a few days here and in Chiang Mai in the north to discover what these might be.

Meantime I had four hours with luggage but no room.

"Perhaps I could take breakfast?" I ventured.

"I'm sorry," he said, "The restaurant in the morning is open to residents only."

"But I am a resident," I argued

"Not until I can register you with a room, I'm afraid" the young man kept his poise.

"I could pay extra." This went against the grain, and in fairness I had had a little breakfast on the brief flight over, but it was the principle.

"There is a pleasant cafe down Kowloon Street" he smilingly suggested.

"OK, but what am I going to do before 12 o'clock, anyway?"

"Well, sir. What do you suggest?"

"That's where I was hoping you might be able to help," I replied with just a hint of sarcasm.

" Perhaps you would like to make use of the rooftop swimming pool."

"Well that would certainly be good for starters. But don't I need to be a resident?"

"Not you sir, I will look after your luggage, you can access a towel to the left of the elevator doors, and I will message you when your room is ready."

So I spent my first hours in Bangkok snoozing in the sunshine and admiring its modern skyline. A boy came up at 10:30 to tell me my room was ready. I took the lift down "Elevator" Tsk.

Once rested I left to take in the sights, the most popular of which is the Grand Palace, home to the Thai royal family since 1782, on the shores of the Chao Phraya river.

At first I was denied entry. I was wearing shorts and bare legs aren't allowed, apparently. I delighted the palace guards by retrieving a pair of long trousers out of my back pack and pulling them on.

Suitably attired, I entered the outer court. There were manicured shrubs and trees, and a variety of buildings all around with narrow golden pagoda style roofs.

I first visited the Temple of the Emerald Buddha, in a golden stupa style building. As you might imagine the centre point and main feature of this quiet, darkened chapel is a statue of Buddha, in jade with golden clothing, seated lotus style on a raised dais. Very beautiful, and a sacred protector of the country, but I couldn't help bringing to mind Dan Dare's green nemesis, the Mekon.

I returned to the Outer Court to enter the Middle Court where the residential and state buildings are housed. At the centre is the most important Throne Room with ornate gold and bejewelled adornments everywhere. Of course this was the major public area where the King gave audience, and judgements could be handed down from his exalted position on a wonderful throne.

The Inner Court was much smaller and were the private apartments and courtyards where the King's wives and children were kept, educated and entertained. I couldn't help but wonder whether it was here Anna taught the King how to dance all night. It was certainly where Anna got to know the children as they marched to meet her.

South of the Royal Palace is the Temple of the Reclining Buddha, probably the most important temple complex in Thailand, it certainly houses the most images in its buildings and courtyards, over 1,000. Around the balustrades is a bas-relief encyclopedia and there are cloisters with plaques depicting scenes from the Ramakien, Thailand's very own Hindu epic (remember Prince Rama with his army of monkeys?).

The focus of attention is the 50 yards long reclining Buddha, housed in a darkened building but adorned with gold, he is accompanied by his auspicious symbols, flowers, dancers, white elephants and tigers to prepare his entry into Nirvana. He is actually lying on his side, propping up his head on one elbow. We all do it.

The cynic in me has often wondered whether they decided on a reclining Buddha because it is much easier to build and house than a 50 yard upright one.

It had been a wonderful afternoon of history and culture and aesthetic beauty, but my day amongst Bangkok's finest was only half over. After the reclining Buddha I took to the water, always a favourite. There was a small wharf and a kiosk selling tickets for a rice barge cruise, with refreshments. Two hours on a boat. Hold me back.

The barge was pleasant enough, with a canopy for the sun and comfortable wicker chairs. The cruise began at a flower market with wonderful sweet aromas and colours especially of the discarded floating petals. We chugged slowly north past all the temples and palaces I'd visited that afternoon, but wonderful to see from this perspective. We chugged on and saw more of Bangkok's riverside life, from domestic residences to shopping malls, temples to pagodas, and other river craft plying their trades, from barges like our own to fishing and retail canoes.

Then we came closer to shore and navigated up one of the many canals. There were more fruit and flower sellers, women in their coolie hats sculling along. We came closer to a small village temple, then another and another. I couldn't believe what I was seeing, I couldn't quite understand the phenomenon of the temple fish. So I composed this:

The Riddle of the Temple Fish

Rivers have always been an important source for civilisation. The Tigress and the Euphrates bounded the biblical Fertile Crescent. Only a mile or so either side of the Nile as it flows north through the Sahara Desert can be seen agriculture and the cities of the Egyptian empire. Europe has the Rhine and Danube, London the Thames, and here in South East Asia there is the mighty Mekong.

203

The Chao Phraya river meanders through Bangkok, and has been its lifeblood for many centuries. People have traversed it, lived on it, traded on it, ate from it and emptied their rubbish into it for generations. Years before roads surpassed it, canals were built from it, and these irrigated its agriculture. The river not only supplied the people with its fish, it created its crops which also fed farm animals, and allowed the city to not only support a burgeoning population, but also trade with the wider world.

Ultimately the river is the source of Bangkok's wealth. With growth and wealth comes art and culture and religion, and all along the banks of the Chao Phraya, beautiful temples have been built for the people to follow the teachings of the Buddha.

In modern times leisure and tourism have come to the river so people can race their dragon boats, view the city from a relaxing cruise, or visit the floating markets. As I wandered the waterways and enjoyed its temples, I discovered and was amazed by the phenomenon of their Temple Fish.

Outside these temples almost geometrically perfect is a square patch of water which is teeming with fish. They shoal hugely, and at first it is easy to see why. They are fed by the monks. But this is not the only reason the fish congregate here. In the grounds (watery) of the temple, hunting and fishing is not allowed.

The fact that fish gather here due to being fed and not killed sounds quite reasonable and logical, but how do the fish know? Surely when eggs are laid and fertilised they scatter throughout the river, and the ones that survive could grow to adulthood anywhere. So, do they find their way back to the temple at which they were conceived, or adopt any temple? And is this an evolved instinct, is it now in their genes?

How can it be evolved? That would be the equivalent of every Christian being drawn inexorably to the sanctuary of a church from birth.

Returning to the feeding by the monks. Yes, rice is thrown to them, they do feed in a frenzy from where it lands on the water. But this is within throwing distance, at best just an arc, from the shore, or jetty. The phenomenon of the gathering of the fish as I have said is geometrically perfect. Draw a line from the boundary walls of the temple at right angles straight into the river, and that is a boundary. Inside this line fish teem; outside the line, empty water. And after a reasonable distance into the river of about 15 yards. an imaginary line can be drawn to connect the two perpendicular, and once again, inside the line the fish shoal whereas outside, anywhere towards the middle of the river, no fish. And there are no nets, no physical boundaries, just apparently psychological ones Given that the scattering of food is just that, a random scatter, you have to conclude that the assembly of the fish tight inside the square must be to escape the rod or net.

The question appears to be; have these fish evolved into spending their whole lives in this dense formation, or is it learned behaviour passed on from generation to generation, which logically ultimately becomes evolved behaviour? And how did it start? Did one fish pass onto its mates the news that not only is there a free lunch to be had within the confines of this human building, but also there is a marked absence of those hooks and nets that appear to carry away so many of our kind to some unknown fate? I would have thought, viewing the nature of the feeding frenzy, that the lucky fish that had stumbled upon this serendipity might keep the bonanza for themselves.

And how long did it take these super intelligent fish to stumble upon the nature of these safe havens? And while we're at it, there will of course be those that believe without question that this phenomenon has been brought about by the Buddha himself. Spiritually these creatures have been drawn to the protection of the deity. After all, in the journey to nirvana all of these fish are simply reincarnated people, and the reincarnated state recalls the knowledge of their past existences.

Buddhists, and indeed Hindus also deify the dogs and monkeys that set up home in their inland temples. They are revered so much that worshippers feed them. Call something a god, then feed it and, lo and behold, it becomes a god; a self-fulfilling prophecy. Does the same apply to our temple fish. Perhaps it does. But I still think there is a riddle here, a mystery, a conundrum; an enigma. It is the classic chicken and egg situation. Which came first?

To further muddy the waters (as it were) in recent years locals have been buying fish from the fish markets, where they are sold live, and then releasing them into the temple waters, thereby instantly affording them god status. And this for fish which had previously been mere mortals awaiting the dinner plate. The purpose of these good deeds is to exorcise bad spirits and bestow good luck on the fish saviour and his family.

And so here is another question. Do the rescued fish, introduced thus, remain within the confines of the temple, where they will be safe and fed, or do they wander back into the river system, to possibly be caught again and re-deified (or eaten)? There could be a study; evolution versus instinct; creation versus human intervention, even nature versus nurture. It wouldn't matter anyway. They'd probably just blame it on climate change.

*

My tour on that slowly chugging barge came to a premature end with the glow of the river lanterns beginning to twinkle and reflect on the water. On board I had met Jan and Margareta from the pretty Dutch town of Valkenburg and they invited me to join them the following day for a trip north to Kanchanaburi. I jumped at the chance. Meanwhile we made our way back through the busy narrow streets of bustling Chinatown, stopping occasionally to sample street food, although I have to admit I shied away from the fried insect type (surely just a joke played on tourists) and kept to the deep fried vegetable dishes. The banana was my favourite. Between courses we would pop into a bar for an ice cold beer or two. By the time I reached the hotel I had had at least six of each and was ready for my bed. Tomorrow, The Bridge On The River Kwai.

After an early breakfast the minibus picked me up for the two hour trip north to the town of Kanchanaburi. Jan and Maga were already on board, and during the trip we shared our knowledge of what we thought we were about to see. I'm only two days from experiencing the history of one series of atrocities, and now we were going to experience the scene of another atrocity-laden chapter in the history of this region.

In 1942 the Japanaese recently having entered the Second World War invaded the islands of the Pacific and Indian Oceans. In South East Asia they worked their way up through the Malay peninsular after the capitulation of the heavily defended British possession, Singapore. We gave up without much of a fight, which hadn't endeared us to our captors whose code of honour dictated death was better than surrender. They now had thousands of prisoners of war, including many civilians (see Tenko).

The Japanese conquered Siam and marched north into Burma, forcing British, Chinese and loyal Burmese troops and thousands of refugees back into India. They took Burma in May 1942. History shows that we rallied and after many close-quartered, fierce battles, were eventually able to push the Japanese back into Burma. Here Orde Wingate's Chindits gradually eroded the Japanese hold on the country and they were forced into retreat. The British recapturing Manadalay in March 1945. The bombs on Hiroshima and Nagasaki brought the whole thing to a halt soon after, but we had already defeated the Japanese.

Just one of the many stories of this campaign involved the river Kwae-yai. The Japanese had extended their supply lines into Rangoon, which had now become stretched. They needed to build the Thai-Burma railway to transport troops and supplies. One of the major obstructions they needed to overcome was the river and its valley, so had to build a bridge and embankments on a ledge through the valley.

The story, which was made into a film starring Alec Guinness, however apocryphal, was that POW's were forced in awful conditions and in the face of cruel torture, to build the railway and its bridges. The Colonel in charge decided the British POW's should work hard and efficiently, building a perfectly engineered bridge, which would maintain their morale and save their lives. However allied commandos were deployed to destroy the bridge and set their charges. Colonel

207

Nicholson, all British stiff upper lip, spots the wired explosives and warns the Japanese overseers. When he realises he has jeopardised the war effort and the lives of the commandos he falls on the plunger himself to destroy the bridge and the supply train.

Cue a marvellous 1957 film which topped the box office.

I hadn't known of the Dutch involvement, so Jan and Maga told me about the Dutch East Indies, what we now call Indonesia. These were the subject of the Spice Wars fought around the 17th and 18th centuries when the British, French, Portuguese and the Dutch vied for control of such islands as Java, Borneo, Sumatra, and east to Timor and New Guinea. The value in those days of spices like pepper, cardamom and nutmeg was huge. So much so that when only one ship survived,laden with spices, out of a fleet of five, and after suffering the death of Ferdinand Magellan, no less, the expedition was still deemed profitable.

When the Japanese invaded these islands, the locals were conscripted or forced into slavery as labourers and comfort women. The Dutch, even though now part of Nazi Germany, were taken as prisoners of war (there was no Vichy style treaty). These also played a huge role in story of the Thai-Burma railway.

We arrived into a hot and steamy Kanchanaburi mid-morning, and it only seemed natural that we first visit the edifying and elegiac JEATH Museum. Here we learned that over 90,000 people were killed during the construction of what became known as the Death Railway, mostly Thai and Burmese slave labourers. The 13,000 POW's who perished included over 5,000 British, 2,700 Dutch and 2,500 Australian

We came out of the museum, back into bright sunshine to see the river itself, brown and quite swollen at the end of the rainy season. The bridge has variously had nine or eleven spans and stands on concrete plinths set into the fast flowing river. It is only partly original, but it is a railway bridge. We walked across and back and found ourselves at the station, Saphan Kwae Yai. We bought three tickets for a few Thai Baht, only about 20 pence, and waited for the train which I thought would just take us across and back.

Our journey turned into something quite extraordinary.

A diesel train pulled up with about half a dozen blue and white open carriages. We climbed aboard, took our wooden seats and with a hissing of steam, and creaking and clanking, the train set off slowly, inexorably, heading for the bridge. I sensed I was taking part in an historic re-enactment, a world moment, a bucket list moment. I was taking part in something I knew I would never forget.

To be fair the seats were superfluous, no-one sat down, we were all hanging out the windows.

After no more than a minute we were on the bridge, the echo sounds of the clanking now bouncing off the metal girders, and the swirling brown waters of the Kwai beneath. On the other side the train chuffed to a halt, and I fully expected it to reverse and repeat the experience. But no, the train set off again, and we entered the jungle on the other side. Soon we were on a wooden trestle arrangement, the cliff to the right, and the river below, and I began to realise the building of this section of the railway had not only included the bridge, but also the Kwai valley, and here there had been different engineering problems facing the constructors, to build a railway to run alongside a sheer cliff face. At times the railway appeared to be running in midair, such was how it had to be built above the jungle.

We continued through the jungle, the river still below us, and at one stage the train almost came to a halt. A railway employee explained that at this point the safe speed was less than 5 miles per hour, and we were welcome to walk alongside the train if we wished.

Try and stop me. The three of us leapt down onto the rickety trestle, as did virtually every other passenger, it was as if we were shedding our weight to give the engine a better chance. At the top of the incline we all clambered back aboard and continue the journey, where to, I hadn't a clue. Weren't we due back at the minibus?

Presently the rolling stock hissed into a siding and everyone descended the train and followed a gravel path down the hill into the jungle to an open air restaurant where we were greeted by smiling staff who beckoned us to sit down at the tables on the long benches, and indicated a hot buffet which we were encouraged to begin devouring. There were noodles, and rice, and chicken curry and vegetable curry and papads and bowls of fruit, and jugs of water.

It was a very pleasant meal, all the more satisfying as we hadn't a clue it was on the itinerary. We hadn't even realised there was an itinerary.

Once people had completed their meals they were led out of the restaurant and down to the riverside where a series of thatched rafts were moored. When it came to our turn we sat down on our bench whilst our captain shoved off. At this point the river was much calmer and green in colour, reflecting the dense jungle on either side. When we reached the middle the captain, a slight man wearing blue shirt and shorts put away his pole, squatted in the bow and gently rowed us downstream. It was a very gentle cruise, extremely peaceful, just a babbling of water and birdsong to accompany our drift. "I suppose we're not going back on the train, then" I ventured.

The captain gradually guided the raft into the opposite bank where some elephants were tethered which we were evidently expected to ride. We were led onto the bank and up onto a platform and an elephant manoeuvred herself alongside. The howdah consisted of two seats either side of her great back with a fringed square roof in maroon and gold cloth. Jan and Maga took the first elephant. I was on my own, so took the next for myself. The mahout handed me a small bunch of bananas and no sooner had my charge begun our journey than her trunk reached around for her first offering. I was only too pleased to share.

Our plodding journey took us down the right bank of the river, through the shallows. Another very pleasant half hour gently swaying to the gait of this marvellous beast. What could possibly come next?

And there they were. As our elephants strode out of the water onto a shallow bank and we descended the howdahs, dragon boats were waiting. These are narrow canoes with an outboard motor mounted on a long pole extended beyond the stern, so the thrust propellers are in fact six feet away, behind the boat.

We got into the boat, one behind the other, and our operative started the engine, brrrba brrrba brrrba, then the revs increased, and the bow was thrust out of the water and high into the sky as we were propelled down the river at breakneck speed. Well it felt like breakneck speed, probably no more than 10mph, but our white knuckles were employed on the gunwales.

We had switched to this type of craft as the river was speeding up, and we needed the control of the motors. With the warm wind sweeping Maga's hair into my face we sped up the river, jungle rising on both sides. Suddenly it opened out and we were back at the bridge. The driver banked hard right and the boat grounded itself up onto the bank, almost beneath the bridge itself.

I was fully expecting to be approached and charged for what had been a most extraordinary excursion, but no, the lad shook our hands, we exchanged our thanks and walked back up the hill in the direction of Kanchanaburi.

Jan conjectured that perhaps the money he had paid to hire the minibus must have included the whole package. Well if that's the case, we agreed, then this was a wonderful package indeed, at no more than 25 Euros each.

Our final visit of the day was to the rows and rows of white stones marking the final resting place of all the poor people who had suffered so and had failed to survive the building of the Death Railway. Although it declared itself a Commonwealth Cemetery, it included many Dutch graves. As we wandered solemnly among the graves, I was a little surprised that young Buddhist monks, with their shaven heads and orange robes, were running around the cemetery, playing hide and seek. Too disrespectful.

We located our minibus driver and slept all the way back to the capital.

That night the three of us once again enjoyed the hustling, bustling streets of Chinatown. We encountered no prostitution, no drugs, no ladyboys, no porn shows, and not a great deal of drunken misbehaviour. In amongst the bright lights, sizzling-smoky street food, and lively bars, most folk just wandered aimlessly, enjoying the far eastern delights of the open air markets and shops. There was just this Dutch pair and a Brit letting everyone down drunkenly regaling the crowds with Queen tracks.

Chiang Mai

The next morning I flew north to Thailand's second city, Chiang Mai. Overnight, the old King Bhumibol died aged 88, and plunged the country into mourning. He had reigned for over 70 years and his passing left Elizabeth II as the World's longest serving monarch.

I checked into the Park Hotel where a very subdued desk team welcomed me with the news that there will be no music, entertainment or alcohol in the hotel as instructed by the government for at least a week. However breakfast will be served from 6:30. My first thought was that I would be able to cope, there are always ways of finding a beer. But no music and entertainment would hit clubs and restaurants. There would be thousands of back-packers throughout Thailand who'll wonder what's hit them.

I was about a mile from the walled city, so after settling in I made my first orientation walk, and was immediately shocked. In truth the taxi ride from the airport had set me up. This was a big city, a big, modern city, sprawling with modern buildings, dual carriageways, flyovers and modern architecture.

For many years I had wanted to see Chiang Mai. It had always been advertised as a hill town, gateway to the hill tribes. Therefore in my mind's eye it was on a hill, a small settlement with perhaps one dusty main street with a few tracks off, a couple of run down hotels, and maybe a bar or two. What I found was very different.

Most notably the city is located in the wide plain of a valley. From the

212

roof of the hotel I could see distant hills in all directions, but nothing daunting.

I walked towards the old town and there were modern shops and offices either side of the road. I was constantly invited to partake of a massage by the very friendly tightly saronged girls who were seated outside their salons buffing their nails (their business not affected by the mourning, then). There were posh hotels, my own, The Park was far above my usual standard. I discovered temples, bars, restaurants, and street vendors everywhere. And I found an electrical shop, useful as I had left my phone charger back in Bangkok. Instantly for a few Baht I could reinstate communications and a camera.

I arrived at the walls of the old town. Inside it is arranged on a grid system, 700 years old. On every street, on every corner, there is a temple. Just wandering down the first street I came to, there were four temples before the park gardens at the end. I wandered into all four, and each one had the same reassuring features. On entry, in the main courtyard you heard the chanting, could smell the incense and see the orange-clad bald and many bespectacled monks busying about. There were stupas and golden Buddhas. Every so often bells would chime. In one, when the bells sounded a dog would whine with every peel. In another a microphone had been placed to amplify the chanting. Unfortunately another dog lay beside it and barked constantly.

The park was a delight, inside the west wall, it had a picturesque lake with colourful gardens , ornamental bridges and topiary. At the north end was a huge beautiful temple housing all of the above, including the dogs.

I eventually found a central square and enjoyed a stir fry lunch at the 48 Garage, a bar restaurant based on a converted VW camper van. The ice cold beer in the hot sunshine was as welcome as it was surprising in the current mood. The Scottish owner told me that if it was difficult to find a drink, it had nothing to do with the King's demise, but because it was the last days of Buddha lent.

"If you're struggling, I'm always open" he said in a strong Glaswegian accent.

I left the old town via the main gate and crossed the bridge over the moat. You cannot cross a bridge without stopping at the centre and looking at what it is a bridge over. Here the moat was dark, reflecting the green trees and sky, there were flowerbeds on the city side and trees planted on the new town side. Three other roads converging on the main gate, creating a cacophony of noise; cycles, motor-cycles, tuk-tuks, cars, buses and trucks battling for access and parking with tourists, locals and street vendors. A lone police officer stood on a central plinth desperately waving his arms about and whistling to try to create some semblance of order amongst the hooting traffic.

I was shocked by the clamour and dived back into the old town to find a travel agent.

"I'd like to visit the hill tribes, especially the Karen people," I asked.

"We can go next week, but they are closed now because of the period of mourning."

The Hill Tribes are indigenous people, and as such they see all others as being usurpers of their land. There has always been a fragile peace between the different factions, therefore the city officials fear that unrest may be stirred up during times of stress. The death of the old king is seen as one of those moments, thus the hill tribes have been closed to tourists.

"But I came to Chiang Mai to see the Karen people."

"Sorry, but there are other excursions we can offer you."

That was why I found my second day in Chiang Mai sitting on the wall outside my hotel at 8am waiting for a pick up which came an hour late to an excursion I hadn't really set my heart on.

The previous afternoon I had returned to the hotel via tuk-tuk, always an excitement, rested then walked back to the 48 Garage for dinner and drinks.

Back at the "dry" hotel the key clerk thought I might like to visit the

214

shop opposite. I hadn't noticed it before, but the shopkeeper had put two tables and chairs outside his shop. I spent a very pleasant, warm evening chatting to the locals, and watching the world go by in the company of several large bottles of ice cold beer. We toasted the memory of the old King. That's how it should be done.

The next morning, before my excursion there was breakfast, sadly a western style buffet. There is sometimes something special about being able to breakfast alone. And that is usually in the form of ear-wigging, sorry, accidentally over-hearing.

On the next table were seated two middle aged ladies, both British, I'm guessing Southerners.

"Ere, Jackie, 'ow did you find your light switch?"

"Eh?"

"I wandered round and round, beer in 'and, couldn't find it"

"Find what, Wend?"

"Me light switch. Turned out it was outside me room. What floor you on?"

"They have running water, you know"

"I know, come and look at mine, me toilet don't work."

"And electricity. Oo'd a believed it."

"And I can't use me shower."

"How wonderful. A girl cooked an omelette for me, you know."

"I was followed yesterday, them Buddha boys."

"Just too quaint."

So I'm sitting on the wall outside the hotel in the warm sunshine awaiting my excursion bus, recalling this surreal conversation and the latent racism. They're monks!

(I know that in English the term monk refers to a holy man, and indeed I had already experienced rather less than holy antics at the

Kanchanaburi cemetery, and there are also reports of violent clashes between Buddhist monks and Muslims in this part of the world, so they are possibly not a pious as we are led to believe.)

The bus arrived, I boarded and greeted my fellow excursionists. There was a Chinese lady and her teenage son (I hope), two South American lads, Peruvian and Venezuelan who appeared very much in love, and two Danish girls, Anna and Ingrid, who as soon as they realised I was English, complained about how expensive London is.

I agreed and explained how most Brits avoid the capital because of the crowds, hassle and expense. At least they have Wetherspoons now, I said.

They asked about it, and I explained about Tim Martin and his chain of pubs selling cheap beer and inexpensive meals, with simplicity at the core of his business model.

Then I told them the tale of when Tim was at school and the careers master had told him he would never amount to anything, which was why Tim had named the chain after him, Mr Wetherspoon.

The day went well, if it was a little touristy and exploitative, but we had lots of laughs and enjoyed the people, the countryside and the animals.

It began with a 90 minute drive south down into the arable farm land, then we turned up the Teang river valley. Presently we came to a camp and were introduced to the elephants who lived there housed in a large barn. Inside the barn we climbed a platform to mount the elephants, one at a time, seated behind their necks. They took us on a journey up through the jungle then down alongside and into the river. It was a lovely experience, especially with the myriad of large colourful butterflies. (There are a variety of rhyming animal groupings; birds and bees, slugs and snails, cats and dogs, lions and tigers and bears, oh my!, its such a pity that Elephants and Butterflies just doesn't go. Too clumsy, lacks alliteration).

My elephant's name was Hanna, she was 48 with pink ears. Many believe, possibly quite correctly, that these elephants are being ill-used, and that this cruel exploitation should be stopped. As I have argued in the past; if it was not for the tourist industry then there would be no use for these magnificent creatures. They work, pay their way, and therefore they exist. The alternative is probably not worth considering.

Dismounting the elephants back in their barn, we were then punted down the river on bamboo rafts through small but giggle inducing rapids.

Lunch of vegetable curry and rice was taken in an "indigenous" village, which we then walked around. Our guide explained the hierarchy of the community, how the houses were built, what the peasants did for a living, how the family unit operated, and so forth. Slightly disappointing, all we saw was a pig. I was hoping for the Karen.

Why did I want to see the Karen? They are famous for the multiple brass rings that the women wear around their necks, making the necks look very long, but in fact the rings force the shoulders and rib cage lower. Many of the tribes are refugees from Burma where they are not treated well.

The final part of our day involved a short trek alongside paddy and cornfields to a waterfall where we swam and experienced the rushing of the water. A powerful jacuzzi.

That night I dined at the Riverside ("No live music, sorry!") with Anna and Ingrid. Very pleasant, but the main feature, a waterfall was so noisy it drowned out any conversation. Walking back to the hotel, still shaking my head and saying "Thank you, no" to all the massage girls, I bought a roadside roti with chocolate and banana, absolute heaven. Finally I set myself up outside my favourite shop in Chiang Mai to watch the world go by.

Back in my room I wrote: *"Sadly due to mourning and Buddha Lent there is more atmosphere on the moon at the moment, thank goodness I'm off to Burma tomorrow. I feel sorry for any late arrivals."*

I woke to catch the sunrise and spent all morning wandering around the temples in the old town. At midday I had a bus to Chiang Rai.

Not far out of Chiang Mai the bus stopped for lunch at a restaurant named "Cabbages and Condoms" The unusual name was to promote that use of the latter, should be as common as the cooking of the former. SDI's and unwanted pregnancy are a real problem here.

Our next port of call was the White Temple. A more striking and unusual building I can't think I have ever come across. Ostentatious, pretentious, the adjectives don't come to mind to describe this piece of architecture which has been constructed solely to assure the philanthropist builder everlasting life.

Billions of Baht have been invested in the gleaming entity. If there is one word which could accurately describe it, it is busy. There is just too much.......flourish going on.

From a distance you see it and it looks like a Buddhist temple, but white, and very pointy, every gable, side, and all vertices are shaped and embellished, reaching to heaven. You come closer and cross the bridge and the moat is made up of countless hands and arms reaching upward, desperately beseeching release from hell. There are mythological creatures everywhere, all aflame, all grotesque.

Inside murals are depicting the most unusual icons, from Michael Jackson to Spiderman and Donald Trump, from the Twin Towers to the Terminator, from Harry Potter to Hello Kitty.

Walking around, I couldn't help thinking that Christianity had been given Michaelangelo, Da Vinci and Gaudi, here Buddhism had embraced Stan Lee's Marvel Comics.

Maybe I was being too harsh on the creator, billionaire Chalermchai Kositpipat, and his Wat Rong Khun. After all it brings in plenty of tourist Baht (but not too much, he doesn't want his contribution diluted) and it is a very modern building in a religion where the ancient is revered. I thought it was a fascinating Disneyland, but far be it from me to criticise modernist religion.

I overnighted in Chiang Rai, a pleasant town with a very attractive central square which contained several restaurants. I seated myself at one, ordered myself a pint of Leo Beer and chose a Northern Thai Chicken Curry from the menu, a local speciality. I don't like to judge regions on the food of one restaurant, but this was a poor experience.

Lunch at the Cabbage and Condom had been gelatinous noodles, there had been the overkill of the White Temple, and now I am delivered of a dish of watery sticks. Honestly, it was boiled chicken in water (not even a broth), and floating amongst the sticks were bits of bark. Are they taking the Mick, I thought. Burma can't come quickly enough.

I wasn't there yet though, there was one more tourist visit, the Golden Triangle. And it was worth the trip.

Here was the confluence of the mighty Mekong and Keong rivers. There was also a striking 69 ton seated golden Buddha, a small temple and a museum. This featured pictures of Karen women alongside the biggest catfish ever caught here, fully seven feet long, and probably the largest fresh water fish in the world.

I spent some time wandering the pathways up, into and around the hot steaming jungle which featured beautiful flowering trees and shrubs, and finally came to a high platform. Here was northern Thailand; a sandbank and forest opposite and to my left was Burma, and across the Mekong to my right, the coast of Laos. The area gets its name from the powerful and wealthy drugs trade that used to be prevalent, now happily defeated. There is new wealth, however, across in Laos can be seen a huge golden temple, but it isn't a temple. It is a casino built by and for the Chinese.

I boarded the bus to its terminus at the border town of Mae Sai, like so many border towns, crowded with traders, money changers, chancers and the various detritus of humanity. Through the interminable bureaucracy of passport control, and on the other side, Tachileik, similarly populated, where I was due to meet my guide for Burma.

Inle Lake

Ei was holding up a board with my name. She had to hold it high as she was tiny. In a country of small people, Ei (pronounced I) was below average height, and slightly built. A beautiful young girl of about 25, with a short dark bob, blue sarong and pink satin jacket, she introduced herself and led me out to a minibus already containing seven people.

"Ok" she announced, "We are off to the airport for the flight to Heho, where we will drive to Inle Lake." I noticed she had a cream spread on her cheeks, palish-creamy yellow, like over-applied sun cream.

It was only ten minutes to the airport for the internal flight. Like many countries with underdeveloped infrastructure, flights are the easiest way to go any distance. To Inle would take over 15 hours to drive. In Burma planes are used like buses, hop-on, hop-off.

Burma, or Myanmar, I'm still not sure which they prefer, has only recently opened to tourism. Granted independence in 1948, it has been under military dictatorship since 1962. The opposition leader, Aang San Suu Kyi, spent many years under house arrest, but was allowed to fight the 2015 elections, and won office. She is seen as Burma's Nelson Mandela, and is revered countrywide as "The Lady". She holds the Nobel Prize for Peace (awarded 1991) but still struggles to hold the country together as it is a hotch-potch of hundreds of indigenous tribes.

The eight of us introduced ourselves while Ei busied with passports, visas and tickets, and after a couple of beers we walked onto the tarmac and into the aeroplane.

80 minutes, and on the other side, in the delightfully named Heho, was another minibus and we climbed aboard for the hour drive to Inle and the simple Hu Pin hotel. It was after dark when we arrived and once checked in Ei took us a walk around the small town to a Chinese restaurant where I ate a delicious fish. Straight away I had fallen in love with Burma, easy to travel through, friendly people, good food, and the beautiful Ei, my very own "Lady"

I had noticed that all the women and young girls we had seen had the same cream on as Ei. I asked her about it.

It is Thanaka cream, she told me, and has been used by Burmese women for over 2,000 years It is worn not just for cosmetic purposes, but also it cools, protects from both sun and acne, and gives a smooth skin. The paste is created from the wood of several trees and can be applied as a large circle on the cheek, or in patterns, sometimes also on the nose, and sometimes also worn by men.

Over dinner I began to get to know the people with whom I would be spending the next few days. There was Leigh and Kate, newly weds but in their 40's from Kent; Sandy, a scientist from Warwick; Simon and Penny a permanently bickering couple from Bury St Edmunds; and Jackie and Wendy, the two women from the breakfast table in Chiang Mai. Deep joy.

Having not seen the town, arriving after dark, I was up for the dawn and climbed to the roof of the hotel. Inle is a colourful, one storey town encircled by mountains. From here I couldn't see the lake for which the town was famous, but there was plenty of low lying mist in the direction of the sunrise. I guessed that was the water.

After breakfast Ei led us along a dirt track to a jetty where a dragon boat awaited. We began by phut-phutting slowly through the town's wood and bamboo buildings until we reached the reeds and our driver opened up. In no time we were on the open water, zooming past fields of floating hyacinth, greenery all around set in an amphitheatre of mountains. We flew past fishermen and other boats, skipping over their wakes. There were dozens of boats on the water heading in our direction, and as we arrived at the starting line, Ei told us today was the annual dragon boat races for which all of the villages from around the lake, the Intha people, provided competitors.

The Intha people have developed a method of rowing used nowhere else in the world. Standing up (so they can see over the reeds), one leg is wrapped around the oar, and the boat is propelled with the usual dipping in and out, often with arms akimbo, or free to do other tasks.

Each racing boat is at least 35 yards long with steerers, bailers, drum beaters and about 40 pairs of rowers. Watching them row, steadying themselves with their inside arm, speedily in perfect harmony, was quite impressive, and we saw several practise runs before the races proper began.

There was an interminable wait in the strong sunshine, as we shifted uneasily to gain shade, and I noticed several drones buzzing around. (Months later I found out that Dara O'Briain and Ed Byrne had been filming for their televised documentary, hence the delays). Then with a great shout the races began.

There was whooping, hollering and chanting as we watched four sets of duels. It was awesome watching nearly 100 men all in stroke on each boat with the strange hand, oar, leg, body twist movement. They all returned in various states of victory from wherever their goal had been.

With the racing finished we visited a stilted village for tourist stuff which I usually try to avoid. First, how they make boats, second a silk workshop, seen it all in China, third a cheroot factory.

I hadn't smoked for ten years, but was persuaded to take a drag. It hit the back of my throat like a sledgehammer, and I coughed profusely, which I was really pleased about. What if I'd enjoyed it? Best decision ever to give up.

During these yawn inducing interludes I busied myself looking for spiders, and there were some really big mammas sitting on webs slung between the stilts. Good old arachnophobia, good old exposure therapy.

Lunch was excellent. Stir fry at the wooden table, with rice and beer; overlooking the lake and reeds in foreground, mountains in the background, waterbirds, sunshine on the water, what could be better.

All back on the boat, and we were shown floating farms of tomatoes and other salad crops, very successful, and never flooded. We entered a river which feeds the lake and chugged upstream for what seemed hours in the afternoon heat. Suddenly the banks opened up and we were eventually able to disembark at the In Dien Temple complex.

There was a steep staircase up to the main temple, but on the way, oh my word, over 3,000 stupas, a veritable army, a maze of regimented golden towers. Some were gleaming brand new, others weathered, and yet more returning to the jungle, all entertaining dancing butterflies.

The older stupas were brickwork and dome shaped, and these were those most showing signs of wear. The more modern had a slimline bell shape and these were the most gleaming. Each stupa represented a family, almost in the form of a mausoleum, Ei informed us

If you could describe organised disarray, this was it. Higgledy-piggledy stupa world. This was definitely an alien experience, and with the lake and mountain backdrop, surreal.

Our driver really opened the throttle on our return, an invigorating white knuckle journey across the placid lake at sunset.

That evening we found a lively balcony bar, ate a meze of curried nibbles and drank copious amounts of beer whilst a live band strutted their stuff. A welcome change from the dour mood of Thailand.

The next day was simply one of those you have to occasionally endure when travelling in a developing country. Sometimes things happen on the road at home, you take a detour or a diversion, add a little to the journey, moan a bit, but there's no harm done. Not in Burma.

We were taking the mainly downhill road west to Bagan, seven hours at the most. Start early enough and you can be there for a late lunch. For some reason the bus wasn't there at six, so we went back into the hotel to partake of a more leisurely breakfast. Seven came and went, so I took a stroll down to the little harbour, just to keep the legs moving, and at eight, we were finally on our way.

There were marvellous views of the mountains until we were deep into the forest, then eventually down onto the lush plains. My impressions of the small villages and towns that we passed through was that there appeared to be more money here than you would have thought for a country which has languished behind its own iron curtain for nearly five decades.

Then the bus came to a halt, and we slowly realised the only vehicles coming the other way were those further along the traffic jam who had given up and turned back. The news filtered through that a tanker had come off the road and it would be blocked until a helicopter could be deployed to clear it. So our bus also reversed and we returned to a village we had just passed through and found a bar that could feed the group. The grateful owners rustled up sweet and sour fish with chips and beer which helped us sleep the afternoon away.

The delays helped the group to get to know each other more. Leigh was a retired army colonel now using his disciplinary skills in human resources. Kate was a judge, a director of public prosecutions, "Sounds far more interesting than it is." They're both on their second time around and support Italy in the six nations, "Easier to get tickets to all the games, and the Italians love us for our support." Sandy was actually a Sandra, a published chemist working for TDK, with a 16 year old son at home. Jackie, a wildly enthusiastic Greggs manager from South London, was the only smoker, for whom we had to stop every so often to light up. Wendy was a shy traveller who takes a simple, naïve, almost patronising joy in everything she encounters. It was difficult to get to know Simon and Penny, their constant petty squabbling was quite embarrassing. It could also be their own coping strategy. I find it much easier to be single and insular on a trip like this.

We eventually resumed our journey, but didn't roll into Bagan until past eight. Over 12 hours on a bus, and my ankles were heavily swollen. Our hotel, the Thazin Garden was very plush, with both a swimming pool and a monument stupa in the gardens. Dinner was wasted, still full from lunch, no opportunity to work it off, you see.

Bagan

I was up early for a swim, and in the early morning light saw dozens of hot air balloons flying over where we were heading later. After breakfast there was a short drive to our first pagoda. It is remarkably beautiful, but in the scale of things nothing special. What was special about this pagoda were the steps on the outside leading around to the roof.

From the top there was the most amazing scene across the Bagan plain. Rising out of the jungle were hundreds of pagodas and temples, each one competing with its neighbours for attention, such was the beauty of their designs. And in this wondrous scene were structures as far as the eye could see in any direction. And at this hour of the morning, with the steam still rising from the jungle, it gave the scene an ethereal air.

Once Bagan had been a huge city. Built on a curve of the Irrawaddy river, it was the capital of the Pagan Empire, the first to unite Myanmar. Between the ninth and thirteenth centuries over 10,000 stupas, temples and monasteries were built here. History tells us that subsequent kings always tried to outdo their predecessors so they have left for posterity the most magnificent architectural structures. The Mongol Empire finally put paid to the Pagans, and in subsequent centuries the plain of Bagan became more of a centre for pilgrimage. Hence we have over 3,800 buildings left for us to marvel at today.

There was nothing to do here but just drink it all in. The warmth of the the sun, the gentle breeze, the silence, occasional murmur of insects or distant birdsong. The blue sky with a climbing sun, the green shimmering jungle, and the towers and pagoda roofs, sometimes golden, reaching to the heavens all around.

Once we had drunk our fill, Ei led us to the Golden Pagoda situated in the bustling heart of the complex where we took tea in a dusty, smelly market. A little reality check. We went on to a pagoda with wall paintings and drawings from the twelfth century depicting stories and fables from the Buddha's life. Finally we visited the Ananda Temple, one of the most sacred in Burma, the temple of the four golden standing Buddhas (two replaced when lost to fire). All were over 30 foot high and facing the cardinal points of the compass. The place is described as the Westminster Abbey of the East, although I can't believe that that is much of an accolade.

Ananda was built during the reign of King Kyanzittha, and completed in the 12th century. Looking at the huge, beautifully golden architecture, and wandering the corridors of gilt and artistic reliefs, statuary and decoration, you have to marvel at the advanced state of this civilisation, existing while we were slaughtering each other at Hastings, or in the Crusades. Then you learn that the king had the monks who had inspired the architecture killed to preserve its uniqueness. Nothing much changes in the world of man.

Lunch was taken back at the smelly market, and it was a buffet of several "interesting" dishes. We picked at them nervously with Leigh declaring that they were "Only just on the edge!"

I swam and sunbathed for a while in the afternoon, then became bored. I was frustrated at not having experienced enough of Bagan. There was the stupa in the garden, but surely more could be seen from the rear of the hotel's grounds. So I laced up my boots and set off to explore.

From the rear of the hotel there were fields of corn which led down to a stream. I crossed the stream and found a small pagoda, just standing there. I moved on, taking a track to the side, wandered through a wood and found another pagoda surrounded by eight foot stupas, which were beginning to return to nature, tree roots emerging. I walked on and came upon a small village; children playing, mothers working, and youths hanging around eyeing me suspiciously. I greeted everyone warmly and continued on my way.

I discovered more buildings as I wandered from field to field, evidence of ancient tombs and family mausoleums, and eventually decided to make my way back. I reckoned I hadn't walked that far, and my sense of direction told me I needed to head to my left. There were tracks leading around the fields, but I had gone fairly deep into the valley. The corn was over six feet high, so I couldn't see above that, and where there was no corn, the woodland was thick with few paths.

It gradually dawned upon me that I was lost. I followed various tracks going in what I thought should be the right direction, and suddenly they would split and I had to make a decision, left or right. Or the track might come to a dead end and I had to retrace my steps. It's not like at home where you can virtually guarantee that one track will lead to a wider one, then eventually a road with signposts. In places like this you can walk logically, make wise decisions, take the best, most common sense route, and still find yourself deeper in the mire.

I came upon another village, different from before, I think, but with the same sort of people, especially youths eyeing me suspiciously. I thought about asking, but asking for what? I think my hotel was "The..." something, but couldn't be sure, and nobody spoke English anyway. I decided to tough it out. Surely I'd come across it …. soon.

As I took the dirt track out of this village, trying to look confident, I heard a motorbike start up behind me. The motor phut-phutted and closed in on me, I stepped to the left to let it pass, but it continued to idle behind me. I once again came to a cross track and as I hesitated to make a decision the motorbike came up behind me, sped past and carried straight on. There were two youths on the bike and the pillion beckoned for me to follow.

I did so. What else could I do, but where might they be leading me. We went through a copse, passed a pagoda and turned left, then right and up onto a wider track. The pillion pointed to his right, and there was my hotel. I waved gratefully and the bike sped off.

I showered, and celebrated my little adventure with a couple of beers in the garden as the sun sank in the west across the plain of Bagan.

The next morning Ei assembled us for an early breakfast in the hotel's beautiful garden and we admired the balloons ascending. They were so close you could sometimes hear their burners as they rose into the sky. It was the only sound, and it was the most beautiful of breakfasts.

We were approaching the part of the itinerary I had most anticipated (not knowing anything previously about Inle Lake or Bagan). We were going to Mandalay. As magical a place as you can conjure up in the mystical east. To be "On the Road to Mandalay" It is Kipling, Orwell, the Empire, Shangri La, Gunga Din, Mowgli, Sinbad, Sheherazade, all rolled into one. But we weren't to be 'on the road'. We were going by boat.

As we left the hotel I looked back and on the sign beneath the name of the Thazin Garden were the words; "Sweet Welcome to Fairy-Land of Wonders". Indeed.

We came to the beach of the Irrawady River, about to begin a leisurely cruise, 160 miles upstream.

Our boat was perhaps 60 feet, red and white with a green canopy, and with two decks. The lower a galley and dining area, the upper for relaxing and sleeping. There were wicker chairs with cushions, on the upper deck and the group settled into their selected seats as the skipper cast off and we headed for midstream.

Our first objective was to sail under the vast bridge that spans the river here. It looked like the river could be up to two miles wide. I had experienced a previous river cruise, along the Nile, which is rarely more than half a mile wide. This makes both banks visible and communications possible with farmers, fishermen, sailors and villagers on both sides. Here, midstream was away from everyone, so we needed to be nearer to the banks to observe river life. We headed for the far side, the west bank.

Soon we were waving to barefoot children who were running to keep up, fishermen casting their nets, and women busy with the laundry. We passed the occasional pagoda amid the thick jungle. It was interesting to see the Royal Palms, standing out high and proud above the canopy. The first couple of hours we spent very little time seated in our comfy chairs, much more interesting to lean over the rail and take in life on the river.

Presently we were called down for lunch with the ubiquitous bowls of rice, accompanying papads, rotis, and curries, and fresh fruit to finish. Excellent home cooking. The crew of three were made up of a captain, chef and a crewman who did all the odd jobs for them and us, including serving the beer from a massive ice box.

Soon after lunch we tied up at a village and clambered up the muddy bank for a wander around. This was probably the poorest place I can ever remember visiting, The villagers had nothing but their mud huts and primitive cooking utensils. All cooking was done over an open fire. Children in dirty rags ran alongside us, there were chickens pecking at the dust, and very possibly the biggest, fattest black pig I had ever seen, laying on her side with vast rows of underused teats. The village industry was making pots from the river's clay, and there was a demonstration of this, as there always has to be for tourists. The opportunity to purchase souvenirs was very low key, and we were assured that the few Kyat notes which were handed over would go straight to the local shop (wherever that may be) to be exchanged for beer.

Back on the boat and our own beers (probably costing ten times what locals pay) were flowing to ensure the rest of the afternoon could be spent soporifically nodding in our wicker chairs as the river and its life floated by. Such is a river cruise.

With the sun going down and the clouds above the horizon becoming more pink, we began seeing animals in them. There was an elephant, a dog with floppy ears, a pink flamingo on one leg, a pink tiger, no, more like a lion with that mane. The clouds evolved into other animals or shapes. The elephant became a rocket ship, the dog turned into a dolphin. I was reminded of ice cream castles in the air.

Then with the sun gone and the sky darkening, the stars started to appear, the first, as always, bright Venus, the evening star.

"Ooh! Is that the Pole star?" Jackie asked enthusiastically.

"No. That one's in the south, behind us. When we see the Plough, Big Dipper, Ursa Major, Great Bear, Saucepan, whatever, then the two end stars point up to the pole star, it's not bright, but it always indicates north the way we're going. I'll show you."

"Always the teacher, eh Geoff?" teased Penny.

And I clammed up, suitably embarrassed.

We were lucky, there was no moon, and the stars came out in their multitude. I showed them the Milky Way and explained our position on the edge of the western spiral. There was Cassiopeia, the Seven Sisters, Cygnus the swan, and indeed the Great Bear. We followed the end two stars up to the Pole Star, in the north, shining over Mandalay.

Bright Venus was by now beginning to set, and as she settled lower in the sky, I spotted a phenomenon I had never seen before. I was shamefacedly excited.

"Look everyone" I could hardly contain myself, "at all these stars, up in the firmament, shining their light on us from thousands, maybe millions of years ago. But that is all you see. And here is Venus, virtually our nearest neighbour, a fellow planet, and the light it shines is from our own sun, reflected to us. And there it is, on the water, shining across the river, like the moon would do."

The silver light of Venus was indeed shining across the water. I was just too ebullient.

And then, as we were all gazing up at the sky, a shooting star swept over, the first of four we saw that evening, but a perfect encore to my lecture.

The captain began looking for a sandbar to moor onto for the evening, but a combination of a black night and high waters were thwarting the search. So we were called down for dinner whilst the engines still rumbled, which was less than conducive to enjoying a peaceful, relaxed meal. The crew removed the wicker chairs and set up our mattresses on deck whilst we ate.

When we had finally found somewhere to anchor, it was nearly time to turn in, but the captain insisted we had a campfire on the shore (it must have been in the advertising blurb) and we disembarked briefly to enjoy the flames.

Personally, I was looking forward to the silence of the night. Once the flames had died away, the lights switched off, and the soft snoring of my shipmates prevailing, this was my moment.

I lay with my legs raised, trying to reduce the swelling of my ankles, watching the stars move slowly across the sky. The Plough moved around, keeping the pole star constant. Orion rose around two am with its easily identified three star belt and one of the brightest stars at its corner, the wonderfully named Betelgeuse. There were more shooting stars, but the weather was changing. I could see and hear thunder and lightning in the distant east. I must have slept fitfully, waking as dawn broke, which was cooler and cloudier. I stretched my legs out on the sandbar before the captain fired up the engines and we cast off around six.

Fried banana and coffee for breakfast. Sometimes it is the simplest things. There was little elbow room for a wash and brush up, it was difficult enough last night with the tooth brushing. At times like this you appreciate a hotel room, shower and all.

The morning passed simply enough, more villages, fisher folk, children playing in the shallows, mothers washing, buffalo lowing. Jungle, sky and water; jungle, sky and water. Quite soporific, dozing in the sunshine as there was not much sleep last night. Every so often a temple sticks up out of the canopy, but there was little to disturb the peaceful monotony.

Mandalay

Lunch comes and goes and we were nearing Mandalay. We sailed under another huge bridge and past the ancient cities of Sagaing and Inwa. The glittering, golden stupas and temples were a wonderful sight on the hillsides above the river.

We continued straight past Mandalay however, and the captain moored at Mingun. Here we would have the opportunity to visit the Whitewashed Pagoda which represents Mount Meru and the Seven Seas, the giant 90 ton Mingun bell, and what Ei described as the world's largest pile of bricks. She may well be right.

The pile of bricks was the Unfinished Pagoda which was 'incompleted' by the eccentric King Bodawpaya at the end of the 18th century. It would have been 500 feet high had it ever been finished, but it was never intended to be finished. Legend dictated that with completion the king would die. So he deliberately slowed down construction. He was also a clever king as the building, reaching over 150 feet occupied thousand of prisoners, keeping them busy and unable to revolt. Damage by earthquakes, the latest in 2012, meant it cannot be climbed.

Back on the boat it was a short trip into the Mandalay dock where we said goodbye to the crew and took taxis to the Marvel hotel in the city centre, built above the railway station.

The brief journey certainly managed to burst my bubble of a magical city. It was busy, beyond just bustling, noisy, and polluted. The main streets were wide, but choked with traffic and litter. There seemed little about this city to write home about.

It had gone dark once we'd showered and met up for dinner taken in what could have been a Chinese restaurant anywhere in the world, with its waving golden cats, pagoda tapestries and plain tables.

Later I caught up with Kipling's poem which had attracted me (the irony hadn't escaped me that I had arrived by river and would leave by rail). A British veteran yearns for his sin free posting to meet up with his Burmese beauty; a sweeter maiden in a cleaner, greener land. He recalls the spicy garlic smells and tinkly temple bells, "where the flyin' fishes play, on the road to Mandalay".

The next day, keen to be won over by this lyrical Mandalay I booked a taxi to see the sights. Captain Jacko and Judge Kate tagged along.

Behind the modern city, the low rise colonial architecture and simple streets were much more agreeable, and our first stop was at Lake Taungthaman, in Amarapura over which spans the famous U Bein bridge. It is a favourite of tourists, therefore we had to run the gauntlet of trinket sellers to reach the security protected bridge.

It is a narrow teak footbridge, nearly a mile long with over 1,000 pillars, and 480 spans. There were covered pavilions for resting and sheltering, but the most evocative images were of conical hatted peasants walking their cycles. The bridge overlooked a hive of activity, flocks of ducks and geese, children flying kites, fishing canoes and farming activity where the low lake exposed rich soil.

Thoughts strangely escaping, the promenade reminded me of the wooden rail bridge over Mawddach estuary which connects Fairbourne to Barmouth in mid-west Wales. Both lovely strolls.

At the entrance to the U Bein there is a small pagoda, and most people just use its car park for access to the bridge. Before we re-joined our taxi we peaked inside. We couldn't have foreseen this. Within this small, overlooked temple were 28 beautifully mirrored columns, reflecting the blue and gold decorations into infinity, overseen by a benign and youthful, smiling Buddha. One of those moments you cherish.

Our driver then took us to the Shweinbin Monastery and a change from the usual douse-everything-in-gold philosophy. This is totally teak, and the wooden colours, smells and cushioned acoustics lent a very different atmosphere. Still the same carvings and statuary, but it was hushed. There was a quietly chanting congregation and it felt as if everyone was just saying "Shush!"

Finally the Royal Palace, an impressive four miles square. Surrounded by a huge moat, this is mostly reconstructed from the original teak which was "carelessly" burnt down by allied bombing in the Second World War. It had been a British fort for 70 years before the Japanese used it as a supply depot. I don't think "careless" comes into it.

What I really enjoyed about the palace (we hadn't the time to go inside) was the view up to Mandalay Hill. Forest and golden pagodas all the way to the summit, a vision of Burma.

We had a 4:30 train to catch, so returned to the Marvel for a late lunch on the fourth floor overlooking the town centre. Descending to the platforms I guessed a buffet car or restaurant may not be a priority on the overnight Mandalay to Yangon sleeper. Cold beers possibly at a premium, so I quickly found a shop to buy a couple of bottles of local whisky.

Once on the train, in two four berths, night fell quickly so we broke out the scotch. After the party, at least we had no problem sleeping on the uncomfortable couchettes.

Before the drink took over and we became a dancing mess (eight people seated in a railway compartment is just about manageable, dancing in one, not), the evening had begun with a discussion about the nature of Britishness.

I've always thought we are a strange race, which struggles to have a clear identity. We are Great Britain, three countries on one island, or the United Kingdom, four countries (and another one) on two islands. We have one government for all of us, but the smaller countries have their own. We have a common language, law, education and health service, with some slight variations. We haven't been conquered for over a thousand years (My brother still hates the French. "But they were Normans," I tell him. It's no use, you can't use logic with intolerance), and for most of the last 500 years we have created and led the greatest empire the world has ever seen. The sun never sets on it. The British Empire has evolved into a Commonwealth of friendly nations headed by the world's favourite royal family.

It is in sport that the cracks begin to appear. We can't be one nation in football, but we are always the UK in the Olympics and European and World athletics. England sing the National Anthem, which also belongs to the Welsh and Scots and Northern Irish, who have to sing their own in soccer and rugby (except for the Irish who then join together with the Republic). We play abroad in rugby as the Lions, the whole of the British Isles. In golf we are European against the Americans, and in cricket it appears anyone can play for England so long as they sing Jerusalem.

In our isolated railway carriage we became more parochial in our stereotypes. All people south of Watford apparently are southerners, extras for Eastenders who constantly shout at each other with comments like "Get outta my 'arse," and "You're not my faaaamly!".

Oop north they're from Coronation street or from across the Pennines in that other country, Yorkshire. People in East Anglia or the South West are inbred while those in the North East go out in all weathers in shorts and vest and are Geordies. Scousers only wear suits for their court appearances, and everyone who lives a rural lifestyle shags sheep.

Personally I'm grateful Crossroads bit the dust years ago, as Amy Turtle and Benny tarred us all with Brummie accents. Being from the Black Country we get very sniffy with that one.

But then snobbishness rears its ugly head with education, whether you went to public school, or grammar school or just a bog-standard comprehensive; if you studied at Oxbridge or a red brick polyversity. And suddenly the conversation has dipped into the class divide, another very British trait.

We ended up on football, as many discussions inevitably do, and derby rivalries. That's when you realise that it's not the Russians or Chinese who are the enemies, nor even the Americans. Sir Humphrey in Yes Minister claimed the French to be our only perennial enemy. He was also wrong. The real enemies of every Brit are the people in the next town, or village , or even street. In fact, we hate everybody, especially neighbours. And that was where the argument ended.

A good laugh was had by all, but the whole conversation had gone right over poor Ei's head. She just grinned and was happy that her group were getting along.

To finish Jacko told us he once knew a Glaswegian in the Scots Dragoon Guards, something of a rarity in itself. He had confessed to being intolerant about just two things, "I detest racism, in all its forms, it is a disgusting malevolence in today's society and should never be tolerated."

"What's the second thing?" Jacko had ventured.

"The English, I hate the English, bunch of southern softies who think they are so superior. Hate them, bloody English."

I told them of a friend who thoroughly enjoyed the film Braveheart with Mel Gibson as the medieval Scottish freedom fighter, William Wallace. "Only one thing wrong with it," he'd told me, "The torture scene at the end is too short!"

Then we started singing Flower of Scotland, and that's when the dancing began.

Yangon (Rangoon)

I was first awake, just before dawn. I had a thick head and the compartment smelled of whisky and stale curry. I dressed and ventured into the corridor, opened the window and stuck my head out for some deep breaths of fresh early morning air. I wanted to see the people and the Burmese countryside waking to greet another day. It didn't disappoint.

We were now in the south of the country having followed the Irrawaddy river valley, and it was low lying. The houses we dawdled past were on stilts, as were the villages. There was litter everywhere. It gathered wherever there was still water, especially beneath the stilts, giving the place an air of filthy stagnation. The Burmese have adopted the western throwaway consumer habits without putting in place systems to collect and recycle.

The people appeared happy enough. Adults and children alike smiling and returning my waves. The fields were flat and bright green, the low sun playing tricks with the shadows of the crops. Every so often a farmer would be guiding a team of oxen, ploughing, with ducks waddling alongside or egrets fluttering behind.

You are never far away from seeing the golden tower of a stupa poking up through the canopy or standing alone in the green sward. Then the roads, with the barrier down and a group of locals waiting to cross. Schoolchildren, usually in pairs, a brother and sister perhaps, holding hands. Hand carts, empty for the moment, being held by conical hat-wearing peasants, anxious to load up for market. Motorbikes, mopeds really, with unisex crash helmeted workers off to the office or shop, left foot on the ground right hand ready to rev up. They're all waiting patiently for the carriages to pass, with me sharing our one moment in time.

We stopped briefly and I bought three samosas from an old man selling them out of a huge brown paper bag. That was breakfast sorted, and we rolled into Rangoon, now named Yangon at 8:15.

Ei has a minibus waiting which takes us to the Panda Hotel, merely time for a wash and brush up before we meet up at a Lucky 7 tearoom, apparently a favourite with the workers, for another breakfast. This one included sticky rice, quite a dish. You peel back the banana leaf to reveal a lollipop shaped lump of rice glued together. Bite into it and it has a sweet taste and texture, excellent to eat by itself, or dipped into savoury, like curry, or sweet, like chutney.

We wandered the city centre, moving from modern shopping mall to squares with statues and fountains, to the People's Park, a lovely green space with lakes and ornamental trees. There is a ban on motorcycles in Yangon, but the streets were still choked with cars and vans. The park was a welcome relief.

Now however it was time for the highlight of our time in Burma, Ei had assured us, and after many days of Buddhist monasteries, stupas, and temples, not even I was prepared for the majesty of the Shwedagon Pagoda. Ostentatious, is not the word. The Shwedagon has been designed by someone who has taken every great pagoda that has ever been created and instructed the architects to improve on them.

We entered up a stairway guarded by two huge seated lions, to Singuttara Hill. There was the usual security and checking of tickets, then we learned the bad news. There is a dress restriction, which I'd not experienced since the Royal Palace in Bangkok. But this one didn't state what we could not wear. In order to visit the Shwedagon, men must wear a Longyi, the full length maxi skirt which is the traditional Burmese dress. The women had great fun wrapping and dressing Jacko, Simon and myself.

It is the size and extent of the place that is so jaw-droppingly impressive, skirt or no skirt. It is 100 acres, that is 50 football fields, of gleaming, spotless marble flooring, with golden god-like statues in every conceivable dancing pose, all looking up to and worshipping over 1,000 Buddhas. The scale and opulence just beggar's belief, and it is publicised as the biggest temple in the world.

Where there aren't stupas and buddhas and gods and goddesses, there are lions and tigers and elephants; all wonderfully decorated and bejewelled, glittering in white and gold.

It was hot and humid, the sun beating down relentlessly. I'd had little rest in the last 30 odd hours, and every so often I had to stop for a breather in the shade of an ancient banyan tree. I would then set off refreshed to marvel at even more ostentation, with the whole edifice defining that word. At the centre, visible for miles around, is the 326 foot high spire, marking where a stupa has stood since 600 years before the birth of Christ.

Back in my room I managed a couple of hours rest before deciding to wander the streets. The Panda hotel is in a residential area of the city, and there were several smaller roads off the main street. I felt I could have a first glimpse of urban life, Yangon style, and this is where I had one of those lightbulb moments, an enlightenment which should have come earlier, much earlier, in India, Sri Lanka, Cambodia or Thailand.

At the head of every junction there is a small shop, a mini-market, and down each side street, some market stalls selling fresh fruit and veg. Here is where people meet and gather and gossip. But further down the street, life reverts to the village, and in the village scene, no-one goes indoors, except to bed.

With a steady evening temperature rarely going below 24 degrees, everyone sits in the street. Children play in the street, Mum cooks in the street, folk eat in the street, neighbours gossip in the street. All tables and chairs are in the street. You are not alone, the community is out there with you, in the street. And that is how you spend your evening.

People in South East Asia have no need for televisions and soap operas and miniseries, for they never have any reason to stick themselves indoors (Except when it rains, swift downpour, then back out into the steam). Life is lived in society, in community, and in so many ways, that is how it should be. It is very easy to envy this lifestyle. Especially since I am flying home tonight, back to the gogglebox and the enclosed living room.

The group had a final meal together and said goodbye to Ei. Various people are catching various flights to take them to other parts of the world. I'm not one for long, lingering goodbyes. Parting is such sweet sorrow, as someone once said. I'd rather say "Goodnight", perhaps allow myself a little hug, and then just not be there at breakfast. And people could wonder about me and gossip about me or just forget me, I don't really care.

I didn't, and I do care. I said my farewells, after all, we had shared special times together that you will never forget in a lifetime. But I had an 11:30 taxi. As I drove out of Yangon at midnight, people were still gathered outside their homes, chatting and laughing and joshing. I would see the dawn on the other side of the planet, in a different world.

The Shwedagon Pagoda

Vietnam

From Mekong to the Red River

Had I been born in America, I could have been conscripted to fight in the Vietnam War in the late 1960's. Or, to be more precise, probably not, as I was white and middle class.

As a teenager at college I do remember quite vividly the images of the war, the first major conflict to be televised.

- Squadrons of B52's unleashing millions of tons of bombs onto jungle, with deforestation a last resort to try to deny Ho Chi Minh's Vietcong, any hiding place or route to attack American positions

- G.I.'s smoking pot through the barrels of their rifles

- Hippies putting flowers in those same gun barrels

- Street fighting in the city of Hue during the Tet offensive

- Lines of refugees retreating with donkeys and carts, being strafed

- Platoons of troops advancing with tanks and flame throwers

- The My Lai massacre

- The All My Loving documentary showing prisoners being gunned down in cold blood

- Forests erupting in plumes of Napalm fire, or was it Agent Orange

- Protests outside the White House

- Kissinger and Le Duc Tho in Paris negotiating for peace

- The ignominious escape from the roof of the American Embassy

Then came the Boat People refugees, and all the time Monty Python was stealing young students' attention. Surreal times.

Over the years these images have mixed with dramatic cinematic reconstructions of the conflict; from Platoon to MASH (purportedly the Korean conflict, but we knew!), The Deerhunter, Good Morning Vietnam and Apocalypse Now. Oh the Horror. The reality and fiction appeared to merge. There was a hit song informing us that the average age of the combat soldier was "n n n n nineteen!" And even my favourite opera, Madame Butterfly was transposed into the hit West End musical Miss Saigon.

As I travelled from the steamy south; from the Mekong Delta, through Saigon (Ho Chi Minh City), to the demilitarised zone and the 17th Parallel, to the cool and rainy north and Hanoi, I encountered many people. The tourists I met were mainly European, and, as I term them, Commonwealth; Aussies, Kiwis and Canadians (precious few Americans) the question was nearly always the same; "Why have you come to Vietnam?" For me it was to witness the history, both recent and ancient, and to experience the reported beauty and contrasts of the country, and especially to meet the people emerging from the conflict, rising from the ashes of that terrible war. For everyone else? "Seen it on Top Gear, mate". At least the spirit of Monty Python still lives on.

Getting There

On an anonymous Thursday sometime in November, over a month before I was due to travel, I was visiting a family friend in hospital with mum, and receive a phone call (withheld number).

"Hello?"

"You apply for visa to visit Vietnam?" the clipped, rather high pitched caller requests.

"Yes" I confirm rather anxiously as the penny dropped.

"You pay wrong money" he informed me, brusquely.

"Oh, I'm sorry, I must have misread the instructions" I apologised.

"You pay thirty six pounds. Now!" came the insistent, shouted demand. And I felt I had been ordered to play Russian Roulette.

*

It was Epiphany, 6th January and 12th night, so decorations were coming down. I had chosen poorly; a Friday evening to travel by train from Euston to Heathrow. Fifteen interminable stops during rush hour, and not a seat to be taken. I have to sit on my backpack. There were some conversations, but only those where the participants were confident no one could listen in. The languages appeared Russian or east European.

I had to overnight in Heathrow in a functional Travelodge, for a morning flight to Kuala Lumpur. But the overall feeling was that I was already in Asia. All the men on the bus were Sikh, the shops run by Hindu families, the businesses Muslim and the houses owned by a combination. Neighbours that would not live next door anywhere else in the world, all happily displaying their exuberantly lit Christmas trees in their front windows.

Next morning at Terminal four a pushchair skins my left ankle and I stab my finger with an errant toothpick, before I settle into my seat for the 6,750 mile jaunt to Kuala Lumpur. Universally known as KL, the capital of Malaysia, recent host of the Commonwealth Games and proud owner of the Petrolus Towers. I transited through a rather wonderful spacious airport with its very own rainforest experience. Mind you, a beer costs a small fortune just like airports all over the world.

Only a brief stopover before the flight to Saigon, renamed Ho Chi Minh City, but still called Saigon. Passport control was a breeze and my luggage first off the carousel. First through the exit, I was confronted by a veritable sea of faces waiting to welcome family, visitors, business people, et al. A distinguished bespectacled gentleman in a floppy khaki sun hat held up a piece of cardboard box with my name scrawled upon it.

That was how I met Mr Hoa (pronounced Hwar), a fifty something balding Vietnamese academic with a long pigtail permanently coiled up inside his hat. With a huge grin he beckoned me towards a taxi and advised in his quiet, inscrutable manner, whilst clutching my elbow and reaching up to whisper in my ear, that I perhaps find "fi' dollar" for a suitable tip for the driver.

Already I felt comfortable with my guide. We shared a century of years, but what different lives they had been which had led to today's convergence.

A Day in Saigon (HCMC)

It was mid-morning in Saigon. The official name is Ho Chi Minh City, but it doesn't matter how much that giant of Vietnamese history is revered, it remains Saigon. For me it is the middle of the night, and I have lost a night's sleep. Hoa chats as we negotiate the wide, French influenced boulevards. They appeared to be choked with clouds of beeping, buzzing motor cycles.

They fill the roads and crowd the pavements, moving in random swarms (I could see why Yangon had banned them). Cars seem few and far between, and look like beetles being carried off by ants. I was desperately tired, and thankful to finally pull up outside a city centre hotel. Narrow in frontage, deep and eight storeys high, it was typical of the modern business buildings of the city centre.

My room, on the seventh floor, and the lift is being used to take bags of concrete up to the eighth floor for repair work. Little chance of a nap then.

After a couple of hours of fitful and noisy rest I popped out to become a millionaire. Staying on the same block (I couldn't contemplate trying to cross the roads yet), I found an ATM and drew out three million Dong, about £100, and 20K to the dollar. This is a useful benchmark when haggling, surveying a menu or contemplating tipping.

Haggling is a strange thing. We generally don't do it at home, but it appears de rigeur in many places around the world. I am always amazed at how wealthy westerners insist on haggling even for paltry amounts. I met an Australian estate agent who specialised in disposing of Melbourne properties from marriage break-ups. He took great delight in arguing down the girls who would go from table to table selling trinkets and pictures. They would start at 50,000 Dong, but he would not rest until he had knocked them down to 15,000, about an Australian dollar. He would swell with pride as the peasant girl left to feed her family.

Newly wealthy I took lunch at a pavement cafe and noticed a group of about a dozen British women. They had a local male guide sporting an Explore tee shirt. Explore Worldwide is an adventure company which specialises in small groups. I had used Explore several times before, so I thought I would make conversation.

"Hi, how are you enjoying Vietnam?" I asked.

"We've just arrived from Cambodia" said one.

"Aah!" I raised my eyebrows, "Been to Angkor Wat?"

"Yes, we were there two days ago."

"Brilliant isn't it". Then I just innocently ventured, "You're an all girl group, bit unusual?"

"You have a problem with that?" came a strident contemptuous sneer from one end of the table.

Back off, back off now, I thought, and swiftly returned to my noodles.

I decided I had to get around, so needed to practise crossing the road. Not to overstate this, but the traffic was horrendous. There appeared to be no lane discipline and every single space is filled by a motor cyclist buzzing along; stop start, stop start, often mounting the kerb and weaving around pedestrians to cut off corners. This aggravates the problem as pedestrians are having to avoid parked vehicles as well as kerbside vendors. There must be some order in this apparent chaos however, as accidents and collisions seem scarce. The answer was not far away, as I stood at the kerbside waiting for a gap.

Just standing there you will never get across. You have to choose the right moment and launch into the traffic, and amazingly, just like wading into a river, the bikes magically flow around you. Keep looking left and make your way gradually to the middle, stop, then look right and trusting in the Lord, launch yourself into the throng coming the other way, and slowly but surely make your way to the other side. You do get used to it, but the first few times you turn and punch the air on safely reaching your destination; the far kerb. "Woo, hoo!"

Hoa would sometimes lead me across, and like some sort of mother hen he would hold his outstretched arms out to try to tell the traffic to calm down. They didn't take a blind bit of notice of course, but it was always fun following a flapping Hoa across the road.

I was impressed by the amount of greenery in the city. The boulevards were tree-lined, mahogany, I was assured. Hedges and shrubs were tidily topiarised, and boxes of flowering plants were evidently well-maintained. The roads and paths were clean, with few potholes or uneven flags. The only problems were the occasional eruptions where trees, especially kapoks had overgrown their ramparts with flying buttress style roots to trip up the unwary.

This is a typical socialist city where everyone has a job, however menial. There was a strange ambiguity however. The shops and streets were still festooned with Christmas decorations even though we were now past Epiphany. This teeming, steaming metropolis had Santas, reindeer and snow scenes everywhere. The reason for this apparent oversight is that the Christmas lights are kept on to celebrate the New Year, also known as the Tet celebrations, around the end of January. It is unusual though to see Christmas decorations (sponsored by Heineken) amid beautifully colourful flower beds.

I rejoined Hoa in late afternoon outside the impressive Notre Dame Cathedral. A lovely man, but I was beginning to doubt his value as a guide when he told me the impressive red brick edifice had been built by the same people who had built its counterpart in Paris. Impressive as the building was, and I knew that all of its materials had come from France, there's almost a millennium of years difference in the building of the two. 1163 and 1863, so seven hundred years actually, but Quasimodo was definitely not a contemporary.

French architecture is apparent throughout the city, but it was the street life I enjoyed most. Every inch of pavement is a market place and if they're not making and selling creations, they're cooking in woks over calor gas fires, and serving meals and drinks on children's plastic furniture. It was so vibrant and alive.

There was much new building as well. A reminder that this is a tiger economy. I believe that countries like Vietnam, making cheap but good quality products to sell to the prosperous West, can only be good for a global economy.

We walked on to the Opera House, majestically pink in the dying sunlight, which was modelled on L'Opéra Garnier of Paris. Suddenly the tiredness of reverse jetlag overwhelmed me, so following a very brief meal of traditional rice vermicelli, I made my excuses and had to return to the hotel.

I took to my bed at only 9pm, but my night najjers struck (they usually only strike at altitude) and my mind raced with the weird, wonderful and downright scary.

I woke and peered outside. Down at pavement level there was a taxi office and young men seated on their haunches playing cards and chatting and drinking Ca-Phe; small, strong coffees taken with condensed milk. I looked at the time; one in the morning. I was all over the place.

My mind drifted to Mae West, who I had read had the philosophy of answering every request with "What the Hell!" I mused that this was an excellent response to shall we climb that, or bungee jump there, or go down those rapids, or leap across this rock; but further thought that perhaps she might have been referring to other excitements.

Then I contemplated the nature of guerrilla warfare (for such is the way your mind jumps about in dreamland) and how it can never be defeated by conventional forces. Ho Chi Minh had said that he may lose ten for every enemy life he took, but he would still win. The many headed Hydra. Cut off one and nine replace it. (My mind was racing now). Today's terrorist is tomorrow's villager, elder, mother. This afternoon's ploughman is tonight's commander. Look at Nazi atrocities failing to defeat legitimate resistance. The My Lai massacre, U.S ignominious defeat; Iraq, Libya, Syria, Afghanistan. When will we ever learn? Regular army can only use up (consume!) IED's. Shock and awe to win hearts and minds just breeds distrust and betrayal. The killing fields of Cambodia. US policy sowed the seeds of Pol Pot. Stupid, wicked, evil politicians sending young people to alien places to inflame violence, invoke hell, and create death and destruction on such an industrial scale. Blood on your hands. Blood on your hands. And the laugh is we continue do it. Do they still love the smell of napalm in the morning?

I woke in a sweat. Breakfast soon, I hope.

There was a reminder at the breakfast buffet, of French colonial rule; baguettes, croissants and pains au chocolate.

Feeling refreshed, even after a troubling night, I boarded a bus with Hoa and looked forward to the 70 "clicks" drive to the Cu Chi tunnels, a war museum. On route I enjoyed a puerile little game of spot the unfortunate business name. So many of them seemed to be called some variety of Phuk Yeu or Phong Pu.

We were soon out into the countryside and I could study the agriculture of this part of South East Asia. Unusually it is not dominated by the paddy field. There were fields of wheat and corn, orchards of fruit, and vegetable plots behind the buildings which lined the main road. The side roads were populated with bikes and oxen. People; pedestrians, workers in the fields and cyclists were all wearing the iconic conical hats, the nón lá.

We turned off the main highway and took a straight road through featureless countryside until reaching the small village of Cu Chi. We disembarked the bus and I could hear the distant sound of automatic gunfire. Atmospheric, I thought.

We were in a forest, but one where all the trees were of the same height and girth, and I was reminded that because of deforestation, no trees were older than 50 years.

We were led to an open shed to view all manner of ingeniously designed and wickedly spiked booby traps, and an insight into this type of conflict. They were not designed to kill, but merely to maim and entrap, so that the cries of the unfortunate would bring help. That was when the ambush was sprung.

A uniformed youngster shows us a camouflaged tunnel entrance, and a typical guerrilla booby trap.

Next we visited the network of tunnels, such a thorn in the side of the "Washington DC aggressor". I've noted that they are rarely referred to as Americans; more often simply "the enemy". Tiny entrances were wonderfully camouflaged, as a uniformed boy suddenly appeared from out of the ground. There is thought to be over 2,500 miles of tunnels which some believed at the time to link the North to the South via Cambodia. It is now known that this was a localised 75 mile network. The Vietcong (Charley, or Gooks as sometimes referred to by Hoa) didn't come from the North, they existed in the South.

Agent orange, napalm, tanks, bulldozers, dogs, sewer rats (commandos), blanket and cluster bombing all failed to defeat this peasant army of girls and boys. They hid in these tunnels containing kitchens, hospitals, and command centres (from which the Tet Offensive was planned and launched) by day, and sometimes days on end, then emerged, weak and diseased, but strong enough to wreak havoc on the enemy.

I entered one tunnel and crawled about 50 yards until claustrophobia forced me out.

We were given a presentation (how the propaganda has reversed), shown how rice paper was made, visited a tank (left to rust where it had been immobilised), and browsed around the souvenir shop. Then I saw the counter which confirmed the sad truth. The gunfire I had previously thought to be atmospheric was real. You could actually buy live ammunition, choose a gun (at a price) then unleash it at a firing range. And there was no shortage of wannabe shooters.

I had always thought that museums like these were preserved as anti-war memorials, with the message of "Lest we forget", and here was the glorification of using deadly firearms. I was shocked and saddened.

I was happy to leave this place and return after lunch to Saigon to visit the Reunification Museum. This modern, luxuriously furnished presidential white house with its extensive lawns, was the scene of the dramatic end to the war when a North Vietnamese tank crashed through its gates on the 30th April 1975.

We had a delightful little girl guide (not the scouting type) and I had to ask a question. "When the tanks moved in and the Vietnamese flag raised, was the place ransacked?"

"No. They may have moved some stuff around". Her reply was suitably understated and splendidly delivered with a little bow to acknowledge the pigdog imperial westerner's stupid enquiry. I smiled my gratitude as I realised that, with the American presence gone all they did was rearrange the furniture.

In the bowels of the palace museum were some rooms with blown up photographs of important moments from the war and a plaque which listed the numbers of non-Vietnamese who fought in their war. One notable exception; none from the UK. Commonwealth and European countries, yes, but no Brits. The reason for this was that Harold Wilson, our Labour prime minister at the time refused to bow to US pressure to send troops. This much maligned pipe-smoking, gabardine-wearing socialist hero; how many young men's lives did he save?

It makes you think. The reason that Wilson is not revered and remembered with pride, could be that he failed to kowtow to the so-called special relationship.

Then I looked at the USA's statistics. Of 500,000 troops sent to Vietnam, they lost 10%, 50,000. A further 10 %, another 50,000 committed suicide after their return. Half of the remaining veterans, that's 200,000 men, were unable to find regular work after the war. They were stigmatised and discriminated against because of their traumatising experiences.

That evening I dined with Steve, an ex-oil industry operative from Aberdeen, and Katie, a Geordie surgical nurse who wants to emigrate to Melbourne because of the appalling treatment of nurses in the NHS in the UK. Leon, the aforementioned Aussie estate agent informs us that Victorian Nurses (those from the state, not Florence Nightingales) have recently been on strike for better conditions.

"Is the grass really greener?" I asked Katie.

"Maybe not", she agreed, "but the weather's better than Newcastle, and you can go in the sea without it freezing your butt off" she countered.

"So how many great whites have been spotted off Whitby?" I replied, and the banter continued.

We had fried chicken on a bed of leaves with rice and copious beer for a few thousand dong. That night I slept better although the ghosts of Cu Chi haunted for a while.

The Mekong Delta

Following a baguette and coffee breakfast there was a 90 minute drive south and I was on a minibus joining the tourist crowds. We stopped at a coffee house which doubles as a marble statue factory and there were thousands of them in all colours but mainly white, and ranging from jungle animals to Greek gods, from front room ornaments to huge garden sculptures. Travelling light allows you to not even consider having to make a purchasing decision; end of!

End of? That's a strange idiom to have entered the vocabulary. I think it generally means; I can't be bothered to discuss or argue any more, or more likely; I can't think of anything more to add, therefore I have lost; end of! Anyway, the shop claims it can arrange shipping. I just can't be bothered. Shopping is for girls (not got a problem with that?).

Whilst we are on the subject of clichés entering our language, don't get me started on the Get-Go. What an awful phrase to signal the beginning of a project. And the "Can I get..., as in buying a coffee. What awful use of our language.

Then there's the standard greeting in English, "How are you?". This is a genuine question about the state of someone's well being, not their behaviour. The answers therefore should vary around 'very well, well, so-so, or not so well, thank you'. Being "good", has nothing to do with it. "I'm good" should only be the answer when you ask a child how they behave at school. I've said it often before, I hate Americanisms, period.

Soon we were back on the road and heading for the town of My Tho (it's not a big one), gateway to the delta. Here we caught a tourist launch, and en route Hoa explains that the economy here is driven by fish, bamboo and coconut. With a plentiful supply of those versatile products, there is no surprise that this region has been successfully populated for many thousands of years.

The river is brown, full of rich sediment from the north, and we drifted past other craft, floating vegetation, factories and pagodas on each bank until we reached our first destination. It was a palm island full of dark green vegetation and surrounded by mangroves. There was a steamy walk to a bee farm, following irrigation channels full of crabs and mudskippers. The air was alive with the sound of insects, and the sun was hot. Dogs and chickens wandered the dusty homesteads, and there were brightly coloured butterflies everywhere. A buffalo with huge horns was tethered, dozing.

Amid this jungle setting we were seated and served tea, with honey and kumquat. I discussed cricket with an Aussie, always a useful pursuit, and the Aussie was typically robust, "Well, of course I enjoy cricket, mate, but let's face it, it's just a good excuse to sit down, drink beer, and watch tele".

Next on the tourist trail was a visit to a coconut sweet factory where we were shown the manufacturing process, and how the sweets were wrapped and boxed. Everyone was given samples and provided with yet another shopping opportunity. There were also bottles of rice wine containing various pickled creatures; scorpions, spiders, and snakes. I tried the snake wine, it tasted venomous.

Then we had to pair up to be pony-and-trapped to a village where we were given a tray of exotic fruits; dragon, mango, jackfruit and sweet grapefruit. There was a photo opportunity with a golden python around your neck, and we were regaled by a local folk group. It was all very touristy, but also very enjoyable and superbly well organised.

Finally we were taken onto a female rowed sampan and followed a number of narrow channels through the jungle to lunch. After a brilliant meal of which the highlight was a grilled elephant-eared fish, a large swallow-tailed, blue butterfly was fluttering around the table.

"What an exhibitionist," someone remarks.

"Butterflies are born exhibitionists," I replied.

"Actually they're born caterpillars" said Natalie, drily. She was an Aussie too.

I nearly choked on my beer.

Finally we were rowed back to our launch, returned lazily upstream to My Tho, and driven to Saigon from where, suitably sunburnt after a day on the delta, I have an 8pm train to Nha Trang.

Saigon to Nha Trang

There is something special about a sleeper train. There are some fantastic journeys worldwide, and this was the first of three on this trip. There is the excitement of the train's arrival, finding your berth, discovering your partners for the night, taking your meal in the dining car, being rocked to sleep by the motion of the train, and waking up somewhere completely new.

This was an eye opener. We were in a four berth cabin, which for Vietnamese railways is upper first class. Our companions were a middle aged New Zealand couple who were nonplussed by my fascination for travelling the world to see dolphins and whales. "We go to the doorstep overlooking the beach, and they're just there in the bay".

Before taking to his bunk Hoa regaled us with his tale of his one and only excursion outside Vietnam. The bureaucratic procedure was quite remarkable; having to get letters of invitation and references, being interviewed for subversive thoughts, applying for permission time and time over, applying for and being interviewed for a passport, the constant waiting for signed documents to be processed and posted. It was interminable, as was Hoa's tale.

He had been invited by University President Geoffrey Gamble, who as a lieutenant in the US Army had been Hoa's teacher and had helped him get into University and escape peasant life. Once in America Hoa was feted and treated like a celebrity and managed to travel from West to East coast and back again before returning to his family in the Central Highlands.

I decided to explore the train after this and found it to be full to overflowing with northerners travelling home, up from the south, for Tet. The conditions in the other classes were less than wholesome and the "restaurant car" was something to behold.

The seats were wooden and slatted. Some Western wag had scratched the letters VIP above one bench, so naturally I sat there and enjoyed a cold beer. People were constantly arriving to collect polystyrene containers full of slop, such as it looked. Every so often the door into the kitchen would swing open and I would catch sight of three or four people in dirty overalls slaving over smoking, steaming woks; flames were shooting everywhere. It was like a scene out of Dante's Inferno.

The walls and ceiling of the dining car were a dirty sky blue, streaked with dried condensation and caked with grease.

Returning to my luxurious berth about 20 carriages away, meant squeezing past so many families of three or four generations crammed into every space throughout every car. Mums and dads, grannies and granddads seated or sometimes squatting around their luggage, comprising either tied up cardboard boxes or battered suitcases having been passed down through many generations, kiddies impeccably behaved, all friendly and welcoming, a smile on every face. I wondered what they thought of this curious westerner.

Last in bed and first to wake, my body clock had finally adjusted. It was early, still dark, so I crept quietly out of my bunk and opened the door to the corridor. I could tell we were moving slowly. I made my way to a door on the right hand side of the train and pulled down the window. We were travelling north, so I knew I was now facing east, and behold, there was the light of dawn on the horizon, a pink sky, then light blue to darkening overhead with white and grey fluffy clouds.

The scene that greeted me was of farmland, fields with hedgerows and copses of woodland. The fields were flat and flooded, the boundaries slightly raised, occasional buildings, little shrines on hillocks between fields, pagoda style, I knew these were family tombs. In the grey, shadowy light people were already tending the paddy fields, bent double, up to their knees, sporting their conical hats. I waved and they were more than happy to momentarily straighten up, smile and wave back. I drank in the warm breeze and looked to my left; I could see the engine in the far distance and an unbroken line of carriages snaking around a lazy curve. I stood there leaning out of the window. Time seemed to stand still as we moved inexorably on.

Presently the sun shook off its night time shackles and a diamond ring of light suddenly breaks through the horizon. Workers, trees and tombs now had shadows. It climbed until it was a single silvery pink ball and its warmth is on my face, and the paddy fields are glistening and there are phalanxes of white egrets.

We rumbled on through the occasional village whose single road is a gated level crossing, and there may be a group of 30 or so pedestrians, cyclists, motor cyclists, maybe an ox drawn cart or two, waiting patiently for us to pass by.

Then we were back in the countryside and the sun is climbing higher and the train clanks on and I'm grinning from ear to ear as I realise this is one of the most magical moments of my life. I wanted to run and wake everyone up and shout "Come, come look at this." But I was selfish, I wanted to keep it all for myself. They probably wouldn't have appreciated it, anyway.

Nha Trang

Nha Trang arrives, or to be more accurate, we arrived in Nha Trang. Apparently it is one of the 29 most beautiful bays in the World. Who compiles these lists?

We walked from the station to the Viet Dong hotel where we took a large, late buffet breakfast then set off to explore. Left out of the gate leads to the beach and the South China Sea which is dotted with green islands, one of which, Hon Tre, has a huge cable car linking it to the mainland.

I turned inland and visited the Cathedral and for balance the Long Son, or White Buddha Pagoda. There are both a reclining and a seated Buddha as you climb the hill to the top which had excellent views to the hills that overlooked the city itself, and to the sea beyond.

There was much new construction going on, and I was told it was Russian money that is helping to develop this into a world renowned holiday destination. I was keen to snorkel, and this is apparently one of the best locations in Vietnam for coral reefs, so I booked a boat trip for the next day.

That evening I dined on red snapper in one of those restaurants where you can pick your own fish, and I picked a beauty. As I walked back to the beach for a nightcap I passed a floodlit orchestra and choir which were playing and singing for the assembled crowds. All of school age, they provided wonderful free entertainment.

I chose a bar right on the beach and settled down to stare out to sea, a universal favourite pastime, and struck up a conversation with a Canadian family of six. You can tell there is a change in the weather on the cards as the wind has got up, and the breakers were crashing onto the beach. Dad was Dan, a palaeontologist and we were soon talking about dinosaurs and their fossils.

I gave my usual observation on the subject, "It never fails to amaze me" I said earnestly, "that whenever I hear the noise of waves crashing onto a beach, that this is the same sound that the dinosaurs would have heard over 65 million years ago".

"Well, not the desert dinosaurs," Dan appeared to reply seriously, "only the ones in the beach bar; the Pissheadosaurus. Fossils of which have yet to be found."

The next day was my snorkelling trip and I presented myself at the harbour complete with kit. The boat was a typical tourist skiff with toilets and galley below, and lots of plastic chairs on deck with the captain's little wheelhouse to the stern. I was delighted to find that amongst my fellow passengers was Dan's family. Sadly though, it was gloomy and overcast, and there was a mean swell.

Casting off we chugged under the cable car. It was impressive, but my tight itinerary precluded it. The first stop was less than a mile down the coast. I could have walked there, the Trí Nguyên Aquarium. About 30 of us trooped off the boat and indoors into the shell shaped buildings. These housed several huge tanks including many rare species from the South China Seas. And they're all giants with huge bulging eyes. I enjoyed seeing the white tipped and black tipped reef sharks, a leopard shark, the moray eels, and green hornbill turtles.

We followed the exhibition finally through to the obligatory souvenir shop, and outside where there was a huge square tank containing turtles with huge limpet fish taking a free ride on their shells. There was a fair amount of floating litter, and I saw a turtle surface and chomp on a blue plastic bag. I had heard that turtles mistake plastic carriers for jelly fish, and eating them can kill them. But as I watched, there were plenty of curators, none of whom seemed bothered.

We left the aquarium and headed out to sea, and after an hour or so moored at a floating quay attached to one of the myriad islands. As usual I was first into mask, snorkel and fins, and jumped off the back of the boat. The water was warm, but the coral scarce, and the fish just the usual butterflies, wrasse, parrots, sergeants; and not in abundance.

The swell, though not fierce, was menacing enough to threaten to lift and deposit me on various jagged outcrops. That, and the overcast conditions lead to an overall disappointing encounter. But never mind, our next location could be better.

Back on the boat, lunch was being prepared. I was chatting to the other folk on board and could see other boats heading for the outer islands. Another boat joined onto ours, and it was raucous indeed. The youngsters on it had obviously been drinking, and a party was in full swing. There was much singing and shouting of "Hoi!" urged on by the captain over the loud speaker. They all seemed to be having a really good time, but I could only harumph snootily as befits my grumpy old man status. After all, this was a serious diving boat and we were on safari.

We thankfully disengaged and lunch was taken as we weighed anchor and headed back out to sea. Rice, noodles, fried fish with chicken, vegetables, spring rolls, soy sauce; excellent fare. I was really enjoying bobbing about on the ocean, looking wistfully out to distant, wooded, green, hilly islands, when a band strikes up. I was jerked away from my reverie and looked over my shoulder to realise we had joined up with the party boat again in mid-ocean. There was an electric guitar, makeshift drums and tambourines.

The Vietnamese crew were playing, and they tried to get the Aussies up and singing with Men At Work "I come from a land down under...", and it worked. Next they worked on the Brits with Oasis's Wonderwall, which (thankfully) was a little less successful. This was followed by Echo Beach from Martha and the Muffins, for the Canadians, and Dan and his family beamed in smiles as they belted out the lyrics, and the party was in full swing. Two Kiwis were encouraged to do their Haka war dance, and made a superb effort (Kambate, Kambate, etc). One of the crew appeared as a ladyboy, gyrating to much laughter with his grass skirt and coconut breasts. He was getting everyone up to dance (not this GOM). A German couple momentarily lowered the tone by trying the Birdy song, but all credit to the band which rescued the situation with 99 Red Balloons.

Cocktails were announced for all those who entered the water, and there, overboard was yet another crew member tethered to the boats on a long line, sitting in a floating yellow skirt, with a drum of Fanta and whisky with which he is constantly replenishing fellow floaters' plastic cups.

I began to realise I'd probably chosen the wrong boat for a snorkelling excursion around the islands, but this was good fun, and probably worth the $10 it had cost.

We had one more stop at a relaxing beach before returning to harbour, but there was a final act to be played out. Dan the Canadian and Derek, a Zambian farmer had been voted beer monsters and had to have a penalty shoot-out by racing more beer down their necks to the strains of "Get 'em down, you Zulu Warrior".

With darkness falling I met up again with Hoa in the Pissheadosaurus bar and we had a relaxing meal as the great breakers fell onto the beach. We had a 10pm train for Danang so made our way to the station and took our places on the wooden platform parallel to the tracks. This was a relatively primitive railway station with no modern facilities, but the platform was lined with market stalls selling soft drinks, snacky foods, and each with a gas heated wok to cook rice, or noodles, or soup to be taken away in polystyrene containers for the journey. Women of various ages ran each stall and were seated in animated conversation with both neighbours and customers.

With no platform we climbed up into the train which was again full of Northerners returning home for Tet, and Hoa leads the way to a six berth compartment (only ordinary first class this time).

There were two Aussie couples already in their bunks and they assumed Hoa was in the wrong class. "Are you in right place?" they enquired loudly, "This first class. Vietnamese must go other carriage."

I squirmed with embarrassment but Hoa smiled politely, bowed slightly, and explained patiently in English better than their's that indeed he was in the right place as he was my guide. The Aussies were shamed into silence so Hoa took the opportunity, as he was readying himself for bed, to relate to them how, as a 12 year old living in a village in the hills above Danang he was captured by Charlie. He escaped but spent three years hiding out with relatives, gradually making his way south.

He told how he had to hide in huts by day, then in the woods at night. That was when the Vietcong would terrorize villagers, and he had seen people tortured and then beheaded in front of their families for suspected collaboration with the enemy.

After the war, because he had been an escapee, he spent many years as a non-person before finally winning a place at university to become a teacher.

His final act in preparation for bed was to remove his battered hat, and as his pony tail fell to the bottom of his back he took to his bunk and wished everyone a peaceful goodnight.

Hoi An

Again I awoke before dawn and headed for the door window to observe the sunrise over this beautiful land. There was only me and the driver awake. We stopped in sidings for a while. Opposite in the open doorway of a wagon, four wizened old railway workers crouched and smoked, grinning at us with stained or missing teeth.

Moving off slowly with the creaking and clanking of over 50 carriages we were again out into the flat countryside. A water buffalo lazily pulls a plough, a woman straightens up, removes her conical hat and wipes her brow, she looks up and we exchanged waves, and gradually the world awakes. Overhead the clouds were black and foreboding, but in the distance the sun fills the void between horizon and cloud, making for an eerie, unearthly light. The sun flashes off the plumage of various birds, the most numerous of which were egrets.

These small herons are among my favourite birds. They have beautiful smooth, milk-white plumage, and long orange beaks, and stand erect. They are slim, sleek and graceful, taking off, flying and landing elegantly, walking slowly and haughtily. They can be found throughout the tropics and are often visible from the roadside.

Egrets do have one little flaw, however. They don't feed like most herons, although I have seen them wading into shallows, and waiting, quite still for a fish to appear before striking swiftly and accurately for a deserved meal. No, their preferred method is to hang around the backsides of cattle, waiting for the droppings, then feeding on the insects that the dung attracts. Other than that though, surely they are the Kate Moss, or Naomi Campbell of the bird world.

It is always a long morning when you are awake at dawn, and we eventually pulled into Danang station at what seems like lunchtime, but it was only 10am. Here was the American stronghold during their war and we drove past China Beach, which saw the first combat troops land in 1965, and some old disused aircraft hangers. Hoa informs me we are less than 90 "clicks" from My Lai, the village where over 500 innocent women, children and old men were slaughtered in one morning of carnage only two generations ago. More on this later.

Our destination was Hoi An, a UNESCO World Heritage site, a few miles down the coast on the river Thu Bon. This silted up in the 16th century leading to the creation of the new port of Danang, thus preserving the old trading port of Hoi An.

Outside the Lotus Hotel there was a new road being laid so we parked in an adjacent street and walked to reception. "Don't you just love the smell of tarmac in the morning!" some old wag remarked. Well that's that old nutmeg done to death I thought, as we checked in.

Usually I am keen to explore a new town straight away, but I needed some sleep and left it until the afternoon. At the end of the street I crossed the wooden, covered Japanese bridge and was instantly transported to middle ages Asia. To my right was the river with decorated sampans, and on my left a hotch-potch of higgledy piggledy buildings, mainly stuccoed in yellow with sweeping angled rooftops, adorned by red and blue ribbon. There were pagoda temples which I wandered around with lion statues, bonsai trees, and the most ornate decorative walls. Altars were burning incense. At the end of this ancient passage a market was selling wonderful varieties of fish and vegetables.

After the modern cities and train borne vistas, this mediaeval riverside promenade was too much. I had to sit down at a bar and drink beer, which at nearly 12 pence a glass, was wonderfully refreshing. So refreshing in fact I also ordered a curry. "You want hot?" asked the chef peering from behind a curtain. Foolishly I smiled and nodded. After all, I had the cold beer as an accompaniment. So I sat and ate and sweated and hiccuped, and watched the world drift by.

The My Lai Massacre in 1968 had been covered up for nearly six months before the extent of the carnage came to light. The innocents of four hamlets had been machine gunned and blown up by grenades as a platoon of young soldiers went berserk with bloodlust. There followed an investigation, an enquiry and finally a show trial in Washington. The only soldier ever to be charged was Lieutenant William Calley, the platoon leader who had been give the enigmatic instruction that day to "engage the enemy". He was found guilty and sentenced accordingly, but because of the weight of American public protest only served one day in prison. He settled down and became a chemist and eventually sank into obscurity. Ultimately the murders committed that day and subsequent events were judged by the Vietnamese. "In war, these things happen," was their magnanimous attitude.

I dined at the "World Famous" Cargoes restaurant and met up with three ladies who were keen to see the ruins at My Son, so we booked a car and driver from a local travel agent and arranged to meet up the next afternoon.

In the morning, drizzle. The overcast conditions of the previous two days had finally decided to precipitate. I walked for two hours and got hopelessly lost in the new town but eventually found my way back to the hotel to re-orientate myself. I set out again and crossed the river and strolled around a small settlement of mud houses. I swear I heard a little delighted squeal of "Tourist!" and two children raced from their garden to accost me.

With the most wonderful smiles they insisted I buy a little wooden dragonfly which the little girl balanced expertly on her fingertip. I took their photo, and as always they were overjoyed to see their picture.

Later I could only contrast their beautiful, happy demeanour with the image of Kim Phuc, her clothes and skin burned away by napalm. The terror, distress and pain are etched into her face as she and other children flee their burning village.

Kim was not expected to survive but after many operations and a lifetime being known as "The girl in the picture" she married and is the mother of two children, now living as a Canadian citizen and UN Ambassador.

I said goodbye to my happy children, and a little later came back to the waterside where an old lady offered to row me across for 500 dong. She donned her conical hat, for photographic purposes, and deposited her daughter and granddaughter on the opposite dockside before rowing me around for a while whilst I sat and dreamily wiled away this magical moment.

Shirley, Judith and Helen were waiting for me back at the hotel, and we journeyed to My Son (Me Shown). The drive was slow and bumpy on single track roads, but endlessly fascinating as my companions and I were thrown about in the back of the car. Several embarrassing clothing malfunctions, a few accidental gropings, one or two unfortunate fondlings, and a great deal of laughter later, we find ourselves transported through thick jungle into the mountains.

The drizzle continued as we wandered the complex of around 70 ruined red-stone Hindu temples ranging from the 4th to the 14th century and built by the Champa kings, very reminiscent of the Angkhor Wat array, but on a much smaller scale.

Much of this area had been carpet bombed, so the temples have been patched back together as restored ruins, with French university teams carrying on the work. They are strangely named, I suppose for ease of identification, like a battleships grid. So A1 to A10, for example, are of a particular age and level of restoration, as are B1 to B14, C5 to C8, and so on. Wherever you turned there was something of interest, a museum with dated artefacts here, a Sanskrit stele there. There were phallic symbols indicating possible harem buildings between areas C and D, and B52 bomb craters all around.

The whole complex was dominated by two mountain ranges flanking to South and North. Was I the only person to have seen the profile of a face in the mountainside which could have led to this being designated a holy area over 1700 years ago?

On the return journey I sat in the front with the driver to avoid being groped again and that evening I introduced my companions to the hot curries and cheap beer of the Riverside Bar.

After two nights in Hoi An it was time to move on to Hue (pronounced Hwey, not Hugh as Shirley had called it), the ancient capital.

Hue

Hoa had organised transport and a car came to pick us up after breakfast. We drove first up to the Marble Mountain and the caves of Huyen Khong with impressive Bhudda statues. The mountain overlooks China Beach where the G.I.s would indulge in their R 'n' R (rest and recreation). It was a Vietcong hideout, proving again their countrywide infiltration. Ultimately it had been bombed.

Next we drove on to the Haiven (Sea Cloud) pass, which, in between the clouds gave great views either side. I climbed to the topmost point where far below I could watch a long train snake in and out of the mountains, and negotiate a tunnel, there was a trail of steam coming from the locomotive, very 1950's. Beyond the railway lay the serenely blue South China Sea.

Arriving in Hue we immediately headed through the rain to the

Perfume river and boarded a tourist style Dragon boat for the trip upstream to the Citadel. The giant flag of Vietnam, red with a yellow star flew over the entrance. Behind the foreboding grey walls is housed the sadly damaged Forbidden Purple City. There is a huge area of open parkland and a moat outside. Inside it is full of gardens, ponds, bridges, ornate walk ways, statues, steles and pagoda style buildings which were all either mausoleums, royal residences, stables, kitchens, servants quarters and the like. It is a virtual copy of the Forbidden City in Beijing, and was designed by the Vietnamese royal dynasties very much to rival their Chinese counterparts. Much of it is now converted into museums or exhibitions. But most notable is the war damage when the enemy tried to defend their positions against the Tet Offensive of 1968. There had been a lot of close quarter fighting here.

There wasn't much fun to be had this day, what with the persistent rain and grey clouds darkening what is undoubtedly, a very colourful scene. I spent hours viewing the impressive features of the Forbidden City. It took me hours because every time I wanted to walk between the buildings I risked going arse over tit on the treacherously slippery flagstones. Thus I found myself playing hopscotch between pathways with some purchase, or hauling myself along by gripping to the sides of buildings. This caused even more discomfort with the overloaded gutters constantly depositing great cold wet drips down the back of my neck. Deep joy.

Eventually I left the Forbidden City and made my way back to the town centre by walking across the bridge spanning the Perfume River. Such was the extent of the rain, the hordes of motor cyclists had donned huge transparent plastic capes, looking like over sized bubble wrap.

The next day I visited the tombs of the Nguyen dynasty. My driver was a well spoken, polite and knowledgeable young man called Luc. He told me he was an ex-teacher which I found sad. There has to be something wrong with a society where you can make a better living driving tourists around than educating children.

First on the itinerary was the tomb of Tu Duc. Even through the persistent rain you could sense the beautiful tranquillity of the place with its lake, gardens and pavilions. It was so opulent that its expensive construction caused an abortive coup. The emperor preferred to live here rather than in his palace in Hue and he can be imagined, according to Luc, writing poetry and composing music surrounded by his concubines.

Actually it didn't turn out to be his tomb, neither was his harem much use. This sad individual had to be buried ultimately in a secret location because of the uproar his tomb building had created. It was so secret the 200 labourers who created his real tomb were subsequently beheaded.

This was in 1883, for goodness sake, hardly the dark ages. And as for the concubines, his smallpox had made him impotent. He wrote his own tragic and modest obituary which appears here inscribed on a huge stele. His adopted son outlived him by only seven months and was actually buried here.

Luc then drove me to the tomb of Khai Dinh who died in 1925 aged 47 after nine years on the throne. This tomb, completed in 1931, could almost be described as a modern day memorial. It is the last of the grand imperial tombs and commands wonderful views of the surrounding hillsides. There are so many concrete statues of horses, riders and armed warriors, some say it may rival Xian's terracotta army. I think not, and anyway, being concrete, everything is grey.

It is wonderful however to see an undesecrated tomb. Throughout the world there are tombs to monarchs which over the years have become war and time ravaged. They have suffered grave robbers or been sacked by subsequent rulers or just vandalised. Here was a group of buildings and their contents exactly the way they were designed to be admired.

There were rooms full of gold, polished wood, coloured marble, ornate furniture and beautiful decor; every square inch oozed the careful hand and eye of the master sculptor, artist and craftsman.

Finally we drove to the Thien Mu Temple whose centrepiece is a wonderful Pagoda which stands over 70 feet tall, and overlooks the Perfume River. It is a working temple, and there were Buddhist monks chanting at altars, taking communal meals, and ringing a 300 year old two ton bell.

One of the most visited and photographed exhibits is that of the blue sedan driven by Thich Quang Duc, a renowned Buddhist Monk, into Saigon on the morning of 11th June, 1963. He calmly parked in a busy street, got out of the car, and in protest at the treatment of monks by the Roman Catholic South Vietnamese government, he poured petrol over himself and set himself alight. News of his protest and death and photographs of his self-immolation reverberated across the globe and ultimately led to the downfall and assassination of President Diem in November of that year. The same month President Kennedy was assassinated. Troubled times.

After a lunch of beef and pineapple curry it was time to leave Hue, and Luc drove Hua and myself to the railway station where I played the Oreo game.

The Oreo Game

The station had a fairly modern concourse as befits the nation's third city. It was certainly different to the plank of wood affixed next to the track at Nha Trang. But we were to be delayed for about an hour, so I went to the station kiosk and bought a packet of Oreo biscuits. Opening them I sought out a suitable opponent.

There was a different atmosphere here than at other stations. Most of the waiting passengers were families of peasants, with belongings in cardboard boxes tied with string, or packages wrapped in brown paper (I saw a whole motorbike wrapped entirely in brown paper, a work of art). There was a smattering of tourists who were white, round-eyed, taller and very differently dressed and also, with the exception of me, quite youthful. I am used to being gawped at, I am after all, very foreign. It is easy to smile and wave, which of course is the ideal ice breaker.

I chose a ten year old boy who was with parents and siblings seated around on their boxes. I sat down alongside him and took out a biscuit. I held one side by its edge with three finger tips and a thumb, then lightly took the other side with my other three finger tips and thumb. I then indicated to the boy with a mime that the hands are to twist in opposite direction to split the biscuit. The objective is to retain the half of the biscuit which has the delicious cream still attached, and then eat it in one.

I offered it to him and the boy nervously took his half of the biscuit with his small brown hand. I took my half, gritted my teeth and feigned to concentrate very hard on the task. I twisted to the left, the biscuit came apart, we each looked at our remainder. Oh No. I had lost. I threw my arms up in the air in mock disappointment and grinned at the winner. He also grinned, but hesitated. I didn't. I popped my dry half, and he popped in his with the delicious vanilla filling, and we both crunched happily. We played again. Same result.

This had attracted one or two bemused spectators. I took out another biscuit and held it aloft as a challenge. The boy's sister immediately threw up her hand and I beckoned her over. She sat down and I offered her the one side of the biscuit. She didn't need any encouragement or guidance. She had learned from her brother, and battle was commenced.

She held her side of the biscuit, we paused, and both twisted. Me to the left, her to her left, and, Oh No. I had lost again. She raised her arms in victory, grinned and looked around to her parents for acknowledgement. They both nodded and smiled and applauded politely. She looked back at me, I shrugged my shoulders dejectedly, she smiled coyly and we both popped in our biscuits. Me my dry half, she her deliciously covered creamy circle. We played again. Same result.

There was a small crowd of children now watching, and when I pulled out a fifth biscuit there was no shortage of challengers.

Ten minutes later I had an empty box of biscuits and I was surrounded by a group of cheerfully grinning Vietnamese children and their parents. Fortunately it has to be said I am very unlucky at the Oreo game; very unlucky indeed.

Then the train arrived. Time to move on.

Ha Long Bay

We were back in upper first class, and I had a lower bunk in a four berth compartment. Someone pulled out a bottle of whisky (Produce of France), and although it was only mid-afternoon, I agreed to share it. I was in bed for eight and rose before five to leave the train pre-dawn. We were now in Hanoi, well over 1,000 miles from Saigon, and an ancient city. But I saw nothing of it as we were whisked away towards Ha Long Bay and 30 hours on a junk.

My imagination had it not already have been stretched by previous events, could now be racing. But I have learnt to accept approaching experiences to be unpredictable. I just sat back and went with the flow.

We flowed onto an eight lane highway speeding to the coast. Except it wasn't a motorway with hard shoulders and central reservations, it was just a crowded two lane road. On the inside, dusty, non-tarmac lane was pedestrian, handcart and ox drawn traffic, next were bicycles, mopeds and motorbikes, then there were the motorised vehicles, slow vans and trucks, faster buses and cars. Finally there was a fourth lane made up entirely of every vehicle which sought to overtake its slower counterparts. The hair raising factor is that this was always done in the face of the oncoming traffic who were all trying to do precisely the same thing. And this fourth lane was shared with that same oncoming traffic.

It was a recipe for chaos which frequently led to lurching lane changing, Doppler effect horn blowing (a continuous hoooonk, rising to a crescendo as vehicles passed, receding into the distance) and a feeling of incredulity that people have to travel like this. Bring back the trains. The best way to keep your sanity as a passenger is to take your eyes off the surroundings altogether and either immerse yourself in a book (difficult when you are being thrown about) or simply pray for safe deliverance.

Four hours later and we turned out of the maddening chaos into Ha Long Bay and were suddenly catapulted into a world of opulent calm, peace and serenity. The huge, marbled and air conditioned expanse of the terminal building was as nothing to the dock to which it led. This was a perfectly rectangular harbour, flanked on each of its longer sides by four storeys of modern white condominiums. The marina itself was crammed with huge modern yachts, all named Paradise Luxury or some other crass westernised meaningless pap.

My boat was a 16 berth black lacquered piece of luxury, my own cabin a miniaturised 5 star hotel room, and the viewing decks filled with comfortable outdoor furniture of the highest standard. The only drawback as we set sail (Ha, it was of course silently motorised) was the weather. It was warm and dry, but with low white cloud. The sea was a green, milky millpond but visibility wasn't great. As soon as we cleared the harbour, the karsts heaved into view.

Karsts are the wonders of Ha Long Bay; forested outcrops of limestone rising dramatically out of the sea, topped by tropical jungle flora. Around their cut-in bases, weirdly jagged shapes sculpted by the saltwater look like reduced waists. Then each one, or pair or group are named for their unique shapes, like the Fighting Cocks (Ga Choi), or Elephant (Voi). There are nearly 2,000 karsts, some inhabited, over half of them named. There are four floating villages sustained by fishing, several internal lakes, and, almost as spectacular as the towering peaks are the limestone caverns.

It has taken half a billion years to create them and the bay is a UNESCO World Heritage Site. Legend speaks of them being dragon's teeth, spat out like jewels to create a barrier against invading enemies. My immediate thought was; if Slartibartfast (Hitchhiker's Guide to the Galaxy) built Norway, who designed these?

The junk glided through this most surreal seascape to experience a number of little adventures. We moored on Monkey Island and I climbed to the top for spectacular 360 views. Back at sea level there was a beach from which I swam. Lunch was taken on the junk, langoustines, crab, a fishy fish, and a bland chicken curry. For Vietnamese standards, tame and disappointing. There was a stop at the Cave of Great Surprise (Hang Sungsot) where to no-one's surprise we followed a well worn tourist trail through beautifully water-constructed formations. Finally, before night fell the junk's tender took us to Ti Top Island for another scramble up to a glorious peak.

Ti Top was renamed to honour a Russian WW2 hero. Remember, this was North Vietnam and to name an island after a Soviet was their way of thumbing their noses at the Americans. Although at the time of his heroics of course, they were all on the same side.

We overnight softly bobbing around on the South China Sea, and Hua and I shared a lingering evening on top deck in bamboo armchairs chatting easily into the night; so peaceful. Sadly there was no moon nor even any stars, just a black night.

I woke early, and the misty coolness was still with us. Amazing to think that only a week earlier I had been sweltering on the tropical Mekong Delta. Following breakfast two villagers rowed up to us to try to make a few Dong selling souvenirs. No-one's told them we are not allowed to take shells out of their country, neither bring shells into the UK. "She sells sea shells on the..." I began to tell Hoa. Then stopped myself. It was a flat bottomed boat.

Bidding our visitors goodbye we weighed anchor and sailed effortlessly between the limestone monoliths until we reached another cave. One with a difference this time as it led by tender into the very heart of an island, almost like a lagoon or sinkhole, the clearance at low tide being only about six feet. We emerged into a lagoon surrounded on all sides by high jungle. It was a beautiful diversion in what is officially one of the new seven wonders of the natural world.

We returned sedately and serenely to the marina for lunch, disembarked, then embarked on the frenetic journey back into Hanoi. I was flung from my seat on at least four occasions. I won't miss

Vietnam's eight lane highways and its crazy drivers.

Hanoi

Hanoi, Vietnam's second largest city (over 6.5 million people), and its capital now and for most of its recent history. The bedlam on the streets is the most chaotic yet. Imagine the streets of Saigon and its wide boulevards choked with motorcyclists. Now transform that to Hanoi where the streets are narrow and buildings right on top of you, and the population swollen due to the Tet celebrations. My hotel was a nondescript modern building, just north of the old quarter and Hanoi's most famous natural landmark, and its cultural centre, Hoan Kiem Lake.

The Japanese occupied Hanoi when they invaded Vietnam in 1940. However fate dictated they didn't ravage and enslave the people as they had throughout the South Pacific in World War Two. This was French Indochina, therefore under the control of the Vichy French Government. The Vichy French were a puppet of Nazi Germany, which was an ally of the Japanese, hence they were honour bound to take a more tolerant attitude. Vietnam's natural resources were plundered however, so with Japan's defeat and ultimate withdrawal in 1945 the resulting famine killed over two million people. Ho Chi Minh was the phoenix that grew out of these particular ashes, and Hanoi was very much his city.

He had developed his Viet Minh guerrilla fighters during the Japanese occupation, and when the French tried to re-establish themselves after the war, he defeated them. In 1954 Vietnam was partitioned into his communist north and a corrupt but democratic south. The Viet Minh evolved into the Viet Cong and fought the American War to establish reunification in 1975, six years after his death at the age of 79.

There were many legacies of reunification. One was the "Boat People" phenomenon. These were Southern Vietnamese who had collaborated with the Americans and therefore feared for their safety. They set themselves adrift on the South China Sea usually in overcrowded unseaworthy vessels, hoping to be picked up by Australian coastguards and taken in as refugees and asylum seekers. Many trips ended in disaster.

Nearly half a century on and there are still boat people from poorer areas of Asia trying to make it to Australia, but now mostly economic refugees. Vietnam is now a relatively wealthy, Tiger economy, and is keen to welcome back their diaspora. There are Vietnamese communities all over the world, one of the biggest populations being in Switzerland.

One legacy the Vietnamese decided to push aside were the "Amouricans". These were the products of liaisons between American servicemen and Vietnamese girls. Unwanted by the Vietnamese, these "Children of the Enemy" have been adopted mainly in the States by grateful families. An embarrassment numbering around 100,000, Hua informed me that over 99% had been thus allocated.

I had but two evenings in Hanoi, and at dusk on the first Hua took me to the City View Cafe. This is on a street corner, north east of Hoan Kiem lake, and on the fourth floor there is an open air restaurant overlooking the lake, and we could clearly see the red painted Huc bridge (it means morning sunlight) which leads onto Jade island and the Turtle Pagoda. We drank sweet strong ca-phe as the lights began to twinkle around the lake. Even at this early stage, I could see the lake was an oasis of calm in this traffic-choked metropolis.

We dined on caramelised beef in lemon grass with noodles and plenty of Ha Noi beer. I was just about fed up with noodles now. Excuse the pun.

My plan for the morning, armed with the hotel's street map was to walk via the lake to the Botanical Gardens and Ho Chi Minh's Mausoleum. At the end of the street was the Chateau de L'Eau, 18th century water tower, and this was to be my landmark. Left at the water tower takes you to the lake.

I set off, a spring in my step, and wandered the streets marvelling at their other-worldliness, in the general direction of the gardens. I pride myself on my sense of direction, although others say I get lost too often. I feel I am able to orientate myself in the most confusing of city centres. However, today things seemed to go awry because after nearly an hour I found myself back at the water tower.

I struck out again. From the water tower, under the railway, follow the arches then left, right, turn left at the lights to the end of the street, turn right, and...back at the water tower. Try again; through the indoor market, and around the back streets to the lake, over the railway and...water tower.

Eventually in a quieter, more wealthy quarter of the city I found the Botanical Gardens, but every entrance was blocked and guarded by the military in their oversized, flat peaked hats. There are times abroad when you know the camera needs to remain firmly in the pocket, and this was one of them. Be that as it may, I was still able to exchange some nervous smiles with the young soldiers.

The Mausoleum was also closed. But I found the One Leg Pagoda, as my translation roughly described it. Apparently the One Pillar Pagoda is the second most iconic in the country. Impressive as it was it didn't make up for the disappointment of not seeing Ho Chi Minh.

Whilst searching out lunch I passed through a street market displaying wares much different than at home. Cuts of whatever meat in tin bowls in the open air, flies, dust and all; frogs splayed out in grills roasting alongside vertical gas jets; huge fish and bigger eels slopping about in washing up bowls, then being trimmed and gutted whilst still alive. Finally the photo opportunity I was going to show to all my pet loving friends at home; deep fried dog (not that I approve, I definitely do not, but this is their world, not mine).

I ate cheese rolls at a new franchise to me, Papa Roti. I couldn't take to the dog, nor the overpriced Pizza Huts and KFC's which were Hua's favourite and which always seemed full of office workers.

After lunch I visited another oasis of calm; a walled enclosure containing beautifully laid out gardens, ancient trees and at its centre the low slung Temple of Literature, dedicated to a golden Confucius. I learned that Confucianism is a religion second only to Buddhism, and there are all sorts of other ism's. Hoa is an adherent to Ancestor Veneration, as are most Vietnamese, worshipping their forebears alongside Tam Giao, the triple religion of Buddhism, Confucianism and Taoism. And why not, it sounds like hedging your bets in a most meditatively relaxing, reverent and peaceful way.

That evening I was back overlooking Sword Lake from the wonderful City View Cafe vantage point. The lights were beginning to twinkle again when suddenly music flooded the whole scene. A female voice hauntingly serenaded the lake and all its surroundings, so melodious I was lost in its echoes. I drained my exquisitely strong ca-phe with sweet milk. Even the drizzle couldn't spoil the magic of the moment.

Then, for the final time I plunged into the crazy streets of the Old Quarter and bade farewell to Hoa over a dinner of yet more noodles. He was heading back to his family near Hue to concentrate on educating his young daughter, only four. I had 24 hours of flights before reaching London, then six more hours of train travel to home.

After breakfast, the transfer took me over the wide expanse of the Red River to the airport. Suddenly the mist and drizzle lifted, and there was sunshine for the first time since Nha Trang. I was sad to be leaving Vietnam and its friendly people. Hopefully I might catch a re-run of the Top Gear programme which has so promoted this place as a tourist destination. I had a six hour stopover in Kuala Lumpur before my connection to Heathrow. In the rainforest experience in the centre of the airport I met a young American family who asked where I had been. When I told them the wife furrowed her brow, "Hasn't there been some trouble there?" she enquired innocently.

"Yes," I sighed, "but that was a long time ago, and it's all history now"

Namaste Nepal

"Namaste" is the greeting every Nepali gives you, with a slight bow and hands together as we did in primary school for prayer. When the tiniest children greet you on the road in this way, often accompanied by a little giggle, it warms the heart.

There is always a smile.

The Nepalese also gave (and still give) us Ghurkas, the greatest fighting man of modern times. "No better man could you wish to have at your side". Mr Tyler, my year six teacher told me in 1959. Mr Tyler was a veteran of the Burma campaign of World War Two which ultimately halted the Japanese march across South East Asia. He should know.

Also I dimly recalled the mystical poem, a music hall favourite, about the one-eyed yellow idol to the north of Kathmandu, the quest of Mad Carew, and his untimely demise.

My particular motivation for this adventure was to trek the Himalayan mountains, and I had flown to Kathmandu with such intentions.

I travelled under a cloud. My father-in-law was ill, step-daughter heavily pregnant, and Kaz was not best pleased. She was furious. I tried to explain that Ranulph Fiennes doesn't cancel an expedition to the Antarctic because he has to take the kids to school. Families of adventurers have to accept their gallivanting.

Nepal is a landlocked rectangular country, bordered on three sides, west, south and east, by India, which therefore controls all its trade routes. To the north it borders Chinese Tibet which hasn't affected Nepal because there are the natural protective barriers, the Himalayan mountain ranges. China is beginning to have an influence however, as they are financing much of the Nepalese improving infrastructure. Never having been a member of the British Empire, the UK however, and the English language are major foreign influences.

Getting There

The first step, with misgivings, was a taxi to Rugeley Trent Valley, where children were trainspotting, or to be more precise, trainwaving. There are high speed Pendalinos which zoom through here at 125mph, and as the children wave, the drivers blow their horns, then the monsters rush through with a great noise and wind, and it's very exciting.

The journey to Euston was pleasant enough, but from there to Heathrow was a nightmare. It was a Friday evening, and I was caught in the horrendous London rush hour (hour?). I have only ever previously experienced such a crush of people at football matches in the days when we stood in stands. To be so close yet not communicating just feels unreal. What talking there was was in languages I couldn't understand. The most prevalent I thought was Russian, but what did I know.

The flight was via Delhi, and I was impressed with their new terminals built for the Commonwealth Games. There was a wonderful spiritual shop where you sat with your feet dangling in a meditation pool surrounded by smoking joss sticks and life mantras, while a sitar played.

Ninety minutes from Delhi and we descended into Kathmandu, over a lush valley surrounded by steep-sided wooded hills.

I was without luggage. The problem with misplaced luggage is that you don't know it is lost until you have stood stupidly by that awful carousel with forlorn hope, until you are absolutely convinced there are no more cases to be loaded onto it. This done, and along with three fellow disappointed passengers, I had to report to the luggage missing desk.

"The next flight from Delhi is landing soon; it will probably be on that". More misplaced optimism, I'm afraid, and once again the four of us had to approach the lost luggage desk We gave our personal and hotel details, then exitted with hand luggage only. To be fair this is only the second time I have been separated from my luggage in over 300 international flights, and the first outbound.

Some 20 hours after leaving home, I took a taxi from the airport to my hotel, and my first impressions were not good. The roads were crowded, we crossed rivers choked with garbage, myriads of people were at the roadside, sitting, trading, chatting, hawking, gesticulating, begging. It was like India, but noisier, busier, dirtier and a little more chaotic. Hardly my imagined Shangri La; peaceful, mystical, nirvana.

The driver told me being a Saturday it was much quieter than normal. He also informed me that this being the end of the wet season, we were also lucky, he shook his head, the Nepali nod. In the dry season, he explained, the noxious stench from those rivers made them unapproachable from 50 yards either side.

Many people wore masks.

There were also motorbikes. Everyone drives a 125cc with customised horns. The cacophony took a while to get used to.

My hotel was the three star Marshyangdi, in the Thamel district, which is the beating heart of K (being in Kathmandu you are allowed to call it K), with its narrow streets, and endless shops and bars. There was a delightful young doorman in a military style uniform. Each time I entered or left the hotel we exchanged stiff, ramrod straight military salutes, and huge smiles.

Kathmandu

In the lounge I met up with my guide, Dinesh (Dino) who will be celebrating his 24th birthday in the second week. He was genuinely warm, enthusiastic and knowledgeable. He had previously been a porter, assistant tour leader, and manager of the "Famous Farm", of which more later. We were joined by Dave, a tall 30 year old Aussie; and Andrea, also 24 from German-speaking Switzerland. During our first briefing the guy from Yeti Airways turned up for me to pay for my Everest flight. "You should have done it through me", complained Dino. The power of hindsight. Tomorrow will be a tour of the city.

My two young companions were two of the most fascinating characters I have ever met on my travels.

Dave, a Queenslander from Brisbane had already been on the Sub-continent for two weeks; a week in K preceded by a week in Bangalore on business, consulting how to improve that town's traffic congestion using traffic lights. Extensively travelled (like most Aussies), his parents had camper-vanned around Europe in his youth. This experience had helped him in later years become a tour guide around Britain and Europe.

Andrea, from rural Switzerland, came from a farming family and her father was about to go into politics. She was a nurse who had been a nanny to Spanish royalty. She had arrived in K the same time as myself, but was going on to India for a grand tour following this trek. She had given up her job in a Berne hospital, and was taking up a post in a Niger hospital on her return. How brave.

Her English was superb (as was Dave's), much better than her French, she claimed. I was to learn that Swiss German bears very little resemblance to German German. When meeting Germans Andrea would converse in English, as did we all.

Although still tired after the journey, and depressed with the luggage situation, Dave took us to the Garden of Dreams, an oasis of green tranquillity in Thamel. It was twilight, and flights of giant fruit bats were gliding above us heading for their roosts. "Grosse fledermaus" I tried to explain to Andrea. Giant flying mice doesn't translate that well, but it did work.

We joined up with some folk Dave had met, including Mancunian Rachael who was working as a volunteer English teacher (called TEFL). God how I wish they'd had that sort of thing when I was

279

young. I have met so many of these volunteers gaining the most wonderful experience of life. We decided upon an Israeli vegetarian restaurant (Why?) and I had cauliflower pie (Why?). Then we found a bar called The Full Moon, very hippyish, and we staggered back to the hotel at two. Dino had previously warned us to be off the streets by ten, as they could become dangerous. So much for heeding his advice.

Dave didn't make breakfast and cried off for the city tour. I was sharing with him, and he was really ill. Breakfast was a buffet. There is no bacon, of course, the sausage is chicken, and there was mashed potato, but no curry. I was mortified. I love the dahl curry or chana with chapati or roti which is mostly available for breakfast on the sub-continent.

Our little group that first morning consisted of myself and Andrea, Dino, a driver and a specialist city guide. First stop was Swayambo, or the Monkey Temple, a vast Buddhist religious complex atop a hill which many climb but we drove to. There was a brief tour then I struck off to explore. The macaques which are fed and deified here were concentrated around a large pool, and were climbing overhanging trees, diving in, and playing exuberantly.

The Stupas, various statues, outbuildings, and views were all very impressive, but then I stumbled across a special room. I entered and was struck by the heat and smoke of well over a thousand candles, but it was so gloomy. This had to be due to the dirt, grime, smoke and melted wax of centuries. There was also the heavy scent of incense.

Six orange-cloaked, shaven-headed monks squatted as a choir around the Buddha. They were chanting tunelessly to the sound of a vertical drum beaten rhythmically with a curved stick. After several minutes the drum beater stopped abruptly, as did the chanting. Each monk then picked up an instrument, and rang, blew, plucked or beat out one strident note for a few seconds. Just as suddenly they ceased and it was back to chanting to the drumbeat. A truly surreal moment.

Our next stop was the Royal Palace in Durbar Square. It was poignant recalling the whole family had been gunned down in 2001 by the son and heir. The monarchy was subsequently stripped of its powers. There were many pagoda style red brick buildings and a healing post which I rubbed up against hoping to cure my back problems before the serious trekking began.

I saw a fully clad Ghurkha and asked if I could take his photo. He shook his head. As I walked away he called me back. Of course, here, a shake of the head means yes, the Nepali nod.

In the square I was furious when two rickshaws sandwiched me. The traffic generally is awful to deal with as you are constantly being honked at to get out of the way. I had not, I'm afraid, reacted with tolerance or patience, probably still jet lagged.

We went to see The Living Goddess, a child who is whisked from her family to live a monastic life until menstruation when she is thrown back to reality. Maybe I haven't described this quaint tradition in its best light, but I had just been told that next week thousands of water buffalo were being sacrificed for a Hindu deity. You have to keep pinching yourself when in Asia to accept what we would see as barbaric, or at best simply alien, practices. It can take some time, and as yet I still hadn't received my luggage.

Anyway, she was out.

We took lunch in a quiet little restaurant overlooking one of the biggest stupa in the world, the Boudhanath, it is surrounded by fluttering prayer flags, prayer wheels and images of the Buddha. It has huge all seeing eyes, and what looks for all the world like a nose, but actually signifies the importance of One. Here we discovered Mo-Mo's which are small samosas. Small is fine as there are ten to a serving, including raita. Very tasty, and a perfect light lunch.

After luncheon it was off to the Pashputinath temple complex, one of the most unusual places I have ever visited.

The Bagmati, the most holy river of Nepal flows through, and the Hindu temple itself is restricted to the faith. There were dogs, and monkeys, and cattle roaming about; and therefore they are holy. They stick around because of the food offerings, donations for the three million or so gods. These donations are served mostly on the statue laps, or can be left anywhere. For monkeys and dogs apparently, there is such a thing as a free lunch.

I was reminded of the temple fish of the Chao Phraya river in Bangkok. These are deemed holy, therefore cannot be fished. They must know this and that is why they mass there. Same goes for the monkeys and dogs.

The real purpose of the Pashputinath temple is far more disconcerting. There is a bridge over the river. To your right, the south or direction of flow, there are about 12 concrete plinths raised above the steps down to the river. They are the bases for funeral pyres. A body is laid on logs like railway sleepers, which are stacked around it. Following the cremation, the remaining ashes are pushed into the river.

And this is a tourist attraction, very awkward indeed. The other side of the bridge is the body preparation area, where it is washed in the holy waters and wrapped and anointed. Family members gather and sons have their heads shaven. I felt a trespasser. At that moment, gentle rain began to fall and there were distant rumbles of thunder. Morbidly appropriate.

The temple complex also has many Holy Men called Sadhus. These all look like left over hippies, with their dreadlocks and painted faces. They give a holy greeting with one hand, whilst begging with the other.

The Nepalis are quite smug over the irony that all of their waste is pushed into their rivers. And all of these naturally flow south, into India.

Driving back to the hotel I was able to introduce Andrea to some idiomatic English. I managed to persuade her that the phrase "For sure" (a favourite for foreign soccer and tennis stars) doesn't exist for real English speakers, and that should you want to emphasise your agreement with a statement, you should say "Indeed".

"Indeed!" she confirmed, eyebrows raised. "For sure" I joked. But the lesson worked and her English was improved immeasurably.

There was a message back at the hotel that my luggage had arrived, but it proved a gruelling two hour round journey back to the airport, by taxi, to collect it

That evening we took dinner at the Gaiea restaurant around a huge square table. There was Andrea, Dave (still poorly and ate nothing), Dino, Rachael and myself. We were joined by Marco, a young Portuguese Leo Sayer lookalike who was studying Buddhism, Wolf, a Bavarian soap scriptwriter and Jack, a large, balding American whose loudmouth had riled Dave at an earlier time. We soon learned why, Jack was so obnoxious with his red neck opinions, and we lost the will to argue with him. He appeared to heed the message and left early while the rest of us drank and chatted into the night. The beer, Everest and Ghorka were my favourite brands, comes chilled in large 600ml bottles. You don't need many.

East Himalaya

Next day we drove to Nagarkot, a tiny hilltop village to the east with wonderful views of the Everest range, but not for us as cloud was covering the high Himalaya. The views were still tremendous though, overlooking valleys and hillsides way into the distance. The traffic was horrendous leaving K, and there wasn't too much respite in the countryside. The population of Kathmandu valley has risen from half a million to 4 million in 50 years, but there are precious few tarmac roads.

Turning off and heading for the hills was much better and the Hillside Resort, a colonial style four storied hotel, had all rooms facing north, and was very welcoming. Dave immediately took to his bed and the three of us set off to walk to a local beauty spot, View Top.

Looking left out of the hotel to the end of the track there was the aptly named Hotel at the End of the Universe, and we encountered several village children who were all very eager to meet us and have their photos taken. A little further on we came across an amusing but disturbing teenage spat. Set down from the road were a couple of village houses and sat on the one porch, four girls. One was actually stood over and wagging her finger at another, berating her loudly. We imagined they were perhaps sisters. Suddenly the finger wagger flew at the other girl and in a moment they were rolling on the floor each grasping the other's hair, and there was much wailing and shouting. Dino made to intervene, but I held him back. Stupidly my western values worried about the consequence of involvement.

An adult, perhaps mum came out of the house and tried to prise them apart, but one of the other girls shouted at her and she retreated. A neighbouring mum came across and started thumping the aggressor on the back, but the fight continued. We rather shamefacedly turned and left. (Returning three hours later, the area was deserted and there was an eerie silence)

We continued our walk up through a dense forest and heard drumming in the distance. Then we heard chanting through the trees. Turning a corner we saw a group of perhaps ten men dressed in skirts and headdresses dancing in circles and in a circle. They eventually broke up and danced down the hill, jumping onto the rear of a wagon to be driven away. Shamans was the only explanation Dino could give.

Sometime later three o'clock arrived and I realised that at exactly that moment, many thousands of miles and two continents away, and six hours behind, my ex-colleagues were gathering to begin the new school year. I was officially beginning my new career as a retired school teacher. (And yes, everyone you meet still asks the same question, but it is now "What did you used to teach?". The answer doesn't change... "Little b******s!".)

We passed an army training camp before reaching our objective, View Top. Here teenagers were clambering about a ruined watchtower and below a large, noisy group of youngsters were joining in party game activities. It was not unlike a scout jamboree.

There were some stalls and we stopped for a cup of Nepali tea; sweet, milky and aromatic. Sadly there was litter everywhere. We are constantly told that tourists should avoid polluting during their visits to various corners of the world. Most tourists are very aware and careful to 'Take only photographs; leave only footprints'. In my experience it is usually the locals who need educating not to soil their own doorstep.

Later after dinner we played cards and watched the stars and the moths. Thunder was rolling all around and lightning spectacularly illuminating the distant clouds surrounding the Everest mountain range.

"While we've been playing you can see how the Earth has rotated." I pointed to a distant star twinkling above the Himalya, and spoke with some conviction as I tried to educate my companions. "That star over there appears to have moved, whilst the dim one above us hasn't, and it doesn't twinkle which maybe indicates it is a planet. And with its red hue, probably Mars".

My reasoning was impeccable until Andrea said, "Isn't that the light on top of the antenna attached to the hotel roof?" Embarrassment overload. I was not allowed to live it down and Dave was eagerly related the story at breakfast, indeed.

"Why do they only use bend over brooms?" asked Andrea later, "They are too short and must hurt their backs" We were watching a hotel employee. She was bent nearly double sweeping away the moths which had perished during the night, one-handed. Hundreds of them, large and small. Why the small brush? Who knows. Trigger would have been in his element.

It was after breakfast we began our first major trek; down the valley to the temple at Changu Narayan. It is dedicated to Vishnu and dated from at least the 5th century. The walk itself was four and a half hours in beautiful sunshine amongst rural communities. We took farm tracks passing women working the fields, cultivating mostly rice, millet or corn. Once again we encountered many village children, appearing to be walking to school at any time of day. "Namaste. Photo?" There is no standard school time, Dino told us.

285

We saw a number of run down farmhouses which shared the ground floors with their animals; Cattle, buffalo, goats, chickens. The elderly sit above and weave cloth or just smoke and talk. There were exotic birds and butterflies, dragonflies and spiders. We stopped at one farm where I was given some local hooch, direct from the still. It is called Raksi and is made from fermented millet. Millet is a staple here. We feed it to budgies.

The final part of the walk was over pine hillsides until we reached the temple and were given a guided tour. We took lunch as the rain fell. Very pleasant until Andrea was stung by a wasp. Dave was really struggling with his tummy troubles; "one careful step at a time," he confessed. My back was fine. Then we took the local bus to the red city of Bhaktapur and had to pay a $15 tourist tax just to enter.

Within the city walls, Bhaktapur was clean and relatively traffic free. It is Nepal's ancient city of culture, and has art galleries and pottery workshops, as well as pagodas and temples which we spent the afternoon exploring. Our rather excellent hotel rooms at the Ganesh Guest House overlooked the main square and as dusk fell we watched the traders packing away. One old man simply sat by a set of weighing scales for which he charged five rupees to "Read your weight". Dave and I idly began to speculate how he might possibly diversify with a tape measure to measure your height and vital statistics, or thermometer or even sphygmomanometer (blood pressure), maybe an eye chart to read. By the time we had finished he was a fully fledged quack.

We had just set ourselves up for an excellent rooftop drink when the heavens opened and we were forced inside and downstairs for dinner. This sadly was awful. My steak was tougher than old boots and Dave was unable to eat his pasta meal. Prolonging his fast and leaving a rather sour taste of a beautiful place.

In the morning we were woken by dogs, and bells from every temple in the city. We watched the traders setting up, including our own quack, and took breakfast (on a rooftop elsewhere) which proved much better. We ate, enjoying the sunshine, and watched workmen weeding the rather steep roofs as rats scampered in and out of the eaves.

The Famous Farm

We were now as far east in the Kathmandu valley as you can go, so we headed west. This meant going back in to and out of K (traffic nightmare), taking the only road winding up and eventually out of the valley, for the hilltop village of Nuwakot. Here we were to stay at a converted Newari farmhouse called the Famous Farm, which had been taking visitors since 2005. Dino described it as a rustic heaven with a medieval feel. He had once been manager and was greeted like a prodigal son as the three of us took in the rather splendid gardens and views across three valleys and down to Nuwakot Palace.

At our organic lunch we met up with Phillip a tall Aussie/German student, Leonie, a delightfully scatty German and a 19 year-old Brit, Ellie. They were all volunteers at the local school which included a home for deaf children. The two girls were joining us on the river tomorrow.

Seeking adventure I climbed to the highest point behind the farm with Dino. Satisfied with the views we both slid back down precariously in the mud and joined the others for a visit to meet the children at the institute and the school. We made many awkward attempts at signing, at which I was awful, but there was also much laughter mostly due to my ineptitude. Finally we had a wander around the 300 year old palace garrison perfectly strategically positioned.

Dinner was the classic Dahl Bat, candlelit, making it very atmospheric. This romantic gesture wasn't out of choice. Throughout Nepal there are power cuts from six till eight to save power.

I was up at dawn to sit in the garden and enjoy the tranquillity and the birdlife. Sadly we had to say goodbye to the Famous Farm after breakfast, a marvellous peaceful retreat, and we were given tika, dabs of yellow and red paint daubed onto the forehead as blessings for good fortune. I was feeling rather guilty over the death of a giant spider which I had asked Dave to remove. Good fortune was rather lacking on the sole of Dave's size 12's.

The Trishuli River

We were driving down the valley to our entrance onto the Trishuli river for two days white water rafting. On the way I regaled my companions and name dropped shamelessly, about my white-water adventures on the Zambezi below Victoria Falls. I assured everyone that there were rarely fatalities on this type of adventure (a style of humour which got me into trouble when climbing Mount Kinabalu). This didn't phase Andrea, such a strong character for one so young, nor Dave, the quintessential Aussie, but Leonie and Ellie were petrified.

After the obligatory safety briefing and kitting out we entered the boat, a 10 foot inflatable, where we were seated on the hulls with our legs inside. I was given port stroke, Andrea and Dino stationed behind. Dave was starboard stroke, behind him Leonie and Ellie who were to prove as useful as chocolate teapots, but were still excellent companions (easily wound up). At the rear and steering, was Captain Ravi. We would have nightmares over his eerily pronounced, slow but inexorable command of "Forward" for approaching rapids. This would become an anthem for the trip. It was a harbinger of imminent danger, and guaranteed to get the adrenalin flowing.

The Trishuli is usually a class three river which means:

Class III.- Moderately difficult. Numerous high and irregular waves; rocks and eddies with passages clear but narrow and requiring experience to run. Visual inspection required if rapids are unknown. Open canoes without flotation bags will have difficulty. These rapids are best left to canoeists with expert skills.

But at the end of the monsoon season it is swollen into occasional class four.

We would be accompanied by a rescue boat and an outriding kayak.

We set off, and saw a troupe of monkeys walking the opposite bank. Soon we would pass occasional fieldworkers, or children bathing, or mothers washing clothes, we waved to greet them.

"Namaste!" everyone shouts.

To begin with there was much splashing and laughter and banter about "going in". We were relaxing and going with the flow when suddenly Ravi quietly but firmly instructs "Forward". And we are concentrating and paddling towards our first rapids.

Up ahead is a huge boulder which forces an angry wall of white water swirling into the sky, then a descent, right into the jaws of hell.

(time to stiffen the sinews, and summon the blood)

With some experience, I know that it is important to retain control of the boat by ensuring we are navigating through the rapids, rather than allowing the flow of water to control the boat. This means strong relentless paddling whilst being thrown about and bounced around. All of which can leave a crew drained of strength and breathing heavily as they slump over their paddles when the boat gently drifts into the resulting eddy.

Ravi continually instructs; strong right, or strong left, or hold, or down (to avoid being popped out), as churning havoc is navigated.

Coming out of rapids and there is always a collective cheer as oars are raised and high-fived in triumph

During the morning there were many good white water encounters. At one Dave loses his grip and looks about to be pitched into the river, but I propel forward and grab his left foot and Dino hauls him back in. The look on his face shows it was a close thing.

The huge green canyons we passed through were spectacular, and the occasional 200 yard footbridge spanning the river would signal a village approaching. Everyone we see waves a smiling greeting.

We beached and took lunch which was a glorious buffet of spicy meats and fried vegetables. After lunch Ravi told us we faced three grade IV's during the afternoon. Nothing concentrates the mind quite like hurtling towards a convulsing wall of boiling angry river, which you know will both swamp and toss your boat vertical, and all you have for safety is a paddle and a seat on a bouncy rubber ring.

To better balance the boat for the afternoon, Ravi suggested I swapped places with Dino. I was now next to Andrea and opposite Ellie. We negotiated the first two rapids, and they were tremendously draining. Nearing the end of the third and we hit a huge wall, and Andrea is in trouble. I reached to my left to try to save her, but she is pitched overboard and the boat heaves me up.

Suddenly everything is in slow motion as I am prone on the hull, horizontal, half in and half out. I am desperately trying to grasp onto a rope and my mind is saying "Any moment now someone will grab my foot and steady me and pull me in". But Andrea has gone, and opposite me is only Ellie and Leonie. My next thought was "I'm going in".

And sure enough the boat heaves wildly again and I'm head over heels and into the water.

Neither Andrea nor I lost contact with the boat and between them Dave and Dino hauled us in. We lay on the bottom of the boat totally bedraggled and convulsed with laughter.

No damage done. I was however gutted at losing my skull and crossbones, black bandanna. I'd bought it in Lanzarote to replace one I had left in the back of an Egyptian taxi. "Well, I saw it floating off," said Dave, "and it was a snap decision, save you or your bandanna. I hope we made the right choice." As I said, distraught.

The remainder of the afternoon passed off without incident and we made camp on a beach opposite the Ancient Fig village about four. Time to dry off, change and sleep.

Dinner was across the huge footbridge; soup and fried chicken with some well deserved beers. Then it was back to camp for a fire and more beers. The heavens opened but the fire survived for more chat and more beer.

I was up early as usual to drink in the tranquillity of dawn. We breakfasted back in the village and were given a tour. The Ancient Fig village is on the main road from Pokhara to Kathmandu, therefore an important trading post. We were shown the school and given graphic descriptions of the punishments meted out to those who misbehave in class (they only do it once). Outside there had been a monkey tethered to a tree lining the path from bridge to road. We had seen people taunting it as they passed by, and I complained (western values again) about its treatment. On our return to camp the monkey had been untied and taken indoors. We wondered, how long for.

The morning's rafting was fun, with some good rapids, but not as spectacular as the previous day. So it was with a slight sense of disappointment when we beached for lunch and both boats were deflated, and all the equipment packed up and carried up to the road to be taken back east.

Lunch was again excellent, and we were picked up to be taken west. Our pick up, a small Peugeot had a smashed windscreen like it had been hit by a sledgehammer. Before we turned left to ascend into the hills we said goodbye to Leonie and Ellie at Dumre. They were off on their own three day trek.

Bandipur and Pokhara

The Peugeot wound its way up and up, taking on a couple of passengers on the way and negotiating hairy hairpin bends. We ran into a variety of close encounters with goats, cattle, people, water buffalo, and also buses and lorries speeding downhill, until we reached Bandipur.

Bandipur is an historic town with distinctive architecture which commands a position guarding an old trading pass route from India to Tibet, and feels very colonial. Our rooms at the aptly named "Old Inn" were windowless cells. They were only for sleeping, however as there was plenty of lounge and library space with comfortable sofas for relaxation, plus outdoor terraces with magnificent views to valleys both north and south.

Like Bhaktipur the centre was traffic free, brick-paved and clean, with schoolchildren constantly coming or going at whatever time of the day.

We took Nepali tea and were introduced to Bimila, the petite 17 year old daughter of the hotel proprietor, who was to be our guide. She was painfully shy but led us up to a football pitch on top of the hill. Amazing, kick the ball out and it will fall down steep inclines on three sides. There was a good view here of the saddle into which the town has been built, and beyond the far goal, down to the river Marshyangdi, and north-west towards Pokhara and Annapurna. Sadly cloud still covered the highest mountains. Dawn remained the best time to glimpse Nepal's snow-covered peaks.

We then climbed past millet and corn terraces and mobile phone masts to the hospital and Memorial Park at the peak. "What's it a memorial to?" asked Dave. "Dead people" came Bimila's impassive reply.

We descended to a temple around which young boys were playing football. Suddenly our bare legs were attacked by biting insects we couldn't see. Mites or chiggers, but we didn't hang around to find out. We literally hot-foot it back to the hotel to seek chemical relief.

The Old Inn's speciality is a roast dinner carvery, and that evening in full Sikh style regalia the chef stood proudly with giant carving knife and fork, behind a tiny chicken. The creamed potatoes and cauliflower cheese were superb. Dave, who is now fully recovered had double everything. Andrea smiled at his returning appetite and said, "I like it here, indeed!"

I shared breakfast and tranquillity on the terrace with a mynah bird, then it was the short walk to the smashed windscreen, and the journey back down the valley. We were accompanied by the delightful wife of the driver who runs a greengrocery in the town, and was going to Dumre to buy stock.

There followed a three hour drive where we crossed several rivers (and passed the actual village of Ghorka) before arriving at the city of Pokhara. In the exact centre of the country, it is Nepal's second largest city, and a centre of tourism, not just because of its proximity to the

Annapurna range, but also because of its relaxed nature, its World Peace Stupa, and the beautiful Phewa Lake.

We checked in near the lake in the area of Pokhara called Lakeside, and Dino disappeared to organise supplies for our trek which begins tomorrow. We wandered into the town. Every other shop appeared to be selling trekking and camping equipment. Barbers beckoned as my white beard was becoming quite unruly and Andrea hired a sleeping bag.

We found a restaurant for lunch at the beach, seeking shade from the hot sunshine. It was next to a small pontoon hiring out rowing boats. Two single diners conversed loudly in French three tables apart for the whole hour and a half we were there. Neither was eating, both had open books, but the conversation, too fast for me to even gather the gist, was incessant. At no stage did the large, middle-aged, dark woman invite her 30ish, slim protagonist to join her, and at no stage did he intimate he would like to move table. The flow was loud and uninterrupted throughout. We could only surmise they were reviewing the books they were carrying. They certainly had a lot to say.

Our chicken and noodles lunches were pleasant if unexciting and the afternoon was wasted snoozing in the sunshine, but there was hard work to come. In the evening Dino took us to the Boomerang restaurant and introduced us to Susan. He was a thin young man who will be one of our porters tomorrow. It will be his first time and he appears rather camp and wears an Arsenal shirt. I wasn't sure the three were linked. There was a rather forgettable dance show, so we left for Busy Bees to listen to a Nepali band playing seventies music whilst retro hippies gyrated drunkenly. All in all a rather nothing day, epitomised by turning on the TV when back at the hotel, to check out world news on the BBC.

The Siklis Trail

The trek began innocuously enough, with no sign of the drama to come. We boarded a rickety coach which bounced up a river valley for

293

about an hour, before stopping to disgorge us. There were seven porters, five kitchen staff and an assistant guide, KB pronounced Caby. An expedition party of 17 souls.

We set off at an elevation of over 3,000 feet, intending to climb 2,000 feet this first day. Soon the river valley was way below us, the tarmac road a distant memory, and we were deep in the jungle. It was hot and humid and didn't take long for us to be drenched in sweat.

Presently we came upon a tiny village with a school. There were six even tinier classrooms in this dirty whitewashed, mudbrick single-storey building. Each room was only 12 feet square and housed a teacher and about ten children crowded around five old wooden desks with benches. The blackboards were painted over the stucco, and the floors were plain earth. The dust of many years was swept into a pile in one corner.

I was invited into one room and the children stood up to bow. I addressed them in my best teacher voice. "What is your name? How old are you?" Each one answered very seriously and very proudly. These were twelve and thirteen year olds. In another class of much younger children I sang the ABC with them. I was invited to examine their exercise books which were as dog-eared and dirty as the children's faces.

Everyone smiled and as we left I waved my farewells choking back a tear.

At the school gate I pointed out our first leech; a black, two-inch sliver of slime which sniffs and weaves cobra-like at the air. I thought no more of it.

A little later we were seated on a grassy knoll taking lunch in the pleasant sunshine. Cheesy chips, boiled vegetables and tuna with Nepali tea; impressive.

Then it rained, and as Dino had warned, the leeches became aggressive. They get onto your boots and slither into your socks in search of blood. Try to pick them off and they attach to your fingers and hands. Try to flick them off and they just stick "like leeches". They got into Dave's hair and among his toes, they were on my legs and shirt, Andrea seemed immune.

We made camp early evening. The camp and tents were already assembled as we arrived, so we changed into dry clothes and met up in a thankfully dry shelter. Water was boiling on a gas stove, but it was dark and dank, and I fell into a terrible depression. A black dog came over me like I had never experienced and I began to feel panicky.

My terror mode kicked in. I couldn't handle this. The leeches had got to me as completely as if they had bored into my brain. I didn't speak, just brooded. I couldn't imagine walking around camp in flip-flops, going to the toilet, being exposed, sitting on the grass, eating in the dark whilst the nasty little devils latched on any and everywhere to thirst for my blood. I felt sick and thoroughly miserable. I summoned up the courage (is that the right term, or is it the contrary) to speak to Dino.

"I want to go back to Pokhara" I knew we were at an early stage, and I could be dispatched with a porter in the morning.

I forced myself to eat a bland dinner. Soup, chips, and pasta in tomato sauce. I could see the chef was trying to cater to our western tastes, but I want curry, or even dal bhat, the lentil soup with chapatti which is the porters' basic diet. We played cards and Andrea has hands you could only dream of. But my mind was elsewhere. I'd given up. I'm going home in the morning.

Time for bed. We left the smoky shelter and were greeted by the most amazing sight. There, across the black valley, rising up through the clouds, and almost glowing in the moonlight, was a white mountain. Perfectly shaped with its sharp peak, it was an ethereal spectacle.

"Say hello to Fishtail" explained Dino randomly. "There is a twin peak which can't be seen from this side. Machapuchare is a holy mountain, at just under 23,000 feet, its summit has never been set foot upon".

We stared to take in its stark beauty before the clouds rolled in and it was gone.

In the tent I searched around with my head torch and evicted three leeches. I settled down into my sleeping bag and tried to sleep, but my mind was racing. Back in Pokhara how would I keep myself occupied for the next four days; where will I stay, how much will it cost, what will I do, who will I meet, what is that snuffling outside? Why have I freaked out over leeches, it's not as if we weren't warned, it's rainforest after all, jungle, there's stuff lives here, it's their habitat, I'm just visiting. This is an adventure, an expedition, there's bound to be difficult moments, surely they can be overcome. What is snuffling around camp?

Without realising, I had fallen into my "night najjers". I get these when camping, usually on a first night, usually at altitude, and usually when there is no alcohol. Night najjers are some form of nightmare which I experience in the complete belief that I am fully awake, and tonight I have been struck again. The self-imposed depression hasn't helped, and then the rain is hammering down on the tent. I'm tossing and turning. Oh God this is awful.

I became convinced there was a tiger in camp and any moment it will tear into my tent with its great slashing claws and I'll be taken head first by its crushingly powerful jaws. I shrank into my sleeping bag and kept very still for what seemed an eternity.

I was awake and out of the tent early. No view of Fishtail, but the dawn sunshine was warming and bright. I noticed a black spot by my toenail, and scratched at it and pulled out a one inch leech, and there was a spot of blood, but the nightmare was passed. Over breakfast Dino asked what I was doing. Neither of my colleagues looked up from their cereal. I simply indicated upwards. "Good" he said.

Overnight Dino had the porters create some salt sticks. These were cloth pouches containing moistened salt, tied to sticks with which we could reach our feet. "Simply touch these against the creatures as they attempt to invade, and they'll drop off," he assured. And they worked.

Today was going to be a gruelling, strenuous trek. A 5,000 foot climb, almost exclusively uphill. No flat, no down (Good. When you're climbing, any descent simply adds to the ascent) This was going to be the equivalent of climbing Ben Nevis from sea level.

We broke camp and began. KB leads, Dino takes up the rear. We were rewarded with no rain, but we were still in the thickest, greenest, wettest rainforest ever. Magnificent trees smothered from top to toe with thick moss. Little light could penetrate as we plodded slowly but inexorably upwards.

We kept religiously to the centre of the path, as leeches dangle from leaves, weave and pounce if you should brush by too close.

We stopped every ten minutes to check each other for leeches, and brush them off with our magic sticks. Every 30 minutes we stopped for water and to towel off. Constant welcome companions were butterflies, dragonflies and both colourful and tuneful birds. We even saw a brown snake checking us out. Impossible at this height, says Dino, but it was there.

I introduced my companions to a very British custom; elevenses. Just some energy biscuits to go with our water, but a welcome little ritual whilst wiping away the sweat and blood.

We decided to continue and not take lunch until we had made camp. It had become a six hour trek, but the last 30 minutes were the most arduous. How the porters had made it before us I'll never know, but we had to hack through undergrowth and still climb steeply. Eventually we stumbled out onto a cleared summit. At nearly 20,000 feet Tara Top was the highest point of the trek. From here we meander down, but for the next 18 hours we could enjoy our brief pinnacle.

The heavens opened and we took lunch behind curtains of water, before taking to our tents for a well earned rest. We woke briefly to experience another great British institution, or was it simply from the Raj. Tea and cakes, Tiffin at four. As we were seated sipping tea, the clouds rolled away to reveal the Annapurna Range. With Fishtail still prominent, it appeared to be flanked by Annapurna numbers one, three and four. They are in fact much further away because each Annapurna peak is considerably higher than Machapuchare, with number one being over 26,000 feet.

Whilst I marvelled at the magnificent vista, I pondered the prodigious imagination which saw four peaks and named them all Annapurna. I was reminded of the news item I had heard some years ago stating a new strain of Hepatitis had been discovered which had previously been known as "Hepatitis not A or B", but after much discussion the medical community had decided to call it Hepatitis C. Also when Anytown College merged with another local college, and employed consultants who for £20,000 had recommended they rename the new institution The Anytown College. Or are these just silly stories, apocryphal.

Anyway, 48 hours later we spotted Annapurna 29, and decided the joke had run its course.

The moon rose to bathe the mountains in that ethereal light we had seen the previous evening and we took dinner in the cold mess tent. Under candlelight we ate soup, Spanish potatoes, steamed vegetables, pizza and apple fritters. How did they do it? We played cards and chatted into the evening. Generally trekking in the mountains is alcohol free, but Dino had a stash of the local raksi, which was most welcome. We had to clear the tents of leeches before climbing fully clothed into our sleeping bags.

Camp gradually stirs and awakens. I am always first up, even beating the Nepalis. With dawn breaking and the sun rising to my right, I sat and watched the mountains to the North. They change with every minute as the light evolves into the morning, the clouds shape shift and the snows and glaciers swing their shadows around. Behind me, down to the South I couldsee Pokhara, surely one of the most perfectly positioned towns on the planet.

Dave and Andrea appeared, smoke began to drift from the cookhouse, and Dino produced a map so we could position each mountain, and discuss the day's route which will see us achieve the mountain village of Sikles.

We took breakfast on the roof of the world.

Day three of the trek took us downhill. It was treacherous, especially on the wet rocks, and there were several falls, but at last we were able to savour and enjoy the surroundings. This was all jungle, or Tsunkel, as Andrea says. There were many precarious crossings of waterfalls and the maxim was "Attention" as it had previously been "Forward" on the rafting.

The banter was rich, especially during a discussion about the respective meanings and responses when a partner says "We need to talk", a sure harbinger of trouble (as in "You are in it"). I explained that the expression immediately depresses me and I am instantly transported through the past six months, and I rack my memory for any comment or action I have made which could have possibly been unfortunately misconstrued. As the saying goes:

"Behind every angry woman stands a man who hasn't the foggiest idea what he has done wrong"

Dave's response? "Any woman says that to me and its "Ok, goodbye!" Simple as that.

Five and a half hours later we emerged into rain and onto grazing land where the villagers had cleared the forest. Within 100 yards of camp I slipped on a piece of mud and went flying arse over tit. I wasn't hurt, but hugely embarrassed.

Lunch was spam fritters, beans and chapati, and we managed a couple of hours sleep before visiting the village of Sikles, which like many in this region has given many young men to the Ghurkas. The half hour trek was tortuous as we were stiff following our morning's exertions.

Entering the hillside community, which is cut off from the outside world for nine months of the year, there were children playing, women at their looms, and men smoking and talking under their holy trees. Water buffalo roamed the narrow pathways. Everywhere was up or down, no such thing as flat. There was some electricity, quite a few satellite dishes, but no fridges. We took Nepali tea in an ambitious guest house, but no cold beer. We were evidently novelty visitors as there were lots of glances and asides from the fellow customers. These appeared mostly elderly, with wizened faces, few teeth, smoking and sporting nepali biretta-style caps. There was also the occasional child peering curiously through the curtain.

We returned for a dinner of soup, roast potatoes, mo-mo's and pasta. There was some local millet alcohol, raksi, and I won at cards. Now we could see the snow-covered (Dino's definition of a mountain) Lamjung Himal and its glaciers. In bed our sleep was occasionally disturbed by the snuffling, munching and bellowing of the water buffalo with which we shared the meadow.

It was day 4 of the trek, overcast but fresh. Huge green valleys surrounded us and we could see the occasional distant village. Clouds curled around the hilltops. Camp awakens, toilet tent used, greetings issued, coffee given, stretches made, rhetorical questions asked; "Sleep well?" No, no-one does. I need a bed. Some women from the village have set up shop during breakfast and displayed some home-made curios to sell as souvenirs. "It is my only income" they bleat, and we hand over a few rupees.

The original plan for today was to trek down to the river formed from the melting glacier of Lamjung, but last month there was a landslide which killed five people and made dozens homeless. Our scouts report to Dino that the area is still too treacherous to risk, so we decided to stay high and follow the contours of the hills.

Landslides, or mudslides are a constant threat here. Where the forest has been cleared for grazing the tree roots no longer knit the earth together and a good soaking can lead to slippage. There is little terracing, which can protect earth slippage. What there is can be found mainly in and around the villages for growing maize, millet or rice.

And the land does get a good soaking. Every spring the monsoon is sucked up from the Bay of Bengal and deposited onto the sub-continent during the summer months. In Nepal the clouds are driven upwards by the Himalaya and the last rains fall making it one of the wettest places on Earth. On the other side however there is the dry arid plain of Tibet, hence rainforest here and Gobi Desert there.

Roads of whatever quality are either washed away or made impassable by rockfall. Young men work very hard to break those rocks and cart away the rubble so that by January there might be a passage for a 4 wheel drive, or tractor. Some bridges are built to avoid the waterfalls which have sculpted the hillsides, but these are only walkways. Personally I can't believe we see no pack animals. No mules, donkeys, camels, buffalo or oxen. The only beasts of burden we see are people; men and women using heads and shoulders to carry enormous loads. I even saw one man shovelling rocks over his head into a basket strapped to his shoulders! (We encountered one team of oxen pulling a plough, but that was all. Dino could not provide answers).

Whatever is done throughout the year to improve communications for the villages, you can guarantee that it will all be washed away again with the next monsoon. The occasional earthquake is also a threat

We left Sikles, one of the biggest villages, and can occasionally see smaller communities clinging to the hillsides across the valley. There are reminders we are still in one of the remotest places on the planet, which apparently still has some rather unwholesome customs. The hawking and spitting is bad enough, (although I have heard that they think we are weird because of our habit of emptying our noses into expensive handkerchiefs, examining the contents, then parcelling it up and pocketing it as if it were a valuable keepsake). But worse; there are occasional signs which say "Welcome to the Open Defecation Free Zone". It takes a little time to work out, but basically it is saying that people now do it indoors.

The track goes in and out as we round the hills. All of the "ins" have downhill torrents, glacial meltwater, which have shaped these lands over millennia, and we had to negotiate about a dozen of these. Some we can hop over using stepping stones, others had rickety bridges, but one in particular caused some fun.

It was about a 50 yard crossing. A bamboo bridge stood, but looked too risky so we decided to wade. Off came the boots and socks, and slung around my neck, then the downpour started so everything got soaked.

On the other side we dried off as best we could and continued our trek. Unseen, somehow some leeches invaded my socks. They are really quite harmless. They attach and inject an anticoagulant, suck away then drop off when bloated. When we stopped for lunch an hour later I sat on a dry wall and removed my footwear, and both feet were streaming with uncoagulated blood. Dino patched me up as we ate lunch. What an adventure; oh, how we laughed.

Three hours later we were watching a group of lads playing volleyball on our campsite. A group of girls arrived from the local school, and suddenly everywhere was testosterone and giggles. It could have been anywhere in the world when teenagers meet.

Beyond the volleyball court KB was digging a pit and erecting the toilet tent. He had a crowd of about 30 youngsters gathered and watching him work, in awe. Gradually with the darkness, the locals dispersed and we were left to erect our own tents and take dinner, soup, mashed potato, vegetables and spring rolls followed by tinned fruit and custard.

Witnessing a worldwide sport this evening prompts discussions into other sports. It transpires that Andrea has heard of cricket but thinks it is like baseball. Horrified, Dave and I spent the rest of the evening explaining and demonstrating the different techniques of batsmanship, the varieties and skills of bowling, and the strategies and tactics and traditions of "God's own game".

"So you two play for Ashes" We can tell she is unimpressed. Then Dino chips in, telling us of the exploits of the Nepali national soccer team which languishes in the bottom ten in the world. Andrea reminds us that the Swiss, indeed, beat Spain before the latter won the World Cup, and we ended the evening on rugby.

It was the morning of the last day of the expedition, and Dino's birthday. KB assured us it was an eagle owl with its hoots, growls and screeches which had disturbed us before dawn. We thought it had been him.

There were some remarkable views to the south. In the foreground was the remainder of the valley to be trekked, then a sea of cloud out of which a veritable archipelago of hilltop islands emerged, and beyond, the plains of India.

Breakfast was a camping favourite, porridge, and we began our final trek. It was Nepali Flat (bit up, bit down) all the way. We passed villages (sometimes only two houses), livestock downstairs, living quarters first floor; a school which had children arriving noisily from every direction. And there were the usual butterflies, birds and wonderfully colourful shrubs and wild flowers.

"You were born in 1981, weren't you?" I asked Dave, mischievously aware of my supplementary question, "So have you heard of Botham's Ashes?" Oh, it is wonderful thing talking sport, and cricket in particular, with Aussies.

It turns out he hadn't, so I then spent a very pleasant hour regaling him with the exploits of the superman of English cricket as he went from hero to zero, to mighty hero during that most wonderful Headingley Test in the year of Dave's birth. And don't get me started with Bob Willis, bless his soul.

It was hot now, and there were grand views of Lamjung Himal; there, and then gone as the white clouds scudded by. The noise of the crickets was cacophonous. Dino decided to take the quick descent to the river which will cut out the zigzagging around the hills, but means wading across instead of using the bridge. We took elevenses in the cool shade of two banyan trees. You find them in every village with built in ledges, one for the men, the other the women, then set off again following the route of a mountain stream, down to the river.

We entered the ice cold water barefoot. It was painfully slow progress as the stones were sharp, and the flow could easily knock you over. At each island, step back into boots and stride along until the next channel to be crossed. There were ten islands in all, then we saw the coach which had arrived to collect us and our team.

Lunch was chips and spam and it was all aboard for the hour long, rickety journey back along the river bank. As always with coaches in the third world, children run alongside in the villages with much laughter and waving. Back at Pokhara we said goodbye to our seven porters, including Susan who had been mercilessly bullied as he had simply been inept. We didn't think he would be portering again.

I check back into the hotel, showered and spend several luxurious minutes reintroducing myself to a soft bed, squirming unashamedly. Later we walked down to the lakeside to take drinks overlooking the Fewa Lake and Andrea introduced us to Amy, who she had met in an internet cafe.

Amy was also a German-speaking Swiss (how does Andrea find them) and she was a volunteer living in Pokhara with a local family. She joined us and told us how lonely and bored she was. It had cost her over £2,500 for this "opportunity" to work with disadvantaged children. She worked two hours a day, three days a week at the orphanage. The rest of the time she spends isolated in her room. The family is kind, and her digs comfortable, and she is fed well, but they are non-English speakers. And Amy at 19 has precious little experienced to go out and involve herself in local life, which for a female in Nepal, of any nationality, is not the done thing anyway. Some agencies somewhere are making a small fortune out of these gap year enthusiasts.

We dined sumptuously with Dino, KB and the rest of the kitchen staff later at their HQ, which happened to be our hotel. Speeches were made and farewells offered (plus the embarrassing handing over of tips. Brown envelopes are suitably sleazy). Finally we wearily made it to Busy Bees for some live music, but we were too bushed and soon headed home for that sumptuous bed.

I woke early for wonderful views of an old friend. Fishtail was there to greet me. It is no wonder it is a holy mountain for the locals, it looks over you with the most benign countenance. Only Gods can live there. Dave and I walked down to the lake for some last pictures, then Dino piles us into a taxi for the journey to the bus station from where, unbelievably, we can see the whole of the Annapurna range. An unbelievable juxtaposition.

It was an eight hour journey back to Kathmandu passing all the places we'd veered off to visit last week. There was the village of Ghorka, Old Fig village, Dumre and the turn off to Bandipur. Every so often we could see the swirling waters of the Trishuli down to our left. It was an exhausting trip punctuated only by sleep and loo breaks and being catapulted from the seats as the bus negotiated potholes.

We re-entered K and found the Marshyangdi, saluted and checked in. My room this time was on the sixth floor and there was a great roof terrace with 360 degree views of the city and the valley. But without a lift, I had to plan my descents carefully.

We dined at the famous Rum Doodle Restaurant, where traditionally trekking teams sign a footprint which is hung as a mobile, or stuck to the walls. We said our official goodbyes. Within 48 hours I'll be in Blighty, Dave in Brisbane, Andrea in Chetwan and Dino back in his office.

Everest Flight

My flight around Everest was to be my ultimate highlight, the first part of my plan, and the only adventure planned and paid for before coming out.

I was booked on the Yeti Airlines' "Everest Express" which advertises itself as "One of the World's Most Exclusive Tours". There is another airline, Buddha Airlines, and both operate this particular flight at dawn. If a flight is cancelled because of fog or poor visibility, you are automatically booked on tomorrow's flight, which was no good to me for I was already booked to fly home the next morning.

I woke whilst it was still dark, and was ready to leave when my wake-up call came. A taxi whisked me to the airport and I was checked in, through security, and strapped into my seat, 9A by 6:30. The aircraft was a 20 seater green and white Jetstream, there was a crew of three and everyone had a window seat. My fellow passengers were mainly awestruck Americans (they must have been awestruck as they kept saying "Awesome!"), and there was one very talkative Australian lady.

No sooner were we airborne and through the first layer of cloud than we could see Langtang which I mistook for Lamjung Himal, last seen on the last day of the trek. The tiny stewardess was running up and down the aisle pointing out which peak was which. I was on the left of the aircraft, therefore with great outbound views. People to my right were straining to look out of my window whilst still strapped in.

Then we were up through one last layer of cloud and the whole collection of sun-glistened, white, sharp sculpted peaks came into view; from the holy peak of Gauri Shanker to the first eight thousander Cho-oyo, right through to Everest itself and beyond to Makalu. Only Kanchenjunga (K2) was missing from the family. Some of the peaks are in Tibet, but they are mostly shared borders.

Everest, or Sagarmatha, at 8,848 metres (29,028 feet) is wholly in Nepal as Dino and all Nepalis insist with great passion. (A Bollywood film once claimed it to be Indian, which nearly caused an international incident) It is a feature deeply resented in Nepal, that from Tibet you can drive to within a two hour trek of Everest base camp. They don't mention that the Nepalis have actually built an airport there.

We flew closer and closer, and it was my turn to visit the cockpit. The stewardess takes my hand and opens the cockpit door. Bending low, I stepped inside just as the pilot turned into Everest, and I felt as if we were right on top of her and her two sister peaks, Nuptse and Lhotse. It was the most wonderful view from the cockpit, directly down onto the snows. The pilot told me she does this run twice a week and it never fails to inspire her. As I stood up to return to my seat I bumped my head into the ceiling controls. "Please be careful" the pilot asked as she reached up to readjust several of the switches, and it was the next person's turn.

We turned into the mountain range and were now so close to the peaks on the right of the plane, and sod the seatbelts, everyone was up and leaning into the starboard windows. We were flying over the top of them. The closest we came was to the Holy mountain whose approaches were sharp and contrasting. I felt I could step off the plane onto its peak, as you feel with clouds.

All of these peaks and approaches are sharp, not having been weathered. A reminder that they are very young mountains, way younger than the dinosaurs.

And then we had passed and were heading home. Everyone was exhausted in wonderment. We flew down the Kathmandu valley, over Bhaktapur with its brick kilns and terraced hills, and landed. Off the plane, onto the bus, to the departure gate, met by taxi and back to the hotel by 8am. I phoned Dave and Andrea to meet me for breakfast, a buffet which included mashed potato, cauliflower cheese, tomatoes, beans, chicken sausage and eggs.

"Why is it Holy?" Andrea asked. "I'll Google it".

Lunch was taken in a little Tibetan restaurant and the germ of an idea for a future adventure begins to plant itself in my mind. The mo-mo's are deep fried here, much better than the steamed Nepali style, and the honey-spiced bread was delicious.

After lunch we found an Irish bar and watched them beat Australia in the Rugby World Cup. Dave was very magnanimous in defeat. Andrea really enjoyed what she called a brutal sport. I then checked in to my new hotel. I have had to move from the Marshyangdi, a final salute, for my final night and I checked into the much cheaper Pilgrim's Guest House.

They had seen me coming and insisted they had no more 750NR rooms remaining. I must take the penthouse suite for 1,000 NR. With 116 Nepali Rupees to the pound, that makes it just under nine. There was still no lift though and I was six floors up without a phone The rooftop was decorated with pretty pot plants.

In the evening I met up with Andrea and Dave, and we found Leonie and Ellie (from the white-water rafting), and Leonie's big sister Christina who had just arrived from Aachen. We took a pleasant rooftop meal at Helena's, and then on to The Full Moon where I regaled all and sundry with Mustang Sally, Bo Rap and Hotel California. "I am pleased to meet the real Tom Jones" smiled Christina. My beard was full and white now.

We had said goodbye to Dino in the Tibetan restaurant earlier. Now it was time to say goodbye to Andrea and Dave who had become dear friends. Andrea is to go on to Chitwan National Park where she will safari on elephant and see the rare one horned rhino, then India, and finally Niger ministering to some of the poorest people on Earth. They've both had to put up with me and my puerile humour, my constant teasing of Andrea's accent, and attempts to bait Dave over sporting rivalries.

In my penthouse suite I had a restless night with strange work-related dreams and. Panic, I woke and it was fully light. Naked, I ran out onto the roof terrace and below there was the unmistakable bustle of city life. No watch, no phone, and I have a 9:30 plane to catch. I quickly washed, dressed, packed and left. I ran swiftly down six flights of stairs almost tripping over my baggage, and out into the sunlight, and it was 6:15.

Phew, panic over, but one too many beers the night before meant I must choose between breakfast and taxi. I bought three bananas and an apple from the market, hailed a taxi and gave the driver all my final rupees.

Namaste.

P. S. On my flight to Delhi I requested a starboard seat, and had wonderful views of the Annapurna range and I am sure I saw Fishtail.

Security was amazing. At Delhi I was searched as I deplaned, again at the entrance to the terminal, then at the departure gate, again at the bottom of the steps to the aircraft, and finally also at the top of the steps. Welcome to Air India.

P.P.S The pilot spectacularly lifted the nose and aborted the landing at Heathrow, we had to go around again. There was a huge queue at passport control, except for the few Europeans on the flight. That particular advantage was soon wiped out at the carousel which was blocked by all the unclaimed baggage, and I missed all my connections.

P.P.P.S. Oliver, my 90 year old father-in-law was happily fully fit when I returned. Natalie gave birth to my second grandchild, Codey three weeks later.

And Finally

The day I left Kathmandu there was an earthquake which killed four people.

Exactly a week after my Everest experience a Buddha flight crashed in fog killing all 17 passengers and three crew. This was the third fatal crash on the Everest Express in just over a year.

The earthquake which sadly devastated the country in Spring 2015 destroyed many of the villages and monuments I have described.

Mount Everest

Borneo

Rivers, Mountains and Orangutans

I was driving in the 1970's. I owned a light brown Rover 3500, an old man's car, and I was tootling around my territory, the industrial estates of West Bromwich where I visited new and existing customers trying to sell cleaning chemicals for an agent's commission.

I was an averagely successful salesman, knocking on doors, and blissfully unaware in my naïve twenties that sales representatives were seen as unwelcome interlopers in most people's settled work place routines.

310

Most days I lunched alone and my only workmates were the characters I knew on the car radio; Terry Wogan fighting the flab, Jimmy Young with "What's the recipe today, Jim?", and Waggoner's Walk, a sort of Archers light for a lunchtime soap. I also enjoyed Nicolas Parson's Just A Minute and Humphrey Littleton's I'm Sorry I Haven't A Clue.

It was on the cerebral quiz show Brain Of Britain that I heard the question; "What is the only island in the world comprising three separate countries?" To which the answer came Great Britain, which sparks all sorts of interesting trivia as discussed previously, including that it is the country with the longest name in the world, United Kingdom of Great Britain and Northern Ireland. But mainly that it was the wrong answer.

"What about Borneo?" I remember shouting at the radio whilst eating a chippy lunch overlooking the pools and rugby pitches on which I have played many times against local rivals Wednesbury. And it was this that set the wheels in motion to check the encyclopedia once home, and begin a fascination with this, the third largest island in the world (another controversial quiz favourite). Borneo, the home of the orangutan.

There are several islands split into two nations; we know about Ireland, then there is Cyprus which has North and South (not if you're Cypriot), Hispaniola with Haiti and the Dominican Republic, the Papuas of New Guinea and the two Timors. But only Great Britain and Borneo have three. Borneo has the tiny but wealthy Kingdom of Brunei on its north coast, and a huge portion of Indonesia called Kalimantan in the south. It has two states of Malaysia, Sarawak and Sabah to the north and east.

Travel to Sabah, climb Kinabalu the highest mountain in South East Asia, visit the orangutan refuge at Sepilok, explore the Kinabatangan river and dive the tropical reefs around Pulau Tiga Island. My adventure was sorted. I just had to wait another 30 years to realise the dream.

Kota Kinabalu

Sixteen hours in the air including a stop over at Kuala Lumpur (saw the Petronus Towers coming in to land) and I checked into the Beverley Hotel at noon. It turned out to be a large but non descript building in the business district of Kota Kinabalu, capital of Sabah State.

Known to its inhabitants simply as KK my first impressions of the place had not been good. Low rise with some skyscrapers, new construction all around and the occasional aromas of sewage or rotten fish.

I relaxed around the pool in the afternoon to allow time for my body clock to catch up. The sunbeds patio overlooked a litter strewn canal, and I watched egrets fishing and the occasional huge monitor lizard heave itself up out of the stagnant water. Later I wandered a few of the local streets and between the unpleasant smells, amongst both old and new, there was an overriding aroma of pot noodle.

The best of KK was the view from my room on the 10th floor. To my left the misty isles and blue waters of the South China Sea, and to my right the forested mountains of the Crocker Range. Its peak is Mount Kinabalu at nearly 13,500 feet. In the foreground, beyond the canal, streets of stilted housing and the city centre.

KK is a major fishing port so I treated myself to a red snapper dinner with cold beers. I returned to the hotel for a nightcap beer in their well-appointed lounge. I was disappointed, as I always am, with the rip-off hotel tariff.

I can't blame the Beverley, they are simply copying the way business is conducted in hotels (and airports) worldwide. Outside, in a good bar or restaurant I will buy a beer for a few Ringgit, whereas in the hotel, catering for fat business-men's expense accounts they charge not double, nor even treble, but four times the amount charged (at a profit) elsewhere. It matters not that I can afford it, being ripped-off always leaves a nasty taste.

The Beverley redeemed itself with an excellent breakfast buffet and I indulged in my favourite dahl and chapatis. I checked out and found the bus for the Poring Hot Springs, pleased to be beginning my gallivanting. I was excited about my itinerary. I'd waited over 30 years for this.

My optimism was sorely tested however when a two hour journey through the jungle turned into five gruelling hours behind slow trucks in a hot, noisy, smelly bus which rarely afforded the luxury of changing out of first gear. Arrival at the Springs, heralded a welcome late lunch of Rangan noodles, then the opportunity to taste durian fruit, a local speciality which famously smells of vomit, and, I discovered tastes little better.

I had really come for the canopy walk, which with four separate suspensions, all about 100 feet high, was an excellent opportunity to witness the rain forest. Not for those of a nervous disposition, the walkways can sway alarmingly, but the sights, sounds and smells of the rainforest experienced in 35 degree heat and nearly 100% humidity, so high above the floor was something special. The bird calls and monkey shouts were the most apparent. But you see very little. The canopy walk was built in 1990, and the canopy is now 60 feet above your head.

Later I climbed up to a cave, supposedly the home to a colony of bats. Although I saw only a few flitting in and out, the smell of ammonia from the substantial pile of guano at the entrance was sufficient evidence to prove the supposition.

I travelled on to the Fairy Gardens Hotel at the foot of what the hotel called Mount Borneo and dined on drunken chicken and rice, a meal which sounds more fun than it is. I loved strolling in the gardens, away from the city and the choking road. The flowering shrubs and butterflies afforded a welcome diversion, and accordingly with a little help from a large scotch, I slept well.

I was up at dawn and went to the gardens for a marvellously clear view of the mountain I was to climb that very day. Then at breakfast things began to go a little awry.

I was seated at a round table and was joined amongst others by what I assumed to be a mother and daughter, probably late thirties and early teens. In the course of conversation I established that these two Brits were also hoping to climb Kinabalu that day, and we were due to be picked up at the same time. The youngster had never climbed a mountain before and was a little nervous. I tried to reassure her that thousands climb this mountain every year, and there was nothing to worry about.

"In fact," I ended with the little joke I use about the Alton Towers white knuckle rides (which I tell to have fun with the grandchildren), "the instances of people falling to their deaths are very rare indeed." I winked and smiled.

There was a pause and I felt other people staring at me, the mood amongst the cornflakes was changing.

"I suppose that is trying to reassure her, is it?" Her mother spat the words at me.

"It was only my little joke, not to be taken seriously" I replied, taken aback.

"Well you need to be more careful about what you say," and she stood up and pushed her chair back. "Come on, Sophie. Let's go and get ready," and giving me a glare to take the froth of your pint, she turned and they both left the dining room.

Well that little encounter left a nasty taste, and I was made to feel even more guilty when Sophie failed to accompany her mother for the climb. I had preparations of my own to make, so tried to put the guilt to the back of my mind.

Now, I am not a mountaineer. I don't do rock climbing or all that tied together stuff, but I enjoy a good trek, and a challenge, and the views, and the sense of achievement. But I won't pretend it's not hard work, especially when you are mostly challenging yourself, and although there are times of camaraderie, and good conversation, the wall, when

314

you hit it, has to be overcome, and only you can do that. So you also need to be mentally prepared. A touch of guilt nagging at your soul is not good.

Kinabalu would prove to be a challenge. The path was narrow and rocky and very steep in parts. It was the sort of climb that should you lose concentration for just one moment, to listen to that bird, look at this flower or admire those views; you can guarantee you will stub your toe, trip over that rock or stumble down that scree.

It is a two day climb, therefore there was an overnight and you have to carry sufficient gear. It is nearly at sea level where you start, therefore it is hot and steamy and you need changes of shirt because they get soaked with sweat. Later it becomes cold and damp, and those wet shirts are very unwelcome. You have to carry warmer clothing and bedding. My favourite piece of advice for any trek comes from the Hitchhiker's Guide to the Galaxy; always carry a towel.

So, towel, check; dry shirts' check; spare socks, check; fleece and headtorch, check; toothbrush, paste and fresh underwear, check; water, hat and sun glasses check; sweets and packed lunch, check; small bottle of scotch, check (purely medicinal). And we begin.

The lower slopes were easy enough, if hot and humid, I loved the birds of paradise plants, and the variety of pitcher plants, all carnivorous. After a half hour I was beckoned aside to see a rafflesia. The excited little farmer who had caught my attention and led me away from the path explained that a rafflesia is a corpse plant. It is the biggest flower in the world, nearly two feet across, flowers only once every ten years, and gives off the stench of rotting meat. The good news was that it no longer smelt as it had flowered the week previously and was now dead. And that was the good news.

You have to plan your timing of arduous treks, especially in the tropics. The last thing you want to be doing is working at midday, when the sun is at its meanest. And I hadn't timed this well. I'd breakfasted too long, my shuttle had been late, there had been no sense of urgency and I'd taken time out to see the rafflesia. Thus I found

315

myself struggling as the going got tougher and the climb steeper. I found that earlier than expected I had to resort to zig-zag climbing, and resting for longer in between shorter sessions.

The climb was strenuous and strength sapping. I cleared the hot and humid rain forest, then the cooler but steeper cloud forest, then beyond the tree line amongst the bare rocks and low scrub there were two more miles of gruelling stepped trek. This was very slow going and I virtually collapsed into Laban Rata camp after six hours of relentless climb. I'd not experienced anything this tough since Dead Woman's Pass up into the Andes on the Inca Trail. Usually there is a bit of climb, followed by a bit of flat, then climb and flat, climb and flat. But not here.

I made it into a bunk, any bunk, sometime late in the afternoon and didn't emerge until gone dark to join other tired climbers for a simple meal of fried noodles. The accommodation was simple, a wooden hut with dorms and shared cold water facilities. There was a balcony and I saw Sophie's mum sitting there looking out over the shadowy mountain slopes. I thought I had better say something, its never any good bearing a grudge, it just eats away at you.

"Oh, hello. Look, I'm sorry if my comments upset you this morning, they were only meant to be light hearted."

She turned and saw me, and got up to leave the balcony, "Yeah, whatever!" she said disdainfully.

She whatevered me. I'd never been whatevered before, not even by my most difficult year 10 girls. I was left open-mouthed and bewildered.

I slept fitfully and fully clothed in freezing conditions until awoken by the guides at 2:15. A hot drink, snack biscuits and set off again. If anything the going was even more difficult. In the darkness you can see the lights of climbers who set off a little before you, almost vertically above you. A head torch is essential, you need all limbs to climb. In some sections there are ropes to haul yourself up onto the next ledge. Even though it was now cold and damp, with a wind that cut through, I still sweated profusely, which rapidly cools to become even more uncomfortable.

Finally I was beyond any vegetation, within reach of the summit, on a bare smooth granite slope which seemed endless. I recall sitting down, and being quite content to go no further, as people do in the killing zone of Everest, but luckily there were climbers behind me who urged me on, and I hauled myself to my feet and plodded on. All this just to see the sunrise. Remember, the darkest hour is just before dawn.

I made it to the summit with about five minutes to spare and stood on the top of the mountain with about a dozen other hardy souls. Sadly there wasn't the burst of sunshine which can greet the dawn, it was rather cloudy, and the light therefore came up gradually. It was however, quite wonderful to see the world appear below and all around you. It was a very real "I'm on top of the world, Ma!" moment.

There were a few minutes to take it all in. I asked a guide about Low's Gully, the notorious, inaccessible and therefore unexplored ravine which guards the easterly approach. Joking apart, people have wandered into here and never been seen again. The guide pointed it out and shook his head solemnly. Then it was time for the descent.

It was slow going down the granite slope, slippery wet with ankle breaking fissures awaiting any false step. This is always the same problem with descending. The lung-busting, muscle-straining part is behind you, but now the pressure is on the knees, and there is the fatigue factor. Your body is tired, your mind is tired, it is easy to lose concentration, and it only takes a moment.

I teemed up with Reuben, one of the English speaking guides, a lad under 25 with some excellent knowledge. Together we made it back to Laban Rata for a little breakfast and to replenish water. During that descent I lost count how many times I had to stop, disbelieving the scale of the ascent I had made, "How on earth had I managed climb that?"

After the lodge it was still difficult going, with many confounding moments, but we could take our time. Displaying a wisdom beyond his years, Reuben taught me about the Sandakan to Ranau Death Marches.

In 1942 British and Australian Prisoners of War, that had been captured in Singapore were shipped by their captors, the Japanese, to North Borneo to construct a military airfield. They were treated appallingly and had their officers removed during their imprisonment.

When the airfield they had slaved to construct was destroyed by allied bombing in early 1945 it was decided to move the prisoners 160 miles to Ranau. The Japanese feared an allied invasion. The prisoners were forced to march in three batches. All of the men were weakened by starvation, beatings and dysentery. Anyone who collapsed on the route was shot or just left to die. Of the few who reached Ranau they soon succumbed to disease, and those who did manage to survive until the Japanese surrender were murdered.

Over 2,700 men were known to have suffered and been killed in this awful atrocity. Only six men survived, all Australians, and these had managed to escape the marches and had been helped by local villagers. The atrocities weren't exclusive to soldiers. By the time the war had ended it is believed Borneo had lost 16% of its population.

Learning of such atrocities and the extent of man's inhumanity to man in such recent times, certainly puts modern day travails into perspective.

Reuben and I chatted all the way down, helping each other across some of the trickier parts of the terrain, with him also giving me a lesson on the local flora and fauna. So it came as a surprise when an excited little farmer suddenly jumped out to invite me to see his dead flower. No thanks, I said.

I bid Reuben a fond farewell as the bus returned me to my comfortable room at the Fairy Gardens hotel. My aching bones and muscles were badly in need of a rest. And as I lay on my bed, sleep about to overtake, I contemplated whether I had ever known any trek to be so difficult, so arduous, or so strength sapping. Certainly not since Kilimanjaro. Whatever!

Sepilok

The next morning, and I could have done with another day resting, my itinerary put me on a bus for Sandakan, on the east coast, and the Sepilok Orangutang Rehabilitation Centre some miles beyond. There was torrential rain as I left the hotel, which continued for most of the journey. The traffic was much easier this far out of KK, also helped by the conditions, but it was a disappointment that nearly the whole journey was spent travelling on a new, straight road through a never-ending palm oil plantation. It sounds ecologically sound to have a plantation, trees, but this one crop farm, a little like the eucalyptus forests of South Africa, consumes the whole of the landscape, and has displaced the diverse rainforest.

The rainforest provides nutrients for numerous plants, which support numerous insects, which support numerous birds, reptiles, amphibians and mammals. This has been destroyed for the sake of one plant, the palm oil palm. The whole plantation may as well be a barren desert. Nothing else grows here, nothing buzzes here, nothing crawls or flies or sings or flowers. In short, nothing lives here. There is no circle of life

Turning off for Sepilok was a mighty relief as the earth's ultimate habitat returned.

The journey hadn't been a total waste of time. I chatted with a charming couple. Craig, from Bristol was a tall man, not inclined to sports, which was a pity, he looked all the world like a powerful second row. His wife, Alex was the quietest Australian I'd ever met.

We bantered about the joys of being British; our NHS, the Royal Family, our armed forces, democracy, legal and education systems, the BBC. We laughed at how the old enemy, the French were so jealous of our institutions, and how those new interlopers the Americans found it hard to understand our stoicism and sense of humour in crises. We talked about sport and how we had introduced soccer and rugby and cricket to the world, and how our own sense of fair play is wrapped up in the rules and laws of those now worldwide and eminently worthwhile pastimes.

We were insufferable, and one or two of those around us chipped in with their observations. A Spanish couple disparaged the British cuisine, and we came back with fish and chips, and without an ounce of irony, the great British curry.

Someone mentioned the weather, about which every Brit is an expert.

"I know we don't have fantastic weather," admitted Craig, "but neither do we suffer the extremes of hurricanes or earthquakes, volcanoes or tsunamis. We don't freeze below 40C, nor bake above 40C"

I added that we had the Gulf Stream and the Jet Stream, and the four seasons, and temperate, crop growing weather.

"Mind you" I continued, "there was a tornado in Birmingham once. It knocked over a wheelie bin and someone reported seeing a trampoline cartwheeling down the road. That's about extreme as it gets." The bus laughed.

"Let's face it", Craig concluded. "It's the greatest gift God can give. To be born an Englishman!"

I'm sure most of the bus disagreed, but Craig was too big to argue with.

Later, whilst dozing on the journey, I was rethinking this episode and I realised it was the sort of codswallop ex-pats would spout whilst sitting outside a Spanish bar, ignoring the sweet irony they were living in Spain. The more I thought about it, the more I realised I should have taken the role of devil's advocate.

What about homelessness, our underfunded and understaffed hospitals, veteran suicides, record levels of illiteracy, overcrowded prisons, MP's expenses, unearned privilege, institutional racism and "yoof" culture. I could have gone on, but it wouldn't have been funny. Until I thought of the two biggies; cold, wet bank holidays and Strictly Eastenders.

Sepilok has had a bad press, as happens to so many well-intentioned causes. It is a rehabilitation centre for rescued and orphaned orangutans. Their objective is to nurse the injured and displaced back to health, rehabilitate them, and release them back into the wild. Because of logging and the development of the palm oil industry, their natural habitat is being swept away daily. Adults are poached, some youngsters stolen for the pet trade. Hence the need for a charity like Sepilok.

It's detractors argue that the apes are exploited for the tourist trade, and it is possibly true that some orangutans have become too dependent on human contact to be able to be returned to the wild. However the good people of Sepilok are operating in a poor country and against the powerful logging and palm oil companies. They are desperately trying to keep this wonderful creature from the brink of extinction. They should be applauded and supported, not criticised. Let the detractors fund them. And while they're waiting for that, us tourists will do the job.

On arrival we were given a short presentation about the work the conservationists do here. This included the news that as the apes are kept as naturally wild as possible, they might not make an appearance at all. It's not like feeding time at the zoo. Also, they hate the rain, and it was still raining. We were then led a little way through the rainforest, into the reserve and up to an elevated viewing platform.

The weather was awful. It was dark and wet and miserable. The only protection the viewing station gave was from the sun, a porous straw matting. The rain dripped through in big drips. We waited, our focus on a feeding station with fruit and bananas about 50 yards away. There were perhaps 20 of us, all Europeans, silently agonising over whether any orangutans would make an appearance. Our patience was eventually rewarded when an adolescent appeared. He, or she, looked like a hairy, orange old man with a bald head and bulging eyes. At this age it is not easy to distinguish between male and female. The males not having grown those elongated facial features prevalent in an adult male. He can weigh well over 20 stones.

This first one was upside down, having acrobatically arrived hand over hand along a rope bridge. Two more soon followed, and then a fourth, and the group settled down to eat their bananas and bamboo. It was like some ape game of twister the way they contorted around each other to get at the food.

We watched for a while, then some folk began to wander back for the souvenir shop, their orangutan appetite satiated. A few of us hardy souls remained in the rain.

Another youngster arrived, but with two babies clinging to her, and then another adolescent. This last one remained with the babies, all chewing on their bamboo stalks, huddled together against the rain as the other apes gradually melted away, back into the forest. I was last to leave, melting my way, back into the car park.

Kinabatangan River

We were now on our way to Sukau, but the bus stopped at a village called Mile Four for us to take lunch. This was not a tourist haunt, therefore we could take lunch with the locals inside a tin roofed warehouse, seated at long trestle tables. I sat with Craig and Alex and we were given plates of shell-on prawns. You can get into a mess de-shelling and eating prawns, so it was no surprise to me when bowls of hot liquid were placed in front of us. I wasn't going to make the typical tourist faux-pas of drinking the finger bowl, I thought, so began washing my fingers.

"Geoff," admonished Alex, quietly. "This is a poor village canteen in the poorest area of a poor country. Now stop being an idiot, and eat your soup properly."

Feeling suitably embarrassed I ate the rest of a fantastic meal, and returned to the bus which travelled another 30 miles on dirt tracks through palm oil plantations to a jetty on the river Kinabatangan where a launch was waiting to take its passengers to the Sukau Lodge.

The Sukau Rainforest Ecolodge is set back from the river bank on lawns in the rainforest. The lodges are on stilts, making excellent homes underneath for such rainforest specialities as giant spiders, millipedes and scorpions. The reception area, lounge, bar and restaurant were combined in a longhouse, typical of the local Iban villages, open to the elements but with sloping roofs to wash away the rain, of which there are many inches per year.

This was a delightful place to wander around, the riverside itself, up to the lodges and beyond the long room to the edge of an almost impenetrable forest.

I didn't have long to wait for the first of five river excursions included in my package; the Sunset Game Drive. Participants were instructed to meet at the jetty at 4:30. I arrived at 4:25 and there was a yellow eight seat rigid inflatable with outboard motor waiting (I do believe these have since gone electric, but for now, diesel powered meant the rear seats got a bit smelly), and I claimed the front seat. Presently Craig and Alex turned up and they occupied the bench behind me, then four women arrived and got into the back seats. Biku, our driver and guide was at the rear, hand on rudder, with the engine put-putting away. The passengers, and fellow residents introduced themselves, politely. The ones I didn't already know were Rachel, Sue, Nikki and Maureen, all 50 something southerners, I guessed Sussex or Surrey.

After ten minutes or so of polite conversation, we weren't moving, so I asked if there was any hold up.

"We're just waiting for Cynthia, she must have popped to the loo," said Sue.

Mention of the toilet was a mistake. "Oh, I think I'd better go," said Rachel, "And me" said Nikki. And they both got out to return to the lodge just as Cynthia appeared.

We waited another ten minutes and Sue and Alex decided they'd better go as well, and left just as Rachel and Nikki returned.

Craig and I exchanged glances with raised eyebrows. Dusk was arriving, Biku sat impassively and the remaining women chatted obliviously.

Their conversation was quite prim, "Ooh! That's a nice top, did you buy it here?

"Oooh! Thank you. No it was from Marks. I've not found anything to fit since I've been here. I like your bobble."

"Thank you, I bought it in that nice market we went to yesterday, I managed to get four for less than a pound."

"Wow, you'll have to show me where. I love those sandals."

And the mutual sartorial appreciation continued unabated. It was mind numbingly vacant, and my eyes were glazing over, which was not a good thing because it was getting darker and darker.

By the time we had a full complement and managed to set off, the sun had well and truly set, and the chance of seeing any wildlife had vanished with it. Inside I was seething.

We did manage to see one troop of proboscis monkeys settling down for the night, a couple of long-tailed langurs and a tree climbing monitor, but the excursion had lost at least an hour on the river.

Dinner was pleasant enough, but again rather spoilt by the incessant inane chatter about shopping and cosmetics and clothes. The objective of being in a game lodge is to keep conversation at hushed tones so as not to disturb any visiting wildlife. There was no chance of that. I was delighted, however to see a huge bright blue moth alight on the long house wall. Beautifully iridescent with wings at least ten inches across. You don't expect such displays from moths.

The next morning was a Dawn Game Drive and I was present at our launch at first light, and clambered into the front seat. Everyone else arrived with Cynthia last.

"Do you mind if I take the front seat, you had it last night," she requested politely.

"Well. Excuse me! Last night's excursion was ruined because you spent so long on the toilet. Then everyone else had to follow you. Thanks to your weak bladders we were an hour late setting off. By which time we had missed the sunset and any chance of seeing any animals. Now you want ME to give up my seat to sit in the back with all the fumes, when I've been the one who has been continually kept waiting!" I felt like shouting. Instead I just smiled, got out and into the only spare seat, next to Biku and adjacent to the exhaust.

Then Rachel got up, "I just need to pop to the loo, I won't be five minutes.

"Sit. Please. Boat go now," said Biku slowly, in a soft, almost menacing tone. Rachel seated herself, and remained tight lipped.

The boat moved away from the jetty and we sat back to enjoy the trip, Rachel cross-legged. I apologise if this is beginning to sound a touch misogynistic, but it did get worse.

The river had dark, smooth water, overlooked on both sides by a looming forest. At times the branches from the trees of either bank could almost meet. The river's widest point was about 100 yards, and there were lots of little inlets we could travel up and back in our search for wildlife. The early morning mist was still on the water with steam beginning to rise above the jungle. It made for an eerie silence when the engine was cut.

It seemed an age before our first sightings, then there was a small troop of langurs, then two rare, red-leaf langurs and excitedly a pair of orangutans sitting on top of a palm, maybe 200 yards away. We also saw a small monitor lizard, a skink, and another troop of lively proboscis monkeys.

Biku navigated our way into an oxbow lake and we beached for a jungle walk. The essential rules on any wildlife trek is silence, and a slow quiet stalking gait. Any game will hear you before you see them, and any sound or sharp movements and they will quickly melt into the forest and your chance is gone. We may as well have been on a Saturday morning stroll through Petticoat Market, the five women just intent on chatting and giggling.

I wanted to ask why they had bothered to come at all, if their sole intention was to spoil it for everybody else. But unfortunately I was too polite and to be honest very aware I was outnumbered.

The walk was very muddy due to the recent rains and we were warned to look out for leeches, another cause for silly squealing and squirming. In the event all we saw were butterflies and millipedes.

On our return there were heron and kingfishers and dragonflies, but this was all a poor return for four hours on the water and in the jungle. Or maybe I was just feeling a little paranoid because of the antics of the women. We were never going to see leopard, pygmy elephant and sun bears which are all endangered.

Later that day, Craig and myself went with Biku on an afternoon cruise and we saw three more troops of proboscis monkeys, both short and long tail macaques, a fish eagle, magnificent stork billed kingfishers, swiftlets and their nests, and hornbills, the highlight being as Biku called them, "Mrs and Mrs Rhinoceros Hornbill", flying alongside then overhead.

Proboscis monkeys are some of the more unusual members of the primate family. The males especially display large extended noses looking like miniature trunks. And they have none of the acrobatic agility shown by their cousins the gibbons, which are also indigenous. They are a rather sedentary monkey due to their chosen diet. They eat leaves, and you need to consume a huge amount of this greenery in order to extract any nutrition. Hence they sit amongst the branches, chewing rather comically with their huge flappy noses and round, distended tummies. Luckily predators of the proboscis monkey are few and far between.

After dinner we went on River Boat Trip number four, a night drive with searchlight. We saw several owls and kingfishers, a small crocodile and a glimpse of a brown civet, but the highlight was three snakes. Firstly a six foot python, then a black and yellow (signals danger) Rawling's snake, also about six feet long, and finally a huge python. It lay on the river bank, and our light must have disturbed it. It raised its large head, sniffed the air with its tongue and slid away for what seemed an age. It was at least eight inches diameter at its thickest, and Biku estimated about 25 feet long.

The whole night sky was wonderful. All clouds had now disappeared, presenting us with a full sky of stars and the Milky Way overhead. We chugged slowly back to the lodge and were graced with several shooting stars.

Pulau Tiga Island

I left Sukau Lodge the next morning, and as our launch went up river we passed a yellow boat with several schoolchildren going down. Now that's what I call a school run. My destination was Sandikan Airport and four hours later I was flying over the peak of Kinabalu before descending into KK. At 4pm I was on a ferry, no more than a speedboat. It skipped over the waves of the Southern China Sea, through Kimanis Bay, managing to soak everyone, luggage and all. In half an hour it deposited me on "Survivor Island" Pulau Tiga.

The Pulau Tiga hotel was an unpretentious beach dwelling. Just an open air longhouse and a number of simple beach shack rooms. I had a wander and discovered hammocks and swings slung between the palm trees fringing the beach. Around the back of the longhouse were the kitchens and garbage area where about a dozen huge monitors hung around after scraps. The largest was easily six feet from nose to tail, almost like a Komodo dragon. There was a coral reef right on the beach, ideal for snorkelling, and I had a glorious hour in the water before night fell.

Over drinks before dinner I met up with Roger, an amateur dramatics Lancastrian and Carol and Ann, two middle aged Bristolians who worked for a firm of solicitors, "we're both qualified for legal 'sex'," they proudly announced.

I had thought Pulau Tiga must be Malay for survival, but they put me right. Apparently "Survivor" had been a British reality television show filmed here, where attractive young people had to undertake survival tasks in order not to be voted off.

As we went into dinner there was an almighty crash, bang, wallop which had all guests running for cover and I admit I jumped out of my skin. The waiters batted not a single eyelid, apparently noisy thunderstorms are quite common. The resulting deluge was the most violent rainstorm I had ever witnessed. Half an hour later you would not have thought there had been anything untoward.

We took our beers out onto the jetty where a couple of waiters were fishing with rod and line. There was a half moon ready to set which glistened on the water and a sky full of stars, the Milky Way itself stretched overhead. Apropos of nothing, Roger sang and acted "If I were a Rich Man " Tevye's dream and plea to the good Lord from Fiddler on the Roof. We all joined in with the beedle beedle bums and deedle deedle eyes, the two fishermen must have thought us quite mad, but on that jetty, on that island, under those stars, we all felt very wealthy indeed.

I rose at dawn, wanting to be on the coral reef. I found that it extended from the beach like a huge horseshoe. Sadly the previous night's storm had churned up and muddied the water, not great snorkelling conditions.

After breakfast I joined Roger, Carol and Ann for a discovery walk around the island. My legs had just about fully recovered from Kinabalu and the walk had everything the oxbow lake had lacked. This was one of three tiny islands created by an earthquake and volcanic eruption in 1897, yet the forest seemed ancient, some of the trees were breathtakingly majestic. We came across two mud bubbling baths, but I didn't want to smell of sulphur and wimped out from immersion. There was a troop of monkeys, monitors galore, smaller lizards, butterflies, crabs and mudskippers, all backed by the constant screeching of cicadas and almost unbelievable humidity.

We crossed over the centre of the island, past a little wooden research post on stilts which appeared uninhabited apart from a couple of sleeping dogs. The other side of the island was pristine forest and beach, with no human habitation, therefore exhibited the desert island syndrome. Sadly there was a build up of flotsam and jetsam, or less romantically, litter, at the tide line. Despite this we had a dip and a splash and a swim in the warm sea, giving the girls the opportunity to wash off the mud that caked them following their mud baths.

We returned for a light lunch and I spent the afternoon snorkelling on the horseshoe. The water had now cleared and the colours of the crazily shaped corals and variety of tropical fish were once again wonderful.

By late afternoon it was cool enough for another walk and we took the Tiga trail to the north of the island and experienced more of this place's marvellous flora and fauna.

Whilst I'd been in the sea during the afternoon, Carol had had a problem in the room she shared with Ann. She told us that she went to the room to change and there was a strange, mad drumming noise coming from the plastic shower cubicle (I never said it was four star!). She looked through the door and saw a large lizard scampering up and down and round and round the walls in a mad panic. The poor thing, about the size of a small cat, was in a terrible state, and the drumming of his feet just got faster and faster in its blind terror.

Carol contacted reception to come and free the stricken animal, and they sent two boys down to deal with it. Unfortunately the lads hadn't caught the mood of the moment, entered the room and dispatched the poor animal, then grinned with satisfaction as they showed the now mortified Carol and Ann back into their now peaceful room with the blood spattered shower cubicle.

"Funny," said Carol, who didn't seem in the least amused, "how dispatched can have subtle meanings. We wanted the poor creature evicted, and they returned it to its maker. One and the same thing, I suppose."

Other than the slaughtered lizard story the afternoon trek was gorgeous. Monkeys and mud skippers, trees and flowers, white beaches and sea views, sunshine and shade whenever you wanted. Stop and rest and everything is there. Time to smell the flowers.

In the evening after relaxing beers there was a red snapper dinner and we went out to the jetty to serenade the fishermen again. This time Roger led us on a tour of the Glums, Les Misérables. A musical I love, but know too little to join in, and there aren't too many jiggy moments. One Day More, because that's what we had left here, was a little poignant, but his Master of the House even had the fishing lads grinning. And the stars still shone.

Whilst snorkelling on my final day I came across three sea snakes, banded kraits. These are among the most venomous creatures in the world, about a yard long but their heads and mouths are so small, with no discernible jaw line that they can't get purchase around an arm or leg, say. But if you accidentally got your fingers in the way, untangling them from nets, for example, you'd be lucky to survive. I didn't know this at the time, thought they were eels, and ignored them.

Of much more interest to me were the wrasses, squirrels, parrots, batfishes, angels, butterflies, damsels, surgeons, sergeant-majors and triggers. And, joy of joys, clown fish, three families, each a pair, darting in and out of their brown anemone home, nurturing dozens of little black offspring.

I taught Roger to snorkel, he had no idea of the world beneath the waves, and he took to it like a duck to water, enchanted.

I left the island after lunch, a speedboat back to KK then a room at an old friend, the Beverley for a few hours before flying home. Another dream banked, memories galore, and what have we learned?

Never underestimate a woman's need for the loo, her capacity to undermine you, and their ability to take advantage of your courtesy.

On an unrelated note, not all snakes are dangerous, and our other primate cousins, orangutans, gibbons, langurs and proboscis, have a far more raw deal than us.

Finally, that a drizzly Monday lunchtime spent parked up in West Bromwich in mid-winter doesn't have to be the nightmare it sounds.

Not when the likes of Borneo beckons.

Indonesia, Islands and Dragons

There are thousands of islands which link the land masses of Australia and South East Asia. Variously known as the Malay archipelago, or the East Indies, or Maritime Southeast Asia, they have featured heavily in world history since the route was used to migrate man and mammal into Australasia; mammals evolving into marsupials. Some islands are huge with mass populations, many are tiny formations of atolls.

Always interested in the region, I remember reading Nathaniel's Nutmeg by Giles Milton, about the wars between the Dutch, Portuguese and British for control of the Spice Islands of the Banda Sea. I discovered that around the same time the Earth was losing its last dodo, Catholics were plotting to blow up a Scottish King, Newton was publishing his Principia as the basis for the physics of the universe and both the Renaissance and the slave trade were in full swing, the major European powers were fighting over pepper, cloves and nutmeg.

All of these islands of the South Seas were invaded and fought over by European nations who left legacies. The people, their land, trade, religions and societies have all developed and evolved because of these alien incursions. They are at relative peace now, although of course, all islands controlled by larger neighbours have dreams and manifestos for independence. The last major upheaval for this part of the world was the awful Japanese occupation which the Allies fought and managed to overcome by August 1945. Mother Earth still manages to create her own occasional chaotic moments, of course, with typhoons, volcanic eruptions, earthquakes and tsunamis

This is a beautiful part of the world, Bali is an island consistently voted top of travellers' bucket list destinations, and this was as far south and east that I intended to explore for my Asian odyssey. Bali was the lure, but in years gone by when there were maps that couldn't quite encompass the whole of the Earth, explorers gave a special name to the mysterious unknown. "Here be Dragons" they said.

Beyond Bali and Lombok, off the eastern shore of Flores lie two tiny islands, Rinca and Komodo. That is why I decided to make this trip, my epilogue for Asia. For these islands are no longer mysterious and unexplored and you don't have to use wild imaginations. They are within reach, and here, there most definitely are, dragons!

Ubud

I flew into Denpasar and arrived late on a Saturday evening, via Dubai and from Birmingham (Friday 9:45 pm departure). My body was saying lunchtime, but here it was nearly time for bed. A young man was there to collect me, Pieter, dark, slim and handsome in jeans and tee shirt. We drove inland, up to the town of Ubud, the cultural capital, and we chatted. I discovered he was Muslim from Jakarta on the island of Java. His wife was a teacher and together they have a four year old daughter. He explained that although the vast majority of Indonesians followed Islam, Bali was a Hindu island, and Flores, Christian.

Pieter dropped me at Nick's Pension at midnight and told me he'd see me for breakfast. My vague recollection of that dead-of-night arrival was inky black sky above, a bright green paddy field between reception and my room, the all pervading scent of frangipani and the statue of Ganesha in the garden, a familiar friend.

Bali is a similar shape, but a little larger than Majorca. Forested with volcanoes, paddy fields and surrounded by coral reefs, it is a favourite holiday destination for Australians, Chinese and World backpackers. It can be a little lively, with so many young visitors.

Personally I was keen to meet local people to find out a little of their culture. Straight after breakfast Pieter walked me to the Widyaguna School, a small school with 98 children of varying disabilities. They are bussed in from all over the island.

There were other visitors (funding has to be sourced) and the children performed a Tai Chi style loosener before launching into the Macarena to much applause and laughter. We were shown around by Ketut who runs the place with his wife Nyoman. He was particularly proud of his cattle who produced building materials (dung), medicines (urine), gas to power the kitchens and generator, and fertiliser for the farm produce. I sat in on a couple of lessons before Nyoman took groups aside to make temple offerings out of coconut leaves and flowers. It was like Generation Game meets Blue Peter; "Here is one I made earlier, now you make one". I didn't join in. I hate the make-the-tourist-look-foolish games. I don't need games.

It was a lovely morning as Ketut showed us around their home and their family shrine. He explained how every aspect of a Balinese household is in perfect harmony with ancestors, the forest, the earth, and fellow animals. Nyoman told us that the first four children of any family had to be named Wayan, Gede, Nyoman and Putu, but since Bali was becoming overpopulated a two children policy was in force. No more Nyomans and Putus.

I met grandma whose toothless, wrinkly grin and a twinkle in her eyes displayed a mischievous personality, along with her tee shirt slogan "This Boy Loves His Girlfriend Too Much".

We took lunch with the children and waved them goodbye.

Pieter drove me to the town of Tampaksining which housed the Pura Turta Empul Temple. It was quite a climb, but relatively cool under a thick canopy. I love Hindu temples with their pagodas, sculptures, frescoes,and curly, knobbly eaves, walls and gateways. Gods and goddesses spring up everywhere, sometimes fierce, often smiling and always entertaining. I was particularly engaged with one goddess who was suckling a baby, the baby twiddling her other nipple.

Before entry I had to dress in turban and sarong, and climbed to the top of the granite complex to where a spring bubbles up through quicksand which would swallow bathers whole. This is where many people leave their flower offerings, and there were flowers everywhere, adding to the colours and fragrance of the occasion. The temple is one of Bali's most holy and the spring is managed to flow into three pools, the lowest is reserved for penitents to perform their purification rituals. Everyone gets rather wet.

Out of the temple and we descended 300 steps to the Royal Tombs, shrines cut into the cliff side, which dated from the 12th to 15th centuries and were originally excavated by Thomas Stanford Raffles, the founder of modern Singapore. It was a lovely trek down alongside a rushing Pakerisan river, but the buildings themselves, the Gunung Kawi were less than spectacular; just empty, featureless rooms.

However, it was warmer and clammier further down the hill, and there was atmospheric smoke, which didn't seem natural. Then I rounded a corner and saw the source of the smoke was a film crew. Someone was waving a charcoal brazier around whilst a director, camera and sound staff were following a couple of actors in some sort of chase or fight scene. It was all very exciting, much more so than the tombs they were running in and out of.

"Look," I pointed and announced "We've found Baliwood." I turned to the various visitors, smug with my pun. Not a titter.

We climbed back out of the valley, and this is where the souvenir sellers were concentrated, just like the gift shop at the exit of an art gallery. All of the stalls were selling attractive wooden carvings representing features of the islands,; turtles, exotic birds, lizards, and then some which might be from another holiday destination, elephant, giraffe and zebra. Butterflies were everywhere (real, not wooden).

About half way up I stopped for an ice cream refreshment when all hell broke loose at the next stall. An old man leapt to his feet, up turning his chair, and a woman was running around beating the ground with a long broom.

"Snake," said Pieter.

That evening back at Nick's Pension we dined on beer, steamed fish and vegetables, rather exotically spicy, and I had an early night. It had been quite a weekend.

Pieter drove me south-east to Sanur the next morning. Leaving Ubud we drove past a monkey forest. That's wonderful I told Pieter, but surely the whole of Bali is a monkey forest, they shouldn't need a special sanctuary. Sadly not, deforestation, even on the most beautiful island in the world has been allowed to destroy valuable habitat.

Sanur

Sanur was a lively coastal resort and the Puri Sanding hotel a peaceful refuge back from the main road. Many beach locations in Bali have been turned into their equivalent of Benidorm.

"You know Blackpool?" Pieter asked. "The Aussies call it. What is Blackpool?" he asked innocently. It made for an interesting lunchtime conversation.

From my hotel, across the busy road then down a dirt track by the side of the posher hotels, was the cycle and promenade path which runs along the beach. Palms and pine trees make up the most shade for the narrow esplanade (or is it a promenade, or perhaps a corniche, or probably just the track at the back of the beach). Along this were the shack shops, open air restaurants, hotel gardens and temples.

It was a splendid walk. Looking out to sea there was a pretty pagoda on a promontory, evidently favoured by wedding parties for their photographs. Along the beach lay colourful jukung fishing boats, each angled by their anchored outrigger. On the path people strolled arm in arm and nodded greetings with smiles. The surf could be heard as it lapped the shore and the gentle chiming of rhythmic gamelan music helped to create an atmosphere of peaceful serenity.

I found a turtle hatchery and popped in to see some of the larger ones rescued from injury. A lovely reminder of my time in Sri Lanka. There was a temple made completely of coral which had some interesting instruction as to who could not be admitted. Luckily neither was I pregnant, menstruating nor breast feeding, so I was allowed into the "Tample", in which I found some comically obese (male) statues amid the pretty flower offerings.

Presently I turned and strolled back the way I had come. As dusk fell thousands of fairy lights began to twinkle in the twilight adding to the magic of the moment.

That night I ate at the hotel with Pieter, and we strolled down to one of the bars for some beers and live music. Pieter informed me that when we embark on the second leg of my itinerary, we would be joined by a group arriving tomorrow morning. I had plans for the morning so wouldn't meet them till the evening. He proposed we visit a beach front fish restaurant for the evening. OK by me.

I walked about a mile north the next morning to meet the boat excursion I had booked, and to my chagrin there were hundreds of tourists milling around. All with the same thoughts, I thought. Then it became apparent this was the port from where several excursions departed.

I joined the queue to redeem my voucher.

"Flying Dolphin, leaves in 15 minutes. Please take seat and shoes off," She was a pretty young girl who booked me in, and while I waited for computer confirmation, she told me she was a student at the local Udayana University, working here for the season. She wanted to come to England or Germany to improve her English. Yes, I said, either would be good.

The trip was out to Nusa Penida island and was by hydrofoil, so very fast and exciting, flying across the waves. Eight of us then transferred into a smaller skiff for our "snorkelling extravaganza". It was unfortunately pure tourist fare, so you followed the itinerary, despite the conditions. Firstly out to Manta Point to swim with manta rays. There were obviously no rays here, so we just had a 15 minute snorkel amongst other boats and murky waters. Then around to the north of the island and four more dives which were lovely in the shallow warm waters with plenty of coral and small fish, if nothing spectacular. Late on my fingers became really pruned and the little butterflies, damsels and sergeant majors enjoyed nibbling at them. That was the highlight, then another fast and furious "flight" back to Sanur.

Mind you, lunch had been interesting. Each boat disgorges to coincide with trestle tables being freed up in the communal restaurant. Standard chicken and rice, very adequate. I had a stroll around the beach which had huge swings to make your girlfriend squeal, and pleasant shaded sunbeds on which to relax, but the best amusement was to watch the Chinese tourists.

There were a hundred or so, all universally dressed in yellow hats and life preservers, and all lined up in twos in three lines. First onto the banana, an inflatable pulled by a speedboat. Six get on, sitting astride the banana and behind each other. The boat takes them out for thirty seconds and brings them straight back in again. And they loved it, laughing and giggling amongst themselves. Then onto the settee, another inflatable pulled by a speedboat. On this they sat four abreast. Again 30 seconds out and 30 seconds back, and they loved that one as well. Finally onto the jet ski, not driving themselves, but two seated pillion behind the Balinese driver. 30 seconds out and 30 seconds back, and again they were all in stitches. Very easy to please, someone was making a fortune out of these gullible guys.

During the return I met Jack the angry Jock, from Perth, Australia, retired and loving his retirement in the new world. To be fair he was just Jack the Jock until the crew misplaced his shoes and he lost his cool.

I walked back to the hotel along the beach, fairy lights beginning to twinkle again, happy with my sun, sand and swimming day.

That night I met up with the group who would be my companions for the next leg of my journey. We had a meal on the beach, a lovely setting and there were firework displays to enjoy, but the service and fare were not up to much.

You had to go into the kitchen to choose your fish which was priced by weight. It was a take it or leave it level of service. Most of the fishes were big enough to feed the whole table, and I didn't know the group so well yet as to suggest shares, so I had to choose the smallest I could find, which was still well over a kilo (their weight unit) and wasn't half as tasty as a red snapper, always my fish of choice.

My new companions were interesting, There were six women, four older than me, two of whom were self-styled grotty grannies. The one, Jane, dressed herself up as The Old Hag from Snow White to present her friend, Sue, with a birthday surprise. No make up required, just the removal of her false teeth and the addition of a shawl. Frightening.

Pieter had a cultural day planned for us, my last day on Bali. We piled into a minibus early morning and drove through Sanur and along the coast. We could see a huge statue in the distance, and once we had passed the strip of land, a peninsular which houses Denpasar airport, it was obvious that was our destination.

The Garuda Wisnu Kencana National Park is an ambitious project which has had its detractors. Why spend a fortune on this white elephant (green eagle, actually) when there is so much poverty on Bali and in the whole of Indonesia? That was the argument. But national pride, employment for hundreds, utilising a barren spit of land, and the attraction of tourist dollars had been a valid counter. When all the detractors could come back with was "it spoils the natural balance of the island", you know the bureaucrats and politicians have won.

The statue, which is at the centre of the attraction as well as the controversy, can be seen for miles around, especially by people entering the island by air. It is an impressive 400 feet high and features the god Vishnu wearing a golden crown and riding his steed the Garuda. The Garuda in this case manifests itself as a bird of prey with outstretched wings. Pieter proudly tells us it is the tallest stand alone statue in the world, but a higher one was currently under construction in India. To give it some perspective it is 100 feet higher than the Statue of Liberty.

It was a good walk, even in the searing heat, through gardens and amphitheatres, past pools and parks and sculptures. The area is so large, the staff go around on segways. From the plinth of the statue itself the views back across the peninsular were indeed impressive. The cultural park is a centre and an arena for performances of both local and international importance. Iron Maiden played here to a crowd of over 7,000.

Following a picnic lunch we piled back into the minibus for the short trip to the Uluwatu Temple complex on the other side of the isthmus. This Hindu sea temple is perched on a cliff edge, 250 feet above the waves which crash constantly onto the rocks below. The temple itself is impressive but the views from the walls above the cliffs, for about half a mile either side of the temple were wonderful. I walked them from one magnificent end to the other, this must be one of the most beautiful places in the world. And you are constantly accompanied by families of macaque monkeys.

I had followed them on the west side as they bounded along the walls and pathways, babies clinging to their mother's breasts, then walked down to the temple and along to the eastern extreme. In fairness there were plenty of signs around warning to beware of the monkeys, who can bite, and have a reputation for thievery. I didn't expect to fall victim myself, however.

As I walked, marvelling at the views, watching the rollers come in from the ocean and crash and explode on the rocks below, a guard tapped me on the shoulder, "Look after your sunglasses," he advised.

"Sure, OK", I confirmed.

I walked to the end, climbed down some steps to a viewing ledge. "Be careful of your glasses," He had come up from behind me and warned me again.

"Yes, OK!", I replied confidently and a touch irritably.

I came up from the viewing point and he caught my eye again, indicating I hold on to my hat and glasses. Yes OK, I mouthed, and smiled again.

Five minutes later I was looking over the wall again at the view when suddenly something jumped onto my shoulders and a pair of tiny hands quickly, but firmly lifted off my sunglasses, and they were gone. I looked up and there was my attacker, a large monkey sitting atop a tall wooden post, calmly eating my sunglasses.

What could I do? The monkey was looking at me, not gloating in any way, simply waiting for my next move. I didn't realise, but the monkey wasn't really interested in my sunglasses at all, simply that which possession of them can bring. He knows.

I looked around and saw the guard about 100 yards away. I walked up to him.

"Hello, erm, can you help me. It appears that monkey (I pointed at the offender) has stolen my sunglasses. Is there anything you can do?" I was thinking catapult, or shout at him, or throw a stick at it, or something like that.

He looked at me and laughed, "Ah, you are the OK guy"

I nodded sheepishly, and he indicated I should follow him. When we reached the monkey, who had waited with great patience, the guard reached into his pocket and brought out a plastic bag of sweets. He threw the ransom up to the monkey who caught it adeptly, and dropped the kidnapped item to the floor.

"OK?" chuckled the guard, "You sure you're OK?"

"Yes, I'm sure. Thank you. I'll put them in my pocket," and I reached down to recover my property. No harm done, just the soft nose pads chewed off.

You have to be impressed with the intelligence of these primates. There is no malice or violence in what they do, they have simply learned how to steal and barter for treats. Clever!

Over the next two hours I came across this particular guide several times, and each time he saw me he announced happily to everyone within earshot; "Hello, here is the 'I'm OK' guy".

At 5:30 Pieter collected us all together and we took seats in the amphitheatre. Below us a Kecak dance performance was about to take place, based on a story from the Ramayana. Beyond the temple buildings and across the silver ocean the sun was beginning to set.

Almost on cue a Jukung fishing boat sailed across the reddening sun. The anticipation as people took their seats was very real, clear and unmistakable. Tonight there would be fire.

The basic story: Family enter magic forest, wicked king disguised as golden deer separates them and kidnaps beautiful girl. Girl's fiancé employs white monkey to rescue her, but he is captured and tied to pyre, but as the fire is lit he escapes and turns the tables. Girl and monkey flee to safety, evil king burns.

The story was secondary to the spectacle. No music but a choir of 50 semi-naked men seated, chanting and swaying throughout. Lots of costumes and dancing and posturing and acrobatics, with the climax of huge fireballs being kicked all around the stage. Sparks and flames and smoke everywhere. Add to this the classic pantomime fare of booing the baddies, and cheering the goodies, with the white monkey being everybody's hero, and an excellent evening was had by all.

We returned to say goodbye to Bali with a steak meal at the hotel and were up at dawn for the morning flight to Flores.

Flores, Moni

And what a flight it was. From the airport you can clearly see the Vishnu Garuda statue, and as we rose into the air we flew above it, turning then to fly towards Lombok. We landed briefly at Labuan Bajo for an exchange of passengers, then back into the air for an hour, flying over more islands and setting down at Ende on the island of Flores. As we left the aeroplane there were huge murals of dragons on the side of the terminal building, indicating this to be their gateway.

It was a two hour drive up to Moni and the Kelimutu Lakes, so we stopped here for an opportunity to buy provisions. I had seen the peninsular Ende sits on as we came in to land, and it was a very pretty seaside area. However we were well off the beaten track and the town, and as I was to discover the whole of Flores island, is not geared up for foreign tourists. This is no Bali (nor Blackpool).

Over the previous 24 hours I had become better acquainted with the group. We needed to gel as we would be spending the next few days travelling from this eastern outpost to the far west of this elongated island, shaped similarly to Crete. It would be a long time in a cramped, bouncing minibus.

Together with Pieter, myself and our driver Wawen; there were the two self-styled grotty grannies, Jane and Sue, Jenny a single dog boarder from Redditch, Tony, a quiet Canadian widower, Leslie a rather large if stereotypically cheerful lady, and two younger ones; Marina a very pleasant Swiss teacher and Mary, an Australian headcase who kept the whole crew amused.

Marina and Mary had met up on a trip to Kenya some years previously and now synchronised their adventures. Whilst Marina was mousey and retiring, Mary was all bounce and flounce, a ready smile with tousled black hair.

I had noticed more and more women joining these small group exploration tours over the years, a safe and social way to see the four corners of the planet. I have also concluded that in these far flung destinations you either saw young backpackers enjoying their gap year, or adventurers from the grey market. In fact 80% of solo travellers are over 45, with a ratio of two nomadic Nora's to every one gallivanting Geoff. I asked where all the inbetweeners could be found. They're all in Benidorm with their kids, Jane answered.

All of these things we pondered as we sat on the roadside in the sunshine and ate local ice cream. It is a tradition I like to recommend to fellow travellers. Arrive at a new place, try their ice cream. Then Wawen indicated the bus was ready.

It was not far to the hillside village of Moni, but with difficult roads and switchback hairpins climbing up through the rainforest, the going was tough and slow. I loved the mini forests of bamboo we saw, imagine bamboo stalks more than a foot in diameter, and you can guess the giant size of these grasses. There was another feature which struck me, the litter. Everywhere where there was a gap in the forest, garbage had been tipped. It was most unfortunate and a sad reflection on areas of the world we imagine to be paradise, to be blighted by such a modern disease.

There were bright spots, though, some flat areas of shiny green paddy fields framed against the volcanoes we were climbing towards. And I was seated next to our antipodean, Mary, and she took the opportunity to quiz me.

"Hey Jiff. Why do the English live in boxes?"

I tried to explain the need for green belt, the building of housing estates with affordable housing, and that most of the rest of Europe live in apartments.

"So, Jiff, why can't the English eat spicy food?

I informed her that curry was our new national dish, with Balti houses and chicken tikka masala invented in Birmingham. My home town now has more curry houses than pubs.

But her stereotyped image of the English (of course, in common with Americans, she cannot distinguish between English and British, despite being from Melbourne) was ingrained and I knew my explanations had fallen on stony ground when in mid-sentence she suddenly shouted, "Ooh, look everyone, there's an antelope, over there in that field, how lovely!"

I looked. "I'm afraid it's a cow," I tried to let her down gently.

Some minutes later, "Did anyone see my antelope, no-one said when I saw it?"

"Mary, it was a cow," I said.

"Well it might have been a water buck."

"No, Mary, it was tethered, it was a cow."

"But it was brown."

"It was a brown cow."

Mary settled down and sulked.

As we climbed further out of Ende, the roads became poorer, with many landslips Wawen had to swerve to avoid. The only other traffic was either lorries or motor cycles. Cars were rare indeed. We passed small villages of shacks with tin roofs, old folk relaxing in the shade, impeccably dressed schoolchildren skipping along. Lunch was at a roadside cafe, banana fritters in a cheese and chocolate sauce, interesting and not unpleasant.

We finally arrived at the Kelimutu Eco Lodge, on the other side of Moni village. We were nearly 5,000 feet above sea level, in a narrow river valley with beautiful gardens where the fruit and veg for the hotel kitchen was grown. It was an idyllic location. Beyond the gardens, across the river were rice paddies, and colourful hillsides. We were all billeted in tasteful little cottages, and I sat on my porch enjoying the view in perfect peace.

Apparently Jenny was next door and she suddenly appeared on her balcony to hang out some washing. When a mature lady wanders into view wearing nothing but her humongous bra and big knickers you try to look away, but there are some images which once seen, can't be unseen.

We met in reception at 3:30 for a walk around a typical Flores village. Pieter explained we would be visiting the Kelimutu Lakes the following morning.

Out of the Eco Lodge, we walked up the road, down the sides of which gushed the river in two huge gullies, then left into the forest and the small fields in which the homes grew their produce. I was struck by the lack of wildlife, no birdsong. Pieter explained that the introduction of clove trees, cultivated for export, had dried up the soil, discouraging insects, bees, butterflies, lizards, birds and mammals. Well done, civilisation, another eco cock-up.

We eventually came to a waterfall, actually two waterfalls, one of rainwater, one draining the volcanic lakes. Where the waters met, the river became milky white, a chemical reaction of minerals.

In the evening we walked up to the Moni's Place restaurant, an open terrace with a lovely view over the valley. There was cold Bintang beer, and tasty vegetable curry with local ginger and honey, and rock and roll music. The owner/chef was very proud of his 1950's juke box.

The next morning, bright and early we set off from the hotel for the Kelimutu Lakes. We drove through Moni then up and up on a switchback road to the car park. The lakes are pools of different colours that have developed inside three volcano craters next to each other. The colours are reputed to change from reds to blues to black depending on the activity of the fumaroles beneath them. It is no wonder they are revered as heavenly by the local population, a very holy site.

The walk up to the first, the Lake of Enchantment was fairly arduous due to the slope and heat, and we eventually arrived safely but strung out, to see the dark, turquoise waters. There were different shades according to the shadows the walls struck. A sheer rock wall separated this from the higher Lake of Youth which had waters of a milky light blue. At the top of this climb was a platform which had the most wonderful panorama of the whole area. A little further on and the Lake of the Elderly which had much more vegetation growing from its steep walls, reflected green.

I ran from one pool to the next, marvelling at the different shades. Tiny zephyrs created ripples of differing hues amongst the shadows. The way the light glistened across the water reminded me of John Denver's "Sunshine On My Shoulders", a joyous little celebration of a song I would sing to my grandchildren when they were babes in arms. And sunshine on the water always reminds me of them. Makes me smile

I'd been seated on the platform, legs dangling over the edge, enjoying the warmth of the sun and taking in the views, and quietly singing to myself, when Leslie arrived. She had had quite a struggle, needing two walking poles and a lot of guts to get herself up here. She was still cheerful though, just happy to have made it. I gave her a guided tour of the three lakes then helped her up onto the platform and sat beside her.

"Isn't it beautiful," she sighed, "the melodic birdsong, the gentle breeze, the mountains beyond, the colours, the flowers, and there, the sunshine on the water," she smiled.

I stayed with her for the descent, the uneven and loose stones underfoot making it quite perilous. She gave me one of her poles, and we linked arms.

Wawan drove us down to Moni's Place for a lunch of rice and beans with stir fried vegetables and tofu in a spicy tomato sauce. Sounds better than it was, and the chef insisted we drank the local hooch, arak. It tasted earthy. I wasn't a fan

In the afternoon I wandered the gardens then descended to the river and found a rickety bridge to cross. The other side were rice paddies which have to be terraced, so I followed the irrigation channels, sadly choked with plastic bottles and other rubbish. I gradually climbed higher until I had a good view of the Eco Lodge below. I sat down and was joined by Joseph, who farmed this land. We chatted a while and he told me of his ambition to grow chocolate to sell in Ende. He also cultivated fish in his irrigation pools which he sold to the local restaurants.

Back at the river a small herd of cattle had arrived to drink, there were squadrons of dragonflies and suddenly some small lizards scuttling around. That night I dreamed of the forests of Borneo, the proboscis monkeys, monitors, snakes and hornbills. Here nothing in comparison, just two geckos in my room, and swallows at dawn which was cool with a heavy mountain dew.

We were a little delayed leaving the Eco Lodge and got caught by roadworks on the way back down to Ende. Road closures are slightly different here, there's not temporary traffic lights to be erected and operated. The road was actually closed with no possible diversion for two hours. We watched as the huge diggers were engaged building a new road higher up the mountain, and causing great rocks to crash down onto our road. The great swinging robotic arms of over twenty machines made for quite a balletic display, but this was really frustrating, we had places to go. No sooner had we been released to continue our journey than the girls asked Wawen to stop so they could take photos of a paddy field. I bit my tongue.

Bajawa

It took most of the day to reach Bajawa. The journey took us down into Ende and out the other side, along the coast road with lovely views of the Ende isthmus, then a stop for a grilled fish lunch at Blue Stone Beach. Back onto the coast road and the litter on the beaches was appalling, sometimes piled six feet high. My God, what are we doing to our planet.

We eventually pulled into the hill town of Bajawa and the awful Edelweiss hotel when darkness had already fallen. Feeling rather frustrated I just took beer and bed.

It had been a very frustrating day, and when I came to review it I recalled this conversation I had with Mary.

"Hey Jiff." Here comes another silly question, I thought.

"You have any trouble with the blacks in England?"

"I'm sorry!" I could barely believe I'd heard the question.

"Well, in Oz, we've got the Abos, and they can be a big problem. They think they own the place. Then we've got people from Asia, and boat people, and all sorts trying to get in and take advantage of our benefits."

"It's a big place, Australia. Surely there is room for all sorts. And, the Aborigines, didn't they actually own the place before you moved in?"

I told her of a friend of mine, a policeman in Perth, WA. He had a lad on walkabout come and sit in the grounds of his police station. When he and his colleagues tried to move him on, he calmly explained that his ancestors had been sitting on that same spot for thousands of years.

"So Mary, who are the interlopers, and what are borders anyway? Surely they're just an artificial way of keeping people apart."

But I'd lost her. She was talking to Jenny about a failed date she'd had which was all the fault of the yellow jacket she had mistakenly decided to wear.

As the scenery of an obscure Indonesian island sped past I began wondering at the multiculturalism back home, in my own small town. The Chinese take away is run by a family from Singapore who cook my favourite Thai curries. The Indian restaurant next door is run by Bangla Deshi's who love talking about cricket. The nail and beauty shops recently sprung up with their Vietnamese artists. The local corner shops whose Asian families have been so successful that they have sent their children to University and who, guess what, don't want to run corner shops any more. These folks were dumped in Britain when Idi Amin expelled them from Uganda. They'd originally only been in Africa because the Raj imported them to work on the railways. And then there's the Windrush generation of people descended from the slaves that our ancestors took to the Americas out of Africa. We invited them to the UK in the 1950's to work in our factories and on the buses. And latterly we have unashamedly tried to repatriate them as illegal immigrants. Shame on those politicians.

When you start to think about it, you can tie yourself up in knots. When Homo Sapiens left the Rift Valley to colonise the world, should they have had passports. Who let the Romans in, and the Anglo Saxons, Danes, Normans?

Strange the way thoughts can run around in your head when you are bouncing around in a mini bus with a quest to see dragons.

"So anyway, Mary,"

"Ooh yis, Jiff."

"To answer your question. You were probably right. Yellow doesn't suit you."

She seemed happy with that and settled down to look for more antelopes.

It was a bright morning when I awoke in the dreary Edelweiss Hotel.

The hotel might have been dreary, but there were fantastic views from my fourth floor window across the colourful rooftops of the town to the volcanoes beyond. Breakfast was curried tempeh, (soy cakes) and rice, delicious thanks to the Balinese curry sauce.

Pieter explained that today we would be visiting the Ngala tribe. Straight away I thought of the usual national dress, silly dances which they encourage tourists to join in, followed by the obligatory shopping opportunity. I tried to keep an open mind.

First stop however was Walobobo hill, and we climbed to the top, to trek around the crater edge for wonderful views of Mount Inierie, the highest on the island, and the villages built on its volcanic slopes. These were the homes of the Ngala tribe.

We drove from Walobobo to one of these villages. There was no tarmac, just a line of buildings with thatched roofs either side of a wide dirt track. But the villagers were out in force, and not just to see us. Today was a big ceremony to celebrate the creation of a new clan. Marriage had forced a split in the tribe and villagers were assembling from all around to take part in the celebrations.

Everyone was in their tribal dress, and yes, we were invited to take part in the dancing. I declined.

The other villagers, on arrival, were challenged with a war dance. This comprised of much chanting, rhythmic drum banging, bell clanging, and spear waving. The accompanying dance had the villagers in the most decorative head dresses lined up in fives with the rest of the celebrants lined up behind. Then they shuffled, I can't call it more than that, to confront their guests. The visitors had also arrived with gifts, five water buffalo and 50 pigs, (brought in Toyota pick-ups) and we saw them at the bottom of the village in the corral.

We took lunch, seated on the concrete floor of a hut, which was rice with a little tough pork, wandered around to take photos and left. Thank goodness we would not be here tomorrow to witness the mass slaughter of those magnificent animals.

We were driven from here to a model village, Bena. Much the same as the previous, but with fewer people. The only people here were old women making and selling shawls. They grinned at us with mouths disfigured red by the chewing of the betel leaf. Their teeth worn away to tiny red pegs. Pieter explained a shrine in the centre of the village. It was a black upright log representing their male ancestors, and a little thatched roof to represent the female ancestors. It looked like a sun shade. During erection, a live chicken, duck and pig were buried alive with the log to interact with and feed the souls of their ancestors. "If I was one of them ducks, I would give them the food poisoning," declared Pieter. He reminded us he was from Java, a much less primitive island.

We were given some time to explore in and out of the houses, and I wandered to the end of the village. Behind two rows of huts I found some steep irregular steps leading up to a banyan tree. Lovely shade, and you could imagine most visitors would call it a day here and turn back. But not me, I climbed further and found a little Madonna shrine surrounded by bougainvillea. I was immediately rewarded by a huge swallowtail butterfly, all yellow, red, blue and black, bobbing in and out of the pink flowers. Behind the shrine was a small straw hut, with a bench in the middle on which was sprawled an old man in rags, sleeping in the midday heat. I left him undisturbed and stepped forward to admire the view. It was to the south west, down into the deep valley, then up over a range of wooded hills to the silver Siwa sea beyond. It was truly breathtaking.

The old man, having sensed my presence, awoke, muttered a greeting and began to play his bamboo flute. It would appear to be a magical scene, but he played Frère Jacques, over and over. I asked if he could play anything else, but my request fell on deaf ears. Which was a coincidence as he was also blind. We got talking, which was better than his fluting, and he told me his name, Florian, and that he had cataracts. He had been offered to have them removed but didn't trust modern surgery therefore he had chosen to forego the operation to live out his days with the sounds of the crickets, the warm breeze and the opportunity to play for tourists. The beautiful irony was that this most haunting of views had a guardian who was a blind flautist.

I ran down the steps to tell the rest of the group of my discovery but only Jenny and Leslie could be bothered to follow me back up. I couldn't promise them a swallowtail butterfly, but a glorious view and a squeaky rendition of Frère Jacques from Florian was guaranteed. Ding, Dong, Dang.

Ruteng

The next morning we drove west to Ruteng. A good early departure, with plenty of photo-stop opportunities. We initially had to follow the coast before turning back inland through forests and winding up and down mountain roads.

We drove through several villages, and in each there would be a shack shop. I had noticed that outside every shop was an advertising hoarding showing an SAS or Rambo style hunk, gritting his teeth in a variety of action poses, always with the singular message "Never Quit". This is a noble and healthy philosophical attitude to life, you may think. It reminded me of a saying an old friend used to trot out, "Winners never quit," he would say, "and quitters never win". The message is clear that only wimps ever give up. And indeed you can argue this is true if you want to succeed in life's modern rat race. So you feel you can support this message until you realise the product they're advertising is a cigarette.

We stopped for a rather marvellous lunch of Nasi Goreng, the Indonesian staple stir fried dish of rice, chicken, and vegetables. Hot, spicy and tasty. We were at a garden restaurant run by a Chinese chef and his Javanese wife who kept us entertained throughout.

Back on the road and I was aware of another quirk of Florensian life. All houses are single storey bungalows, each with gardens full of fruit and vegetables. At the side of the garden would be the plots of their parents and grand parents, marble tiles marking the graves. They are a reminder that throughout South East Asia, whatever religion has been introduced and ultimately adopted by the peoples, the ancient method

351

of worship, the veneration of their ancestors remains uppermost. And these graves are always tastefully displayed in pride of place in the garden, usually next to the satellite dish.

We rolled into Ruteng, a large town built on a grid system with some contemporary office blocks housing banks. There were also several modern shop windows displaying western mannequins sporting western clothing.

Reminding us that Flores is a predominantly Christian island, we stayed next to the rather lovely white towered, colonial Galeja of Maria Assumpta Katedral, in a convent. Mine was a very simple room (cell?), but outside there were rather lovely gardens, although no hope of a bar. So for my evening cold Bintang beer I found a little place down a side street with a couple of tables outside. I sat there drinking my beer, taking in my surroundings, writing my journal (everyone else appeared happy to spend the afternoon in their cells), whilst three local lads decided to amuse themselves by giggling and pointing at the strange foreigner.

The rest of the group did stir later to join me in Ruteng's equivalent of Pizza Express, I chose a pizza for one. Looking at the size of it I must have been ordering off the children's menu.

The next day was our last with Wawen, who had been at the wheel for a total of over 24 hours on roads that would be lucky to achieve an unclassified status at home, and as I congratulated him later, had not caused one fatality.

Just outside Ruteng is its one claim to fame, the Spider's Web paddy fields. These were only spotted when quarry workers noticed them from the hills above the flood plain, told the villagers of their unusual paddy shapes, who told the council, and hence the tourist board. It is thought that nowhere else in Asia has these unusually shaped paddies.

Years ago, when a farmer from the Manggarai tribe died, his land was shared between his sons. A length of stream was decided upon and a line drawn to the lowest point of the field where the irrigation channels drained. This created a triangle of land to be split between the brothers.

The eldest received the largest portion near the stream, and so on. With the centre point fixed, subsequent generations bequeathed the land using the same guidelines. The result has been to create a huge web of rice fields. When they are at different stages of harvest, the effect is quite stunning. Wawen took us to several spots where we could climb and look down on this remarkable, accidental man-made feature.

With the spider's web behind us all that was left was for Wawen to drive us the remaining five hours, downhill all the way, to the town and port of Labuan Baju. We had been here, briefly five days earlier when our plane stopped on route to Ende. The flight had taken 50 minutes and it had taken us this long to return. Wawen had driven us three hours from Ende to Moni and to the lakes, 10 hours to Bajwan, six hours to Ruteng, and five hours today.

Rinca and Komodo

We boarded our boat at noon; the Binteng Explorer, a 16 berth skiff with captain Suleiman, a cook, and a crew of three. As soon as we left harbour we took lunch on the foredeck, a rather windy but wonderful occasion as we sailed between rocky outcrops, skipping over the silver ocean.

I looked back at the disappearing Labuan Baju and the forests and mountains behind and imagined Florian playing his flute, looking down on us.

It didn't take long to arrive at Rinca Island. The captain anchored off shore (it costs money to tie up at the jetty) and we were rowed ashore in two shifts. A ranger greeted us and explained we had to sign in at the Ranger's outpost. This is a World Heritage Site, and part of Komodo National Park, set up to protect the dragons.

It was hot, cicadas screeched, any breeze was like a wave from an electric fire, and everything felt so dry. The earth was scorched and cracked, rocks as hot as ovens, trees seemed to droop, failing to keep upright in the face of such heat, and the sun was relentless. The shadows cast in the struggling forest an essential target wherever possible. If you needed to stop to speak or listen, to a neighbour or a ranger, you had to dive into shade. The air was so hot it hurt to breathe.

The Komodo Dragon is the largest lizard on the planet, can grow up to ten feet from nose to tail and those youngsters that avoid predation by their cannibalistic parents can live up to 30 years. They live on only four islands, Rinca being one of them.

As the ranger walked us to his station a female, Daphne Dragon, stepped out of the forest to greet us. I'd never encountered a dragon before and was unsure how I should react. I think the others in the group were of the same mind and we looked to the ranger for guidance.

"Don't worry" he assured, "she has eaten and will not need to again for some weeks. She will not attack so long as you do not approach her or startle her."

When hunting, a dragon will stalk and attack its prey; pigs, deer, buffalo, (and humans), killing them within minutes with its powerful jaws and teeth. It then tears off pieces of its kill, swallowing them whole. Contrary to popular belief, they don't bite then wait for the animal to die from sepsis.

Daphne was going the same way as us, so we walked in parallel. She was perhaps ten feet from forked tongue to tip of her tail, and swaggered slowly beside us. When we arrived at the station and signed in we saw five more dragons hanging around the kitchen waste area. "They smell our cooking," our ranger explained. "This is where Daphne was heading"

We took a short accompanied trek into the forest, over a couple of wooded hills and around a waterhole in which wallowed a buffalo. We saw one more dragon, at a nest site, waiting to lay or eat, we couldn't be sure, and there were some monkeys and deer. Wild horses also roam this island, although we didn't see any, probably making it the only place on earth where horses are still prey animals.

"What about wolves and cougars in America?" said Jenny. "And tigers in India?" added Mary. Ok, I conceded, one of the few places.

There have been six recorded attacks this century. A man who fell out of a tree and an eight year old boy were killed, a ranger was attacked by a dragon hiding under his desk, a tourist and a construction worker were bitten, but the most extraordinary story happened in 2008. Five scuba divers became separated from their boat and washed up on a beach. They were rescued after two days, but not before they were forced to repel attacks by dragons, some in the dead of night. That must have been terrifying.

Feeling satisfied with the results of our safari we were ferried back onto the Explorer and Suleiman immediately set sail for Kalong Island. On route we saw how treacherous the waters are around these islands, and therefore how skilful our crew. The ocean has narrow passages to force its way through with its tides. We could see huge waves and swells as the ocean forced its way between the islands, sometimes a huge discrepancy in water levels.

The sun was setting as we reached Kalong, and saw the first of the fruit bats. They were coming out of the forest, flying over us, heading for Flores and their evening fruit feast. These bats are large, up to four foot wingspan, and they were very impressive as they glided over the boat, just above our heads. You felt as though you could reach up and touch them. Ultimately there were thousands, filling the reddening sky heading east. The phenomenon lasted nearly an hour, wave after wave creating a huge cloud, and then the magic was over. Suleiman started the engine and we headed for a sheltered cove for the night.

We dined and drank beer under the stars. There was no way I was going below into a stifling cabin so I dragged my mattress up top. Mary and Marina had the same idea so as the conversations fell silent, there were just the three of us looking out at the universe.

"Jiff, sing us a song, Jiff", Mary's voice whined at me. "Go on Jiff, you've been promising for ages. Sing us a song Jiff."

I protested we would wake the others, nobody wanted to hear me sing, and what's more, I had promised no such thing. But Mary was so insistent that in the end Marina suggested it would be best if I just got on with it. OK. So, with the stars and the location, and the evening and the beer, I was feeling quite romantic. I chose George Michael's "A Different Corner", it being Kaz and mine's 'our tune'. I'm not sure how much Mary enjoyed my extraordinary performance (that's what Marina called it), but she never asked again.

Later, and apropos of nothing, just as sleep was beginning to overtake us, she elbowed my ribs.

"Jiff, Jiff," she whispered, "Why can't I get a man?" There was a pause as I assumed the question to be rhetorical. But then as if to answer her own question she said "And Jiff, why do they call me Mad Mary?"

Dawn swept over us. I hadn't slept, just spent the hours watching the constellations moving across the sky as both the earth spun and the boat turned in the tide. Skipper Sully started up the engines as the crew served us breakfast. It would be two hours to the island of Komodo.

Presently the island came into view and Sully dropped anchor away from the jetty. Komodo didn't seem as forested as Rinca, more a sandy, desert island of hills and scrub. The rowing boat was deployed and a welcoming party of islanders stood on the beach to greet us. This wasn't because we were important foreign dignitaries visiting the island, you understand. Their one ambition was to sell souvenirs, mainly wooden dragons of varying sizes, tee shirts and hats bearing relevant images. Their market stalls were on the beach, and behind, on the gentle slope shaded by the few trees stood their village huts, surrounded by a substantial protective perimeter fence.

We ran the gauntlet of traders, promising to purchase on our return, and followed Pieter who met and introduced us to our guide, Toby. Toby explained that animals on the island kept to the lowland forest, carpeted by dry crunchy leaves, never wandering far from the sparse water holes. Before he could lead us into the forest we came upon a Daphne dragon on the beach who was smelling the air with her forked tongue, no more than ten yards from a deer. Neither animal was skittish, if you approached the deer, once within about ten feet, it would simply walk off to another grazing area. You could also approach to within a few yards of the dragon, which simply ignored the human presence. We followed Daphne as she strolled along the beach, then left her when we came to a bridge to lead us inland.

We visited several water holes, there were plenty of monkeys, wild pigs and more deer to be found. We also saw two Denzil dragons, one sleeping, the other a sorry old soul lying deep in the bush who Toby assured us, had settled down to die. Before returning to the beach we encountered four more Denzil and Daphne dragons.

This was it. This was my Komodo Dragon experience. Absolutely stunning, wonderful creatures, but they are not hidden, endangered, nor difficult to find. Once here, they are there for you to experience. I suppose the main adventure is in the getting here.

We returned to the boat, stopping to purchase trinkets as promised, and Sully took us to a beauty spot on the southern tip of the island, Pink Beach. There were no dragons here but the snorkelling was good, as were the climbs to the cliff tops for wonderful views of the islands of Labuan Baju bay.

Skipper Sully had one more stop for us, Bidadurai Island, the Island of Angels, with beautiful white sands. I snorkelled here for a while, but was aware that just beyond the drop off there was a heavy current threatening to sweep away the unwary. I kept to the shallow coral garden. Even so I was buzzed by a black tipped reef shark. The fish was only about three feet, but could take a lump out of you if you ventured too close. I always take bananas with me to feed the reef fish, which love to swarm around me snapping up sweet pieces of fruit. Barracudas, sergeant-majors, grunts, damsels, tangs, butterflies, wrasses, all swirl around for the treats. I'm usually quite happy to just float and watch, but today I didn't fancy a three foot shark coming up to nibble my fingers, so I quickly disposed of the bananas and left the water. It was time to go home.

Captain Sully returned us to the port and we were taxied to our final hotel, the five star luxury that is the Puri Sari Beach Hotel. The gardens were full of exotically flowering shrubs which were a haven for butterflies, tiny yellow nectar feeding birds, and weary travellers.

That evening there was a sumptuous steak meal followed by chocolate ice cream, and the group said their goodbyes. In the morning I had a relaxing breakfast before strolling through the gardens to the beach for a low tide paddle, and a pre-lunch transfer to the local airport.

The flight returning me to Bali was delayed two hours, but once taken off, the views down to the islands of the Flores sea were stunning. I definitely saw both Rinca and Komodo. We circled three times before landing at Denpasar which gave me more wonderful views of the massive Garuda Vishnu statue. Then it was back on the Airbus for eight hours to Dubai, and six hours to Birmingham, and home.

At Labuan Baju airport a terrified explorer hams it up

Epilogue

My random jaunts through Asia have taken me to 16 countries, flying over 60 times, and using bus, rail, ferry, boat, car, tuk-tuk and rickshaw. I've stayed in hotels and hostels, boats and trains, and slept under both canvass and stars, and travelled countless miles on foot. There have been historic cities and mythological forts, ruined castles and beautiful temples; jungles, rivers, mountains and oceans. I've encountered numerous animals and birds, including primates, cats, elephants, sea creatures and dragons. But most important there have been people. People I have travelled with, eaten with, drunk beer with, shared hotels, campsites, berths and cabins with, and together experienced adventures and my special form of gallivanting. Moreover I have met local people. People who have taught me, guided me, and who have been my friends and mentors. These are the people who have welcomed me into their countries and their lives.

As you travel Asia you realise more than anywhere else in the world, the people, culture, industry and society have all been shaped by their interpretation of their various religions. There have been the adherents to Islam with their marvellous mosques and minarets, mausoleums and mudasars. Less frequently you come across Christian churches and Jewish synagogues. As much as I respect these particular forms of monotheism, and indeed my own, looking at the rest of Asia, perhaps the followers of these particular religions take themselves a little too seriously.

I am fairly sure that those millions who adhere to the religions that concentrate on the state of mind and well-being of the soul are the happiest and most content of people. There is always a smile as they accept their lot and enjoy their lives.

It may seem to be a very simplistic conclusion, but when there is a god for every emotion, occasion, or fortune; or you see your deity as a mortal whose teachings appear a worthwhile philosophy; or you rely on the goodwill of your ancestors' guidance, then your life can follow a pathway of contentment and serendipity.

So congratulations to the Hindus and Buddhists, Confucianists, Sikhs and Taoists of this world. And of course I make this wish for all peoples. May the sun always shine on whichever body of water you meditate beside, and may the light always make you happy.

*****

The following excerpt is taken from my *Random Jaunts Around Africa*, due for publication in 2021

Walking the Great Falls

I decided I wanted to see the World's greatest natural wonders. I had trekked deserts, climbed mountains, flown canyons, snorkelled tropical reefs and gawped into volcanoes. I had tackled forests and jungles, safaried savannahs, steppes and prairies, traversed great rivers, and cruised island chains. I decided that the most spectacular single visit objectives would be waterfalls.

Almost immediately I discovered the world of waterfall wonders was by no means simple. Which are the greatest waterfalls? How are they measured; height, width, flow rate? There are different types including plunge, step, segmented, horsetail, cascade, and more. Most people would put Niagara Falls at the top of the list, but other than greatest number of visitors, they fall well short of any other criteria. A far more impressive array of horseshoe falls are those on the Brazil, Argentina, Paraguay border, on the Iguazu River. Niagara is miniscule in comparison. The highest, Angel Falls, is a mere stream falling off a Venezuelan tepuy (flat top mountain). For most of the year it evaporates before reaching its forest floor. Therefore, and simply because they are near the top of the list of most criteria, Victoria Falls are generally accepted as being the greatest of them all.

Moshi-Oa-Tunya, the Smoke That Thunders were first seen by European missionary and explorer, Dr David Livingstone in 1855. He named them after his queen, and the town that grew up in the 20th century to exploit its tourism value was named after him.

I left Birmingham on a Friday night, and flew via Dubai into Johannesburg. There was an early morning flight north into Zambia with excellent views over the Zambezi river, and after a quick yellow fever inoculation I was met by a cheerful young man, Evans, who drove me the five miles across sun scorched rocky scrub to the Jolly Boys Hostel in the centre of Livingstone. Evans introduced me to the most elegant, tall, beautiful, smiling receptionist. Grace was resplendent in a shining blue green traditional dress and turban. She showed me to my dorm and around the complex, and advised that nowhere in the town was off-limits during the day, but only to travel by taxi at night. I had slept well on the flights, and had neither gained nor lost time as we were on GMT, so after a swim in the pleasant gardens and a brief lunch I set out to explore the town.

Livingstone is a one street town but quite wealthy for a provincial African outpost. There are modern buildings housing banks, businesses and the council offices. On the high street were a few shops which mainly sold essential provisions. The road itself had plenty of potholes and the kerbs were sometimes gigantic where water had caused the surface to sink. Behind the main carriageway was a no-go area for cars, but cycles and motorbikes were able to negotiate the broken roads. In some places they appeared to have suffered earthquake damage the gaps were so wide.

Barefoot children played in the red dust among the overgrown remnants of some attempted lawns, and large shrubby weeds erupted from the broken tarmac and concrete. A misshapen old football was being chased by all.

I wandered randomly and eventually found my way back to the main drag. The shops were small and the indoors kept dark to stay cool. Africa has discovered self service but the aisles are so narrow and gloomy it is difficult to navigate your small trolley. There are still many products sold loose and unpre-packaged; not just fruit and vegetables, but herbs and spices, dairy produce, meat and dried goods. And there are brands we haven't seen in decades, like Tide, Oxydol and Omo. All used to ensure African children are turned out immaculately for school.

That night I dined on pasta and the excitement of seeing the Falls the next day.

I woke early and caught the first available shuttle to Victoria Falls National Park, about a ten minute journey. The car park was already full of vendors selling souvenirs, but I rushed past them to buy my ticket. A short walk on a well marked path through a thicket and I came upon the gorge created over millions of years by the falling Zambezi river. However it wasn't as I expected. Opposite, instead of the postcard image of a wall of water flowing over, there were perhaps a dozen or so smaller cascades. These fell about 350 feet into the rock strewn floor of the gorge and met up with water from the Zimbabwe side to flow out of the narrow exit from the gorge in an absolute torrent. Ahead and on the other eastern side I could see the privately owned Livingstone Island, and beyond that the tell tale cloud of steam, the smoke that does indeed thunder into the gorge.

I walked along the knife-edge trail, marvelling at the diverse colourful flowering shrubs flourishing because of the moisture cloud thrown up by the falls. I reached a bridge. Crossing the bridge I arrived at the end of the track. Still only able to see the steam cloud, and the small rivulets falling into the gorge opposite. This, apparently, was as close as you go in Zambia.

Alone in the early morning sunshine I opened my hands, stared in disbelief, and cried out in anguish, "Is that it!"

Resigned to this being the end of the trail I sat for a while and sketched the Eastern Cataract, took a few photographs, and headed back. At the beginning of the gorge instead of turning right for the car park, I struck out left and reached the shore of the Upper Zambezi. I could see there was a route across the river towards Livingstone Island, and indeed some children were already playing in the pools, alongside mothers slamming their washing against the rocks. They must feel safe, I thought, next to a river in Africa famous for its crocodile and hippo populations.

I began to walk along the edge of Victoria Falls.

No-one had told me that October was the end of the dry season and that the mighty Zambezi is reduced to a comparative trickle. Compared to the Victoria Falls picture book views, they looked like they were turned off. This drawback however presented me the opportunity to walk across the falls instead of just viewing them. I was enjoying hiking alone, and feeling much better about the situation. I leapt from rock to rock, waded across still pools of warm water, and peered over the most amazing drop to the rocks below. There were rivulets gushing over the edge but these were safe to cross far enough upstream.

I came to one such waterfall. To my left it gushed over the edge into oblivion, upstream to my right I could see where I could safely wade across. But I calculated that I could climb across this small torrent. It was too far and too risky to jump, so I simply managed a controlled fall forwards so that my hands were planted on the rock on the far side, now all I had to do was bring my legs across. Too late I realised that I had overstretched. Releasing either leg would result in a fall, there were no nearer footholds to be had, and I couldn't push myself back. I could possibly lower myself into the rushing water and hope for a foothold, but the force of the flow would more than likely just throw me over the side and to certain death on the rocks below. I considered my options. There weren't any. I was stuck.

Not able to go forward, nor even move back, or God forbid, down, I began to despair. I was prone, prostrate, horizontal. Strangely, my mother's warnings came to me "Don't do anything foolish" she would always chastise. I now felt rather foolish. I raised my head to look around, but there was no-one idiotic enough to be walking across Victoria Falls.

Then, about 200 yards upstream I saw a group of people. Two young tribesmen were leading four European women the safe way across the Zambezi. I shouted for help, but my voice was drowned by the roar of the water. I risked loosing my right hand and waving as frenetically as my perilous position would allow. But this was tiring for my standing left arm, and anyway they were walking away from me. I resumed my position and once again weighed up the options. There was nothing for it, I waved again and again calling forlornly for help each time.

I don't know why, but for some reason one of the lads turned and saw me. Without hesitation he nudged his friend and they both set off across the rocks and rivulets. Leaping like sure footed mountain goats, they negotiated the jagged rocks with ease and were with me in no time. The rescue was simple, they held and supported my arms as I stepped across.

"Thank you! Thank you!" blathered the red faced elderly white man to his young black rescuers, boys no more than 13 years old.

"No problem, Sah!" they both said and rushed back to their other charges before I could say any more.

I sat down on my rock to catch my breath and contemplate the fate that could have befallen me. I took in my surroundings. Below my feet, a torrent disappeared over the edge, crashing onto the rocks way below. It joined the swirling, foaming white water of the lower Zambesi and flowed out of the canyon. I looked across to the cloud forest owing its very existence to the spray of the waterfall, and to my right, to the huge cloud over Livingstone Island which is "the smoke that thunders".

"That's where I'm heading now. No more risks," I thought. And chuckling to myself I stood up, dusted myself down and set off again, along the edge.

*****

I hope you have enjoyed Sunshine On The Water, Random Jaunts Around Asia. I'm hoping you'll find my Random Jaunts Around Africa equally adventurous, humorous and informative, and I do hope you endeavour to read them in my final (possibly) book of gallivants. The first book of the trilogy is still available if you haven't managed to catch it yet. Laughter On The Bus, Random Jaunts Around The Americas, is also available on Amazon

In the meantime, if you have any comments about this book, or would like to ask any questions about my adventures, please feel free to email me at geoffleo@hotmail.co.uk or find me on facebook.

I would also appreciate if you could write a review on Amazon. These things mean so much.

Until Africa.

Printed in Poland
by Amazon Fulfillment
Poland Sp. z o.o., Wrocław

65172264R00206